No Gurus Came Knocking

MOLLY LANNON KENNY

"I let my light shine, totally blind to 'above or below.' In my presence, no one will languish in darkness."
~ Molly Lannon Kenny, dharma code

DEDICATION

To my brother Brendan and my student Dani Nova Rose.

You have to grow from the inside out. None can teach you, none can make you spiritual. There is no other teacher but your own soul.
~ Swami Vivekananda

There's a crack in everything, that's how the light gets in.
~Leonard Cohen

Acknowledgements

This book would never have come into existence were it not for the encouragement and stewardship of my beloved assistant, student and friend, Jivanmukta Sarah Ditty. You are a superpower, Sarah, and I love you.

Thank you to my editor, Kelly Birch, who both reined me in and gave me space. Through the process of questioning, considering, deciding, letting go, digging in and yes, fact checking, I became a better writer and a better teacher. For that alone, I owe her a huge debt of gratitude. I am ever more committed to learning, teaching and sharing this wisdom, as accessibly, as expansively, and as accurately as I can.

My deepest appreciation for my student and teacher, Pam Havig. Pam was the one who, when I was once longing for the direct presence of God, put her hand on my head, and without a hint of patronizing or diminishing, said to me, "Molly, do you really think all those ideas you have about Integrated Movement Therapy come right from here?" A deep teaching – Pam woke me up to a direct relationship with the Divine. She taught me to listen for the voice of God – the voice of my heart -- that was always moving through me.

To Robert Svoboda for giving me not one, but two, Jyotish readings, and who, through his other-worldly yet deeply grounded presence pointed me directly back to myself.

To Joseph LePage, for his heart and integrity. I learned as much just from watching you be you than from almost anything you "taught" me. May I offer the same to my students.

To Stephanie Sisson, my dharma sister, for growing up with me.

To Richard Miller for being the first yoga teacher I met who broke the mold of what I thought a "yoga teacher" would look like. Richard's words of wisdom in my dark night of the soul following 9/11 showed me that this path could actually bear fruit.

To Father Richard Rento for his weekly homilies that remind me again and again of the One Love.

To Father Greg Boyle for being Christ consciousness. Father Boyle's stories gave me an even higher bar of expansiveness and grace, and an even greater desire to embody the same.

To Mom and Dad who taught through everything they did, and who gifted me with life lessons that have shaped all that I am. Thank you for being activists and advocates. Thank you for the constant reminders that all beings are of equal value. Thank you for supporting and believing in me, and for all the risks that your love has allowed me to take.

To Sasha, for being my companion, my handler and my co-adventurer. Asmi Tvaya. Always.

To Yogarupa Rod Stryker for truly living his practice. Rod's encouragement and acknowledgement changed the course of my life.

To Robin Reich, my very first yoga teacher, who I met at a gym yoga class in Seattle. As a former workout addict, I'm sure I would have never stayed with yoga if those first classes weren't Ashtanga with a million chaturangas. I followed Robin to her own studio and left the gym, starting my real entrée into yoga at Studio Ganesh. Everything about Robin was perfect for me at the time – her integrity, her kindness, her gentle approach to the sequence, her knowledge. Robin continued to teach me about the practice when she supported me in starting my yoga-based therapy venture, when she sold her studio, when she deepened her studies in Buddhism, when she left the yoga scene, when she reached out to me throughout the years to give me encouragement and love. Robin was the first true yogini I ever met.

To De West for teaching me to sing at the end of class.

Thank you to my friend and colleague, and long-time supporter of my work, who declined to write a blurb for the book, in part because of my "constant focus on concepts like God, the divine, etc." You helped me to define my audience and to affirm my path as a bhakta, and you toughened me up in the best of ways. I thank you for that.

To EB Ferdig, Leigh Drake, RW Alves, Genevieve Hicks, Brenda Bergreen, Rachel Plies, Bess Abrahams, Ana Ruiz and Jaime Bedard, and all of the IMT faculty, for the greatest of all honors - having you call me your teacher. Thank you for caring for me, for inspiring me, for carrying on my work – our work - with truth, love and integrity.

To Veronica "V" Waters Beck and Sally Carley for giving me unconditional love and support through every part of my journey.

To all my staff, faculty and assistants who have grown and learned and loved with me, and who have encouraged my own growth.

And most of all to my students. Without them, I could not be a teacher. Thank you for the honor. May this book offer you a record of our practice together.

And with undying love, affection and infinite gratitude for you, Ram Dass. You are my inspiration and I love you beyond measure. Ram Ram ~ Sitananda

Note: Most names have been changed except those that I was given express permission to use.

Everything within this book - my interpretations, my opinions, my understanding of yoga philosophy, and my understanding of life - is my own work and does not necessarily reflect the opinions of my teachers or editor.

The following essays: Angelina, Dedication Devotion, A Love Song to Devotion, Bottoms Up and the Afterword were not edited by Kelly Birch.

Foreword

As I write this I am sitting in one of the most beautiful places on earth, where the cottonwoods and the pines sing a song of aromatic bliss, and the mountains hold me in their sweet strength. This is a place I love, doing the thing I love — teaching the path I have taken to both new and experienced students of yoga and of life in the hope that they too will discover the beauty of their own souls, the essential worthiness of their own being. In this setting I feel steady and strong; I take the time to reflect on my own life and how I got to this place, both literally and metaphorically. Mine has been a journey of seeking, finding, celebrating, questioning, being, and seeking some more, and it has led me down many roads and to the homes and hearts of many people — teachers, in truth, all of them.

And yet, this has also been a solitary journey, a journey in which I have largely taught myself — first born out of a desire to live a spiritual life, then a desire to prove myself, and then finally, simply the desire to engage in this life, in this world, in the most creative and courageous way I could. Somehow that journey led me to being a teacher, and I can only pray that I am the teacher I've always wanted to have for myself: loving, kind, reflective, grateful, honest, determined, and fierce. I believe that it is in the continued search for the teacher that we remain humble in our not-knowing, and at the same time, we circle fully around to find that the teachings, and the teacher, are within us, if only we can set ourselves in that inward direction. Without an outside perspective, however — someone or something else to guide and question and check us — this inward-seeking may turn egocentric and self-serving. We start to believe we hold all the truth, and that that truth is somehow absolute. We can end up simply reinforcing our own beliefs and our own ego identification, and our inner teacher ends up simply being another lost soul telling us what we want to hear.

For me, my most valuable teacher thus far, in the absence of "the one" (for I have had many), has been a very basic and down-to-earth understanding of yoga and yoga philosophy, most especially the yamas and niyamas — some of Raja Yoga's most foundational precepts. With these ten tenets as my guide, I have continued to hold, observe, and examine most every major struggle in my own life. My gratitude and love for these ten guidelines is immeasurable. And yet, even when I know them by heart, I sometimes need to turn them on their heads in order to keep them fresh and alive, so that they are never relegated to the musty crevices of intellectualism, but instead live lively in my mind and in my everyday life.

With this intention, several years ago I led a retreat on the yamas and niyamas where we specifically asked ourselves the question: what could I do that would help someone else to live by these precepts? For example, how could I act that would in turn ignite within another the spirit of non-violence, or non-grasping, or contentment? As our week together progressed, we continued to hone our findings into simpler and simpler terms — again, moving away from an intellectualized dialectic and toward a real-life expression. At the end of the week, we had distilled this process down to just five words: encourage, acknowledge, love, forgive, practice.

I have used this framework repeatedly over the years and have invited students to also use these words as a guideline for how to meet others and how to be at ease in the world. It is always a feeling of extraordinary wonder and delight when I see myself, and others, using these teachings to create an inner and outer world of love and peace.

Although I continued to seek my very own teacher, my own guide and cheerleader, I also continued on the path of being the teacher, as it was clearly one of my divine gifts, and one that I could use to uplift others both directly and indirectly. As part of my teaching, I began sharing stories of everyday life and how they were influenced or framed within my understanding of,

Saha na vavatu
Saha nau bhunaktu
Saha viryam karvavahai
Tejasvi na vadhita mastu
Ma vid visha va hai
Om shanthi shanthi shantih
    ~*Vedic shanthi mantra*

Prologue

In truth, I have felt the presence of the Divine within me for as long as I can remember. I was raised Catholic, in a very liberal church, with very liberal parents, who invited their children to take the time they spent in church, if not as a wholly religious experience, as a chance in their week to be still and to simply be. I loved the community of our church, and I loved the singing and the music. My whole family loved to sing, and it is not unusual, even now, for us to get together for one holiday or another and to spend an evening singing. One of my favorite songs was, "They'll know we are Christians by our love." When I sang it with my church community, I really believed those words to be true and already felt moved to ensure the truth of that claim through my own life. Even as a child, it seemed to me that there was an essential quality in our religious practice that shone through as pure love. I was taught, through the modeling and teaching of my parents and their community, to be open minded, accepting of all people, compassionate toward the suffering, and dedicated to personal and spiritual growth. But as I grew up and saw more and more of the world, I began to notice the ways in which the Catholic Church could be exclusive and judgmental. I came to see the complexity of the church and its doctrine and delivery, and more tragically, the hypocrisy and suffering often enough perpetrated by that same church. As I reached young adulthood, the Catholic Church, except for its sense of the familiar, no longer felt like the right place for me to focus my sense of the spiritual.

Although I stopped going to church, I never lost my sense of divine presence. I continued to seek faith and community and an external home for this deep, unwavering feeling I had of connection with and compassion for others. I went through a period of visiting several different churches, and I dabbled in several different organized religions and spiritual practices. My favorite of these was probably the African Methodist Episcopal

Church I attended a few times at the invitation of friends. I realize now that it seemed to have all of the elements I would ultimately define as requirements for my own organized practice: a true sense of a living God, an unconditionally welcoming atmosphere, a deep sense of devotion, and a joyous celebration of everyday life. Of course, digging deeper would reveal that it also held some of the very elements I wanted to get away from, including prescribed hierarchy and exclusionary dogma, and as much as I loved my experience there, it would also not become my spiritual home.

When I started practicing yoga, I must admit that, like many other people, it was not for any kind of spiritual awakening, but for fitness and an opportunity to excel at something I seemed to be good at. At the time, I didn't even put together that this new physical practice, to which I was becoming increasingly dedicated, also had within it a spiritual practice and philosophy -- one that I would explore deeply and ultimately adopt as my primary spiritual path.

In fact, it actually came as a surprise to me. Little by little I began to feel both a sense of community and a sense of the Divine being reawakened in me, simply through the practice. My soul had been searching for a home, and my heart was building a house of yoga.

My practice of yoga might be described as an accidental meeting of a physical discipline that was the "perfect workout" and my soul's deep, inborn desire to feel, seek, and cultivate true kinship with others. It seemed like a lucky coincidence that I would find one within the other.

It took me years to refer to myself as a yogi and I still do so reluctantly and infrequently, but this is the faith I understand. This is the practice and philosophy that gives me solace when things are hard, a lens through which to see more clearly when things are complicated, and a sense of great joy and ease in a life full of ups and downs and uncertainties.

I continued to study yoga, becoming a teacher—first of the poses, then of the philosophy as I understood it. As much as the practice and teachings seemed to be serving me and those I taught, I also began to understand the danger in adopting, or attaching too rigidly to, one specific path. I saw that yoga was for me accidental and even, in many ways, incidental, to my true longing for the Divine. I became aware of the potential for any one of us to become more interested in the external concepts and constructs of a path than in the inner experiences that drew us to that path in the first place. In *Autobiography of a Yogi*, Paramhansa Yogananda quotes his teacher with these simple yet supremely important words: "Do not mistake the technique for the goal."

When I began studying the philosophies and practices of yoga in earnest, I was partly motivated by a desire to legitimize the practice to which I had already dedicated so much of my time and my life. Over time, however, the study and the need for legitimacy simply evolved into my own practice, my own lens. It is indeed through this lens that I discovered my true heart's desire—to grow and change and live a life that is sweeter and more at ease than whatever I had experienced before and to take full responsibility for my ability to transform my own thoughts, feelings, and, indeed, my own suffering.

It is a great honor to be able to offer this same perspective, to perhaps influence others in their own desire to alleviate suffering. This collection of essays reflects my life in yoga, including my quest for a teacher. But the teacher never came. No gurus came knocking. And so I offer humbly here the outpouring of my own heart; may it guide and inspire you and remind you that the teacher truly is within.

MOLLY LANNON KENNY

A Note about Terms and Commentary

A note about the Sanskrit terminology in the essays, as well as my commentary and interpretation: For the most part, when I use Sanskrit terms I am referring to the yamas and niyamas, the set of ethical precepts set forth by the sage Patanjali in his eightfold path to enlightenment, described in the classical text, *The Yoga Sutra*. Similarly, on the whole, when I use the term "yoga," I am referring to Raja Yoga, or the "yoga of practice," as explained by Patanjali. Although in some of the essays I describe or define these words or principles, in others I refer to them as an aside or assume the reader will understand my intention within the context of the piece. My definitions or explanations of each of these precepts is based on extensive reading and research over many years, as well as on my own direct experience in living and working with them in ways that have transformed my life.

Because this collection reflects my explorations and personal interpretations, there may be times when my definition of one of the yamas or niyamas varies from that of another source or is defined according to the specific purpose for which I am invoking it; in some cases my definition reflects an evolution of my understanding of the precept over time.

For example, I use the precepts as conversational guidelines, based on yogic principles, for talking about difficult subjects like institutionalized oppression or power and privilege. Following is how I might describe some of the precepts in such context-dependent situations:

Satya — being with what is. Seek first to understand. Always assume others' good intentions. Keep your communications within the context of cultural relativity. Satya also means truthfulness — speak of the experiences of your heart or your understanding, not what you've seen or assumed. Speak of your own direct experience.

Aparigraha—non-grasping. Don't hold your ideas so tightly. Don't assume everything you think is correct or even that you will still think the same thing five or ten years from now.

Shaucha—purity. Speak with kind and clear words. Keep the integrity of your heart, and assume the integrity of others.

Santosha—contentment. You can't change everything. Allow the process to unfold; trust in the process. Find joy in the fact that the conversation is happening at all.

Tapas — determination. Stay with it. Work through, even sit with, your discomfort. Perhaps there is something to learn by not giving up.

Interpretations like these will likely differ from those found in other sources. To my mind, this is as it should be. Defining each ethical precept in a context-dependent way encourages critical thinking, or viveka, described in yogic texts as the capacity for discernment and wisdom. Similarly, when I use the term God, I am referring to my own personal experience and understanding. For me, God, or "the Divine," is the ultimate reality—the all-pervasive force that pulses behind our most immediate sense of reality. In the same way, when I use the terms atman, purusha, soul, Brahman, or even pure awareness, I sometimes use them as nearly interchangeable based on my personal understanding, and comparative study, of them. They are words with different nuances for different writers and contexts, but they all refer to some continuous manifestation of divine presence. In fact, to my mind, they are concepts that ultimately defy language, and trying to home in on one correct meaning only takes us further from a felt sense, an experience, of what those words point to. My only intention through these essays, at all times, is to ignite the reader's passion for these ideas about interconnectedness as a guide to life, community, communication, and relationship.

Although I am passionate in my study of yoga and Vedanta, yoga's historical, philosophical roots, I am not a formal scholar. At the same time, I believe that the knowledge I have to share in this little book, as I understand it and interpret it to you, will be of some service in helping illuminate some of the yogic concepts and philosophy. My beloved Swami Vivekananda writes in his book *Bhakti Yoga – The Yoga of Love and Devotion* –

"… *Ramakrishna used to tell a story of some men who went into a mango orchard and busied themselves counting the leaves, the twigs, the branches, examining their color, comparing their size, and noting down everything most carefully, and then got up a learned discussion on each of these topics, which were undoubtedly highly interesting to them. But one of them, more sensible than the others, did not care for all these things, and instead thereof, began to eat the mango fruit.*"

He continues, "*If you want to be a Bhakta, [a follower of the path of devotion] it is not at all necessary for you to know whether Krishna was born in Mathura or in Vraja, what he was doing, or just the exact date on which he pronounced the teachings of the Gita. You only need to feel the craving for the beautiful lessons of duty and love in the Gita. All the other particulars about it and its other are for the enjoyment of the learned. Let them have what they desire. Say 'Shantih, shantih' [peace, peace] to their learned controversies, and let us eat the mangoes.*"

*E*ncourage

Take a moment to think about all the people you know and all the people you don't know who are walking a spiritual path, who are trying to create change inside themselves, who are seeking teachers, and who have a heartfelt desire to uplift others. Silently send them prayers of encouragement. Think of how the word "courage" is within the word "encouragement," and remind yourself and those others of the great courage that is required to stay determined, even when the road gets tough. Remind yourself and them that it is worth it and that you are never alone in your practice or in your intention.

MOLLY LANNON KENNY

Often when you think you're at the end of something, you're at the beginning of something else.

~ Fred Rogers

MOLLY LANNON KENNY

The Guru is Within

The year was 1999. Our collective addiction to information and fast Internet connections was not yet an issue. The World Wide Web was still an exciting new phenomenon to many of us, a mere foreshadowing of what would become a commonplace resource for finding information about almost anything in a matter of seconds. In those days, we had to turn on our computers, go and make ourselves a cup of coffee or take a shower, and then come back to see our Netscape coming up like an early morning sunrise. This was way before the popularity of Google or the ease of email, a time when we were just beginning to be able to reach out to all kinds of people, often tentatively, a time when we were just starting to humbly ask questions of folks we might otherwise not have the courage or humility—or even the simple contact information—to connect with at all. This was before the brashness and bravado of the whole Internet phenomenon as it would become just a decade or so later, back before we could find any answer or fact with nothing more than a search phrase and a push of a button. A time when, if we wanted a question answered, we would have to reveal our own ignorance on a topic.

This was the cultural setting I existed in with regard to the Internet in 1999, as most of us did, and yet the little hints were there that a mere ten years later, we would all be compulsively checking our emails, our texts, our Facebook pages, our Twitter feeds. I remember one example like it was yesterday. I was employed as a speech pathologist at a large HMO, and our state-of-the-art computers had just arrived. We were all given email addresses, and suddenly we were learning to create and navigate the new rules for electronic communication and information sharing. I remember that every time I received a new email, my computer would make a little sound. This sound became almost a Pavlovian stimulus. When I heard it I would respond immediately with a desire—that I could barely contain—to check and see what was coming to me through the ether. Sometimes, even if I was with a client, I would sneak a peek at the email subject line, just to see if it could wait or if I "needed" to answer it right then. This was also before I had to wear glasses to read the words on a computer screen, so it was easy for me to check the text, no matter how small, and no matter how dark and obscuring the black and green color palettes of the early email interface.

I remember one day especially, when I was waiting for a simple response—a response that would come to change my life. Of course, I had no way of knowing that then, but I am sure that it is only because of the personal nature of both the question (and of its answer) that the response had such an impact. Had I been able to answer my own question through a simple Google search, I doubt it would have set me on the same path. I would never have had to show my ignorance, or my longing and vulnerability, to another person. I would have found multiple responses and reviews and quips and would have been able to sort through the information, find a satisfactory answer, compartmentalize it as I wished, and move on. I would have found my answer, but it would have been superficial. In those days, I could not search for answers in this impersonal and protected manner. Instead, the question burned deeply for me and so did the answer. This simple yet profound question was one I had typed very directly to the one person I knew would know the answer, my yoga teacher.

"Who, or what, is *Guruji*?"

I had been wondering about this for some time. I had fairly recently begun practicing Ashtanga yoga, mainly as a workout that I enjoyed and was pretty good at, and I was just beginning to see that some students took this yoga thing really, really seriously. I had heard them talking about Guruji, and that Guruji was coming, and about who had studied with Guruji and when and for how long. This Guruji person seemed to keep coming up in conversation. Perhaps it was my endless stream of insecurity and the need to fit in, but my ego kept me from just asking my fellow students the same question I finally asked my teacher. The computer dinged. The subject line was "Guruji." It was from my yoga teacher. This I had to read. This, I knew, was important.

"Guruji," she wrote, "is a name some students call their teacher as a term of endearment and respect. In this case, the students are referring to their teacher Pattabhi Jois." Right then, I knew it: I wanted a Guruji. I wanted a teacher to whom I could show my respect and reverence and who could in turn "show me the way." But the only one I knew about was this Pattabhi Jois character, and I knew I had to find him and become his student. He was the teacher of my teacher, and the teacher of the teachers I would later study with. He was the big kahuna, and I wanted to know him too. But how could I make this happen? I started to feel that I had to go to India if I was ever going to be as deep and committed as my yoga friends, but at the time, that seemed impossible. Plus, I kept hearing mixed reviews of practicing with Guruji in India. There were plenty of myths and stories about Guruji — none that seemed to have any irrefutable truth, but that were still intriguing and sometimes alarming. Stories about him making people get up in the middle of the night to practice, about hurting people by sitting on them, yelling at them, pushing people further than they were ready to go. The culture at his school in India was always described as intense. Just as often however, the stories I heard from returning students made it seem equally elitist and shallow. Without any sort of reliable filter for the seemingly conflicting stories I heard, it began to sound and feel more to me like my high school and college years of following the Grateful Dead, with subtle, but apparently very serious, contests of who was the biggest Deadhead, the most hard-core devotee. But, just like in my thirst for Guruji, even with all of the posturing and maneuvering among his students, I still wanted to be a part of the in crowd, to go to the shows, to enjoy all the good — I still wanted the sense of being part of a scene, of belonging, of having some legitimacy, that came with all the clutter.

As time moved on, I became less and less focused on going to India to study with Guruji — it just seemed too complicated, as well as being way outside my financial and practical reach. But now I had the bug. I wanted to join the students who had a teacher, and the only one I really knew of was this Guruji. He was coming to the United States, and wanting to experience him for myself, I knew I would go wherever I needed to study with him. Luckily for me, I didn't have to go far — only to Southern California, where I could combine my morning yoga classes with afternoon surf lessons and make the whole thing into a much-needed mini-vacation from my work at the clinic.

I arrived at the huge rental hall in Carlsbad that first morning, nervous and excited about my introduction to Guruji. I set my mat right at the front of the room and reviewed the primary series in my head. I watched the other students file in, with their standard yoga clothes and accessories, and I imagined their ease in their yoga practice and the culture surrounding it. I watched them set their mats down in just the right place and high-five and hug their Ashtanga friends. I thought I saw some of them with just a hint of a swagger — these would be the students doing the second series. These were the advanced students. I imagined that these were the ones who had been to India and who, after practice, would already know to line up for a chance to sit at or touch Guruji's feet. These are the students who I would watch and follow to try to keep up with in the practice. These were the ones whose practice and demeanor I would try to imitate, striving to achieve the perfect balance of respectful excitement and cool detachment.

As I sat on my mat taking it all in, a very elderly woman entered the room. She was slight yet strong looking, with a perfectly matched velour sweatsuit and head wrap. She strutted in as if she were half her age and walked right up to me. She looked at me sitting on my mat, and then she picked up the mat carefully set down next to mine by one of the other early birds wanting a front row seat and moved it just enough to put her own mat down in its place. I was both amazed and amused at her chutzpah. It didn't seem to me like these star-struck Ashtangis were people you messed with, but at the same time, they were yoga students, and they were here with their Guruji, and they were disciplined and contained — if not exactly overflowing with generosity and warmth. Of course, I would later understand that generosity and warmth often begets the same, and I was not exactly oozing with these qualities either, instead protecting my ego and hiding my own insecurity by being equally standoffish.

The elderly woman situated her mat until it was just where and how she wanted it and then turned to me and with a very heavy accent introduced herself. Her name was Eva, she was 86 years old, and she was born and raised in Israel until her thirties, when she moved to New York City and became a tour guide. She had been practicing yoga for as long as she could remember and had studied with Guruji before. She seemed to know what she was doing — she was "one of them" — and although I was a little shocked and embarrassed by her moving other people's mats, I was glad to have made a yoga friend in this new and somewhat intimidating environment.

Guruji entered the room. Everyone became hushed. "Samastithi!" he barked. We all stood at attention. We were off! — the primary series had begun. I followed along, determined to hold every pose, make every jump-through. Eva held her own. She moved quickly and gracefully, until at one point Guruji came over to her and snapped some instruction or other. She looked him in the eye and said, "Don't tell me what to do, I'm the same age as you are." Guruji stared her down. Eva didn't blink. Guruji walked away, and we continued with the practice. All the way through the closing series and even into savasana, I felt Eva's presence as both a guardian and an inspiration. She had found and chosen me over all the other students. She exerted her independence despite all the pressure to conform to the group, something that seemed impossible for me to do at the time. I didn't know it then, but Eva would be a subtle force in my own growth and ability to stand alone as a yogi and as a teacher. She would not be bullied. When I asked her at the end if she was going to wait in line to sit at Guruji's feet, she laughed out loud. "Are you joking?" she asked. And then she invited me to dinner later. We made arrangements of where to meet. Eva left and I waited in line. This was Guruji. I would sit at his feet.

Molly with Pattabhi Jois

That evening I met Eva at an intersection somewhere near Carlsbad. She pulled up in her huge car, and at first I didn't recognize her. She was wearing a big blonde wig and a much fancier velour sweatsuit. Eva had wonderful stories to tell, interrupted only by her completely insane driving. I divided my attention between her stories and her several near misses — with pedestrians, parked cars, and buildings. As she and I sat together at Souper Salad, she gave me more insight into her practice and her life. She talked about her children, her history, and her worldview, much of which in fact seemed filled with bitterness and judgment.

As we left the strip mall parking lot, Eva backed loudly into another car. Instead of stopping, she sped away. I grabbed the dashboard for my life, sure we were going to kill someone, if not ourselves. "Eva! You have to stop!" I cried. But there was no stopping her. She pulled out of the parking lot and onto the freeway. The car we had hit was in pursuit, and the driver was flashing his lights and honking his horn. I pleaded with Eva to stop, and finally she acquiesced. We turned into a parking lot and Eva got out of her car. The man in the other car jumped out of his, and I quietly sat and prayed for our safe return to practice the next morning. The man started yelling at Eva, "What is wrong with you. You backed into me!" Eva responded even before he could finish, "You backed into ME!" she insisted, without, apparently, even a touch of trepidation about this out-and-out lie. The man stared at her incredulously. Then he whipped around her and opened the car door to where I was sitting, "Is she serious? You saw what happened!" "Yes," I said. "She definitely backed into you. I'm so sorry. I told her to stop, but she wouldn't, until now." I was stuck in the middle between my "friend" and this man who was righteously pissed off. Eva and the man shouted back and forth a bit more, and then finally, seeing that his complaint was falling on very deaf ears, the man got in his car and drove away. Eva got back into her car as if nothing had happened. As we drove on, Eva began to talk about various people in her life for whom she had either great respect or great disdain. Eva was a woman of passion and intensity, which I loved, but she was also someone who saw things in stark contrasts and was not easy to sway to the middle. She made up her mind about people and stood her ground, whether she was even remotely correct or not. For whatever reason, Eva liked me. "Molly," she said to me as I got out of the car, "most people are midgets. You are a giant. Don't forget it." My ego swelled momentarily with her simple yet powerfully spoken pronouncement. I wanted to hold on to the compliment, convince myself that it was true. But I was smart enough, even then, to feel and know the dynamic tension of wanting approval from a seemingly powerful person while recognizing that person's deep flaws. When were the flaws deep enough that they ultimately negated the experience, the attention? I was confused and mystified, and also very immature. I would take the attention and diminish the flaws.

Eva was not like any other old person I had met. I liked her spunk, but I was also put off and dismayed by her totally cavalier sense of anyone else's place in the world. Nonetheless, I was flattered by her comment and looked forward to seeing her the next morning at practice. As I got out of her car that night she reminded me, "I'm old. I know what I'm talking about."

I arrived early again. I was feeling a little more like I belonged. I had watched the whole second series the day before and, with my own agenda to be among the special students, had already resolved that I would move up in the ranks as soon as I returned home. Eva arrived just moments before Guruji. Again, she picked up someone's mat and moved it to place her own down next to me. This time the other students were not so accommodating. I will never forget the young guy who behind Eva's back made the gesture of picking her up and drop kicking her. I knew that what Eva had done was not right, but neither was this response. As much as I was setting my intention to increase my physical prowess and dedicate myself further to this practice and achievement, I was coming to understand that there was a vast difference between my own idealized version of Guruji and his followers and what I was actually seeing and experiencing. I was coming to understand, in fact, that any ideal might be unrealistic, and that there were a lot of different qualities that a person would need to be the kind of teacher I was seeking.

Ekum, inhale. Dwe, exhale. Trini, inhale, Chatuari exhale. I moved through the sun salutations but couldn't shake the image of the man drop-kicking Eva. I couldn't stop thinking about Eva yelling at and lying to the man whose car she had hit or her entitlement in moving people's mats. I kept spinning in my own ego that at once loved Eva's attention and compliments, but also knew they were coming from someone with a very conflicted sense of right and wrong, "good" and "bad." I couldn't settle in to Guruji's yelling and demanding of "no fear." I couldn't make sense of this dedication to the practice and to the man. I was deeply unnerved by the lack of basic respect and kindness I saw around me, of the shouting and shaming by the teacher, and of the apparent complicity of his students. I finished out the week in Carlsbad and returned home.

This Guruji, Pattabhi Jois, would not be mine, but I would remain dedicated to the practice for some time. The idea of the teacher, the guru, faded into the background and I simply did my practice.

However, as Pattabhi Jois often said, all was coming.

Within a year, having continued my Ashtanga practice and advancing through the first and second series, I started to teach the practice to fellow students when my own teachers needed someone to fill in. I had studied with Pattabhi Jois several more times after that first trip, both for the joy of practice and, still, the desire to be legitimized by saying I had practiced with Guruji, but no longer to fulfill the deep longing for my own teacher, my own Guruji, at least not in that person, in that setting.

I was getting more serious about yoga beyond Ashtanga, reading everything I could find about the roots of this practice, as well as books recommended to me by teachers and fellow students. I was learning new words and ideas and feeling deeply drawn to the bigger picture of what yoga could offer. In fact, a year or so after that first Guruji sighting in southern California, I left my job at the hospital. For all of my misgivings about the cultish and unexamined ways that disciples and gurus can behave, I was also meeting many healthy, kind, and dedicated students and teachers. I was learning a lot about myself through my practice, and I was determined to use all the best parts of it for healing both myself and my clients.

As a therapist, I had the idea that there was something I was learning through yoga that was changing my way of thinking, my way of wanting to offer therapy, and even my desire to work in a clinic. It was early 2000 when I created a title and a brochure for my new adventure and began advertising and offering *Integrated Movement Therapy* (IMT), an approach I called "yoga-based therapy," combining my growing love of yoga with my clinical experience and background. I rented a space in a low-income area of town and began my private practice. I was on fire. I spent every day reaching out to folks through the Internet, now relatively more reliable and efficient, or pounding the pavement meeting people, developing my therapy method and my connections. I supplemented my income by teaching the Ashtanga yoga practice I had studied for so long and loved so dearly, despite its potential shortcomings, and I continued reading everything I could about yoga. My yoga practice, in the biggest sense, became my whole life.

I dedicated all of my time and energy to developing and sharing IMT with as many people as possible. I watched as my students quite literally moved through difficult situations due to strokes, autism spectrum disorders, anxiety, depression, and profound loss. I was combining proven clinical methods, my understanding of very basic yoga philosophy, and simple yoga poses and movements suited to the particular individual. As a therapist, I was thrilled with what I was seeing—IMT was unique, it was nourishing, and it worked. I wanted to find a way to share not only the direct experience of the therapy but also the method itself to others in similar fields or with similar orientations to the holistic viewpoint that I discovered through my yoga practice.

Through what then felt like a series of fortuitous events, and what now feels like a divine plan, I came into contact with Joseph LePage, the founder and director of *Integrative Yoga Therapy*. I was fascinated by Joseph's work and would spend hours combing through his website to see what he was teaching, what I could learn, and how I could potentially share IMT through his trainings. I sent Joseph an email asking if I could join him on his next training and perhaps share a small section on my yoga-based therapy method. He replied, saying I could join the training and that he would allow me to talk about *Integrated Movement Therapy* to the students during one of the evening sessions. When I think about this now, I have even more love and respect for Joseph. In retrospect, his response seems unlikely, and I wonder how I would respond to someone now with a similar request. Over the years, I have come to believe that Joseph's response was based on his keenly developed sense of intuition and his connection to grace. Joseph's acceptance changed my life and set me firmly on my path.

Molly with Joseph LePage

I was thrilled. I was going on my first-ever yoga retreat, where people were going to be talking about and learning about and studying yoga together — and I was going to be able to present my work to them. I was also nervous — this was all very new. But I knew it was what I wanted, and it led me into the extraordinary opportunities and experiences that would continue to shape my personal, professional, and spiritual life.

I remember waiting in the Santa Barbara airport for the shuttle to take us to the retreat center. I sat with the other yoga people, with their rolled-up mats and their Om T-shirts, and talked a little about my experience and why I was at the training. No doubt second guessing the wisdom of Joseph's generosity, and feeling unsure in this new setting, I began to rely on a familiar strategy — I wanted people to be clear from the get-go that I was "special," and I was here because I had something special to offer. I believed at the time that they were duly impressed.

I had no idea what I was in for — more learning than I ever could have imagined was on its way. I soon learned that my old strategies would have to evolve and my understanding of yoga would have to expand. I knew that the seeds being planted in this training would grow and transform my life, but I did not yet know how. The very first night at our opening practice, I was mainly occupied with just two things: judging other people's practices and wondering how I could get attention for my work. I remember looking at some of the other students, non-Ashtangis all of them, and wondering how they could do yoga therapy when they couldn't really "do" yoga as I had learned it. I had only ever experienced the physical practice through the Ashtanga method and was still, regrettably, caught up in my competitive nature. I wanted to be seen for my strong practice in a place where it truly didn't seem to matter and in fact was somewhat maligned. How then, would I get the teacher's attention? An opportunity came for me to "shine" when the person who was writing notes on the flipboard for Joseph wasn't able to make it to a session. When he asked if someone else was willing, I immediately raised my hand. I was a good speller, and I would get to be up in the front. With the teacher.

As Joseph talked and meandered through the yoga philosophy and dropped some serious yoga science, I was pleased and proud to be able to keep up, not only with his thoughts but also in correctly spelling much of the Sanskrit terminology I had never formally studied. I rarely asked questions or for clarification — I could not let anyone know that I had so little real yoga background or think that I didn't deserve to be up there with Joseph. The scribing went on. Joseph talked about the kleshas, the chakras, Vedanta, Sankhya, Patanjali, the eight limbs, yoga nidra — more and more new words and concepts for me to keep up with. I wrote furiously, often waiting for Joseph to finish a thought completely and then synthesizing it as quickly as I could. I was in awe of his knowledge, but too self-absorbed to show it.

Joseph had what was, at that time, a unique way of offering his trainings; he would bring in a variety of high-quality teachers to expand on specific areas of expertise. On that first training alone I met Anodea Judith, Scott Blossom, Richard Miller, and Larry Payne. I was excited and ignited by all of them, and through the intense schedule, lack of sleep, and close sleeping quarters, I was beginning to be humbled. I went on to assist Joseph on two further trainings and each time my yoga education was deepened and my eyes opened more. And I kept hearing all of these excellent and deep teachers talk about and acknowledge their own teachers. There was that teacher thing again. Even after that very first training with Joseph, I started to want one again, and this time in earnest.

I returned to my home and studio in Seattle energized and changed. Over the course of the two weeks of training, I had begun to shed some of my posturing and to develop a sense of reverent appreciation for the practice, for the students and teachers, and for "the bigger" yoga. Once I loosened my desire to be identified as special and began to trust in just being myself, the pendulum began to swing heavily to the other side—I began to feel like an imposter in my own teaching. Without the false security of puffing myself up and trying to show off or outdo the other students, I was left feeling exposed and incompetent. How could just being me, with my eclectic education, be enough? I was teaching yoga, but I didn't have a teacher. I knew a lot about yoga, but I couldn't put my finger on exactly how I knew what I knew.

I wanted to find that person, my own Guruji, who would tell me what I wanted and needed to know, who would guide me in my process just as I heard stories of others being guided in theirs. I wanted someone who was kind and patient and generous; someone who was both learned and humble. I'm not sure if I knew it at the time, but I also wanted someone who was my very own, who I didn't have to share, and who, once I had given up trying to prove how special I was, would see and acknowledge me as special anyway. I dreamed of a teacher who would remind me of my own worthiness when I didn't trust myself, when I was unable to see it on my own, my view being clouded alternately by self-aggrandizement and self-doubt. The longing grew steadily deeper until I began to think about "my teacher" all the time, the way you can fall in love in a dream and spend the whole day pining for that love. It felt like both an ache and an emptiness, and as I continued to study on my own and even create my own yoga teacher training, I developed ever deeper feelings of being a charlatan, sure that someone was going to find me out. I studied harder so that I might be able to answer any question asked of me, whether I had the benefit of the teacher or not. If I couldn't find my teacher, at least I could continue to gain information and knowledge that I could share with others. I could continue my own practice, and teach authentically at least from that experience.

Through this steady pursuit of all things yoga, including its academic aspects, I had kept in touch with some of the teachers I had met through Joseph including Scott Blossom. On his recommendation, I was introduced to Dr. Robert Svoboda. This was exciting. Robert Svoboda! The first American to be given an Ayurvedic degree in India. The author of countless books. Scott's teacher—his own Guruji, or so it seemed to me. I couldn't wait to meet him. I was nervous and giddy. Scott contacted Dr. Svoboda for me and made an introduction. Dr. Svoboda would be in Seattle teaching, and Scott asked me to drive him from his accommodations in Seattle to the yoga studio where he was teaching. Even at that time, I knew of Jyotish, the astrological dimension of yogic study, and I knew that Dr. Svoboda was well established in this practice. Through Scott, I asked him for a reading, which he generously granted. I didn't know what to expect when I arrived at Dr. Svoboda's host's house. Dr. Svoboda was dressed in flowing Indian garb, and he offered me a piece of cardamom. I chewed on it slowly, taking in the intense flavors. This was a new level of experience in this vast realm of yoga practice; I could feel it. Dr. Svoboda moved about his room with fluidity and ease and emanated an aura of other-worldliness. He was tall and vaguely effeminate. But that wasn't really quite it. More accurately, it was as if Dr. Svoboda, like the Shiva he frequently invoked by *weaving Om Namaya Shivaya* into his casual speech, actually transcended any sense of "this" or "that," masculinity or femininity, saintly or salty. His conversation was philosophical, irreverent, erudite, devotional—and hilarious. As we chatted on the way to my studio, where he would do the reading, I found myself being my old predictable self again—that is, trying to impress this man with my accomplishments and my knowledge. It makes me laugh to recall this. Dr. Svoboda is not, it turns out, so easily impressed.

He sat down across from me at a little table in my studio's foyer and took out his laptop. I remember watching him as he moved with grace and intentionality — opening his computer, peering over his glasses, his face animated by a continuous flood of expressions, from intensity, to questioning, to skepticism, to dismissiveness, to genuine excitement. Computer technology had apparently advanced enough to do ancient astrological readings, and I was about to have one from the master. Dr. Svoboda told me many things, some of which were too esoteric for me to really grasp and others that were so detailed and practical that I could easily test them against reality. For example, he told me that I was going to be moving out of my house within the next couple of months, which I knew wasn't true; I had absolutely no intention of moving. Although these apparently random predictions were shaking my faith, I still waited dutifully until it was time to ask the one question burning in my mind:

"Where is my teacher?"

Dr. Svoboda smiled. "Hmmm," he said, lifting his eyebrows in the way one might when listening to a child telling a tall tale, "You don't have a teacher?" I was being outed again and was feeling impatient. "No, but I really, really want one," I said, hoping he might at least acknowledge how much I knew about yoga without having a teacher and how genuine and humble I was in my desire; but he didn't. I waited then for him to scold me and remind me that I had no right to have a yoga studio, let alone a yoga teacher training, if I did not have a teacher. But he didn't do that either. He simply stared at his computer screen, cocking his head this way and that.

Finally he said, "Well, your teacher is coming. But you have to keep your eyes and mind open. Your teacher may show up in a very unexpected form. He or she may show up as a gemstone or a bagel, and you will have to be able to see that this is your teacher." "Great," I thought. "Thanks, Dr. Svoboda, I'll keep my eyes wide open and make sure I don't mistake my bagel for just my breakfast." I thanked him, and with that, he stood up and shut his laptop. "I have to get going," he said, and we walked to the car and I drove him to his talk, which I was eager to attend.

I sat right up in front, right in front of the teacher. But Dr. Svoboda hardly acknowledged me, and no one could tell the experience I had just had with him.

Two months later, I moved from the house I had lived in for nine years. Perhaps Dr. Svoboda did have something to teach me. In fact, I had the great honor of inviting him to my new house a couple of years after that first meeting. I remember being so excited and honored that he would come to my home that I cleaned my house and bought him special tea and snacks. Before I could serve him, we moved to my living room and sat down at my table. I asked him again, "Where is my teacher? I have kept my eyes and heart and mind open, but I still don't feel like I know if my teacher has appeared. What if I don't have the clarity? What if I miss him or her?" Dr. Svoboda looked at me directly. "Do you have a daily meditation practice?" I felt humbled again, but not belittled. "No," I responded sheepishly. Dr. Svoboda pursed his lips and slowly nodded his head. "Please don't ask me about clarity again until you have the clarity to have a meditation practice. This is the most important thing in your spiritual life." At that moment I decided I would become a real yogi. I would meditate every day, and my teacher would come. I trusted that Dr. Svoboda knew what he was talking about and that if I would just follow his recommendation, everything would fall into place. He is a man of great honor, knowledge, and integrity. But just as I was so intrigued by him that I forgot to even offer him the food I had bought especially for him, his words and my commitment went out of my head pretty much the moment he flowed out my door.

Life went on. I continued teaching, reading, and writing about yoga. I continued to keep my eyes open, and continued to feel this great sense of loss for something I had never had. I tried to push it away or to minimize it by doing what I could, going to therapy and reading a lot of yoga books, although, ironically, never actually meditating. I felt isolated and inadequate and felt like I needed to do something, not just sit there. How could I gain more credibility? How could I legitimize what I was doing? How could I find my teacher? I sought out every avenue I could to delve deeper into yoga, to be a part of something that would establish me as credible in this seemingly elite world I felt like I had crashed. Having heard of and respected the work of the International Association of Yoga Therapists, I began to create a relationship with them through writing for their publications and attending their conferences. When I applied and was elected to their board, I felt like I had finally arrived.

Now I was really in the big league. These were all people with teachers and, rather than feeling elevated as I had imagined I would, my own sense of inadequacy deepened daily. Through my various affiliations with IAYT and my new interactions with different "sages on stages," as they are called in the biz—the bigwigs of the yoga scene—I constantly heard the terms lineage, tradition, guru, teacher. I found my pendulum swinging wildly again. As I clamored to show my worthiness and intellect and heart, I also heard this: "You are making up what you are doing. You have no right to teach yoga or to sit at this table with us. You are not a real yogi, and you are doing great damage to the dignity of our practice." Whether these were real voices from real people, or imagined voices hijacking my thoughts, the effect was very real to me. I knew that I experienced the promised sense of oneness and peace and connectedness much of the time when thinking about, practicing, or teaching yoga. I knew that I knew some things about yoga, and I understood some things about life and love and suffering and joy and that I could share these to uplift others. But I also knew that I didn't know all the right words, the right quotes, hadn't read the right books. I knew I didn't have a teacher and that everyone else, all these other yoga teachers, seemed to have one.

But I really wanted to make this right. I would ask these "real" teachers about divine transmission, about paths of direct knowledge, about integrity and humility, trying to find a way that I fit in, yet never simply settling in to my own unique experience. All the time, I continued to study and teach.

One winter, IAYT granted me the opportunity to moderate a panel on yoga therapy at a national conference. Although I was excited to be on the panel, I was predictably feeling deeply disheartened by the back-slapping and glad-handing I saw among the invited and esteemed teachers. It seemed, much like my experience in high school, that despite all my best efforts to fit in, this yoga teacher thing would ultimately be an impenetrable club of which I would never really be a part. In high school, I didn't have the right social or economic lineage. In this new world, I didn't have any lineage at all.

Back at the yoga conference, one night at dinner, I had a chance to meet and talk briefly with a particularly popular teacher, without knowing who he was. He seemed to me to be down-to-earth, quiet, humble, and real. I felt like I made an instant connection with him and began to seek opportunities to study with him. I remember leading a teacher training shortly after meeting this kind man — this shantha — and talking to my students about my own search for a teacher. I think I wanted to be transparent — to let my students know that I had not been formally trained, both so that I wouldn't be "found out " and also, no doubt, because I wanted to impress them with my knowledge, in spite of not having the kind of credentials one might expect from someone leading a teacher training. I tried to express my search for a teacher with a balance of self-assuredness and humility. I wanted a teacher because of my own inner longing, but not because I couldn't teach my students well without one. I suppose I wanted them to have a longing too, and perhaps even for me. When I talked with my students about the teacher I had recently met, they were excited for me — would this be "the one"? I felt like the baby chick in the children's book *Are You My Mother*? There was a quality to my seeking that was very much like searching for a lost parent, and my students could feel my yearning.

I signed up for the next time I could study with that teacher and managed to have some profoundly grounding and encouraging interactions with him. He was smart, funny, and kind. I wanted him to be my teacher, but at the same time, I was losing my sense of what I actually wanted. Even as I seemed to be homing in on a teacher, I was at once becoming confused about my motivation and desire. This man had the knowledge and the heart, for sure, but I also came to understand that what I really wanted was an individual relationship, one in which my teacher knew and honored and directed me in a very personal way. That was what I had heard about and what I had read about and what I wanted. In fact, it seemed to me like the only real way of having a teacher.

I had created an ideal for myself, a story I told myself about all of the great teachers and students and their own gurus. Suddenly, it seemed disingenuous of me to accept a relationship where I was just one of many, mostly women, students who seemed to hang on the teacher's every word, also vying for attention and recognition. Yes, this was a genuine teacher, but it was not my image of the guru. While I deeply wanted this ideal — someone who could help to reveal my own truth to me — I began to see in myself, again, that frustrating and tenacious desire to be seen as special somehow. To be the most invited guest. To truly fit in. I was becoming impatient, frustrated, and even disgusted with myself. My longing started to seem pathetic. I started to become less clear on what I was looking for and how I would know I had found it. Although I could understand the value of the teacher teaching to many, I also wanted to feel like "my teacher" would pick and choose students who were particularly ready or qualified in some way to be students. I didn't want to think that my teacher would teach just anyone, as long as they paid the price of admission.

Perhaps in some way, it was like reliving my own childhood, and the struggle between seven of us kids to garner the attention of my very willing, and also often overwhelmed, parents. It was this recognition of my deep insecurity, even after all of my yoga study and practice, that just disheartened me the most. Although I returned home quite happy to know this teacher existed for me, I was beginning to lose faith in "my teacher," the teacher who was coming just for me. I was ready. I'd been ready. I looked into gemstones and bagels and in teachers and books, and thought I had opened my mind to who and how my teacher could appear. Now I could finally just let it go.

During this same time, I continued to work with the International Association of Yoga Therapists, and through that affiliation I was a part of a committee established to develop educational standards for programs that teach yoga therapy. As the many experienced and established teachers worked through the various minimum requirements for the field, I often heard the lament about how few people understood the "real" yoga and how few teachers there are in the United States with the depth of knowledge required to create advanced yoga therapy programs. I thought this might be true, but I also kept thinking about the teacher I had recently met, and all of the many teachers I had known along the way, and my appreciation for the time I had spent learning with each of them deepened upon my reflection. It seemed to me that many teachers deeply understood yoga, even its practical application of a sort of cognitive behavioral therapy and beyond, and seemed willing to share their knowledge with passion and generosity. In my mind, any of these teachers could be qualified to teach the kinds of programs and materials we were discussing. As is my way (I have been writing unself-conscious letters of deep love and appreciation to my teachers, students, family, and friends for as long as I can remember), one morning after a work session and discussion with our standards committee, I decided to reach out to one of these teachers I had come to respect so deeply, to simply thank and acknowledge him for his teachings. I received this in response:

Dearest Molly,

Thanks for this email. I appreciate the kind words and, of course agree about the dearth of authoritative wisdom sources in this country, but it should be said that they are not a dime-a-dozen in India either. In truth, it takes a rare kind of student willing to undertake the process of learning this vast science. Such a student is rare mainly because the teachings themselves cannot truly be studied in the abstract; the student must be willing to grow and evolve along with their knowledge––all of which requires a kind of one superlative, patient, and teachable individual. That is why teachers quietly celebrate when such a student appears before them, ready to learn. You are such a student. So, I look forward to every chance we will have to work together and in which I can add to all that you know already.

In that moment, I was finally acknowledged, finally seen. Someone whom I respected and admired had openly acknowledged my quest, my thirst, and my dedication. It wasn't just about the student seeking the teacher, but also the teacher seeking the student. I felt celebrated. My sincerity as a student was as important as the acknowledgement and approval of the teacher I had been seeking. This became the exact impetus I needed to stand in my own power. This person, this teacher, whom I honored and esteemed, honored and esteemed me back. I didn't need him; I could choose him, and he could, and would, choose me. While his kind and generous words sparked this knowledge, I learned that in fact my desire ultimately had to be met with my own acknowledgement of myself, of my own self-approval and self-love. There was the teacher. Not a gemstone, not a bagel, but my own heart. The guru, I found, truly is within.

MOLLY LANNON KENNY

Ahimsa: Offering the Gift of Connection

The concept of ahimsa (usually translated as non-violence or non-harming), the first of the ethical precepts as described by Patanjali, can be considered the very foundation of yoga; it is the very foundation of all of the teaching in our Samarya Center community.

When we consider these "restraints" and "observances" (yamas and niyamas) as described in yoga philosophy, we may wonder, how do we do we put them into practice; how do we live them? One way of looking at this is to consider that ahimsa is not only about committing to a life of non-harming (or at least committing to thoughtful attempts at decreasing any tendency for harming) but is also about cultivation of the opposite. This idea of cultivating the opposite of disturbing or harmful thoughts is described in sutras 2.33 and 2.34 as a practice called pratipaksha bhavana. With this practice it is further suggested in sutra 2. 35 that in the presence of one firmly established in non-harming all natural instincts to harm will cease. So, if we want to live ahimsa, we are not only invested in what we are not doing, but also in how we nourish, encourage, and cultivate our capacity for love and kindness, so that others too may feel its benefit.

One of the things I love most about yoga is its celebration of direct experience and its clear relationship between the theoretical and the actual. Yoga provides the student with guidelines and practices that are readily applicable to everyday life. For me, it has always been through direct experience, and through using these concepts as a lens and framework for my entire life, that I conceptualize my own life in a way that feels healing, productive, and joyous. I find I am constantly discovering new meanings and nuances within my yoga study and am often surprised by how they emerge to inform my experiences.

Not so long ago, through an intensely personal experience, I realized another facet of ahimsa, and indeed all the yamas and niyamas: that we can not only invite our exploration of these concepts in ourselves but also how we can reveal and facilitate their presence in others.

In the midst of one cold and rainy Seattle winter, I left for the tropical climes of Costa Rica. I wanted to be in the warm sun, but I had an even greater reason for leaving. I had a surprise planned for my Seattle community, and I needed to leave for a bit of time for it to work out in the way that I imagined. I had recently discovered I was pregnant with twins, and I delighted in the idea of settling into my pregnancy in the slow-paced jungles of Costa Rica and of my quiet return with my big belly. It was perfect. I would get to rest and be totally inwardly focused through my first trimester, and then, when I was feeling like myself again, I would come home, having passed the stage of worry and anxiety, confident in the progression of my pregnancy.

But life had a different plan for me. While I was in Costa Rica, I began to sense that something was wrong. I went first to the tiny rural clinic near our home, where I was lovingly reassured and sent home. *Todo esta bien, tienes que relajarte* — everything is OK, you just need to rest. I went home and rested, and I felt better for a few days. I was scared, but as the days passed without incident, I regained my confidence and continued to fantasize with my husband about our new life with our two new babies, just the four of us in our jungle home in Costa Rica. But soon my confidence turned once again to the dark cloud of anxiety and not-knowing, and I returned to the clinic more scared than ever. I was once again treated with sweetness and compassion. *Tranquila corazon, todo esta bien corazon, no llores* — don't worry, dear heart, everything is OK, don't cry. And, next, *tienes que ir directement al hospital en San Jose* — you have to go right to the hospital in San Jose.

Numb, my husband and I made our reservations on the tiny "puddle jumper" plane for that afternoon, and we were soon caught in a riptide of rapid motion from which we could not swim away. From the plane to the taxi to the emergency room, straight into the triage center of the hospital. I was given a blanket, and a young nursing assistant began to ask me questions, patient with my Spanish, with an open heart that comforted me even more than the warm blanket he offered: "We have to wait for the doctor, he is 45 minutes away, but we can take you for an ultrasound now to check on your babies." My husband followed as I was rolled in to the ultrasound room, only to find out what we already knew. The pregnancy was not viable, and I would have to have an immediate procedure to clear the pregnancy for my own health and physical wellbeing.

Everything was moving so fast, and suddenly I was speaking Spanish words I never knew I knew. No, I am not allergic to any medications; yes, I have had surgery before; yes, we have a hotel room in San Jose; no, I do not have insurance. I was filled with fear, loss, and despair and at the same time surrounded by love, understanding, acceptance, and compassion. As the nursing assistant wheeled me into surgery, he took my hand in both of his and looked directly into my eyes without a hint of awkwardness: Toda esta bien. I remember only two things before I went under: another male nurse wiping the tears off of my face and brushing my hair back, and the anesthesiologist saying, "You go to sleep now."

When I awoke, I was immediately aware of this great void in my body and in my heart. And, yet, miraculously, at the same time, my heart overflowed with an equally great sense of gratitude, love, hope, and knowledge of the innate kindness of others.

As the riptide calmed, I had both these thoughts: "This is why you are not supposed to tell anyone you are pregnant before the end of the first trimester," and, "Why not?" And thus began my reflection on these two important questions and on ahimsa.

First, why is it that we often do not want to expose our pain or even to disclose situations in which we may possibility feel pain at some point? Why shouldn't I tell people I'm pregnant? Why shouldn't I share this experience with you? The answers are in many ways obvious and, precisely because we are reluctant to share our deep personal challenges, also grounded in an everyday reality. In other words, we don't share our experience of pain because we don't want to burden others, because we don't want to show failure, because we don't want to be exposed, vulnerable. But why do we feel this way? Because we are afraid of other people's reactions and how those reactions will affect us. Maybe we don't want to be the center of attention; maybe we want to be able to decide when we want to focus on our suffering and when we want to put it away for a while; maybe we don't want to hear other people's stories, solutions, or truisms, or perhaps even their judgments; maybe we don't want people wondering about our lives and what we may or may not do next.

I know that I cycled through all of that. And, I perpetrated violence upon myself by asking myself a barrage of questions: "What did I do wrong, how did I cause this? Why aren't I younger; what is wrong with me? Why was her pregnancy successful when she is not as healthy as I am; don't I deserve this—look at all I do for others—why can't I have this?" But I didn't want to let myself stay there. Those kinds of thoughts, though they may arrive unbidden, do nothing to bring peace and only muddy the waters of presence. They have no satisfactory answers and only serve to add suffering to my pain. I cultivate the opposite of these anxious and agitating thoughts when I simply sit with my grief, sit with my feelings, sit with what is. And I give others the opportunity to do the same when I share my loneliness, fear, or despair. In many ways it is a gift I can offer, in sharing my pain, and my suffering; I give the people around me the chance to also practice sitting with grief, fear, sadness, and what is.

We know that pain is an inevitable fact of life. But the truth is that we can differentiate pain from suffering. Certain events of our lives—a miscarriage, a lost job, a heartbreak, a sleepless night—are indisputably painful. And yet we can learn to bear these challenges with grace when we are offered opportunities to just be with them—not to try to change them, not to push them away, not to fear them, but to simply accept them as a natural part of the ebb and flow of life itself. Just as joy comes and goes, so does despair. This is a lesson that we can practice again and again, until we find that our natural reaction to pain is witnessing it, accepting it, and creating a spacious container to soften its hard edges. This takes practice and determination, but it is indeed entirely possible.

Perhaps we are not very good at being with suffering precisely because we don't talk about it. Perhaps we must learn to tolerate some exposure, some poor attempts from others to console us, some awkward or frustrating moments of disconnection, to get to a real heart connection, to find that place in which we can allow others to help us bear our suffering and in which they, in turn, can get better at this task. What I saw, again, in my recent painful situation, was that when I had no choice but to be fully exposed and vulnerable, all of the people around me immediately and instinctively dove into their deepest well of pure love. In a very dark moment, I clearly felt the radiance of unobstructed, unself-conscious connection holding me up.

The impulse to love is there. The impulse to connect is there. Sometimes we are so guarded that we not only deny each other the opportunity to act on this impulse, but when faced with that moment of being a witness to another person's pain, we second-guess ourselves and allow fear of failure or disconnection to trump our natural instinct to simply be.

The truth is, I did tell many people about my pregnancy early on; my immediate family alone counts as close to 25, so I had a lot of "untelling" to do. As the most immediate sting of loss faded to an early morning heartache and heaviness, I continued to be touched by the simplicity of the responses to my news and by the number of women who had had a similar experience that I had never known about before. A few of my beloved friends said, "I don't know how you feel, but I can imagine"; to which I said, "You too have experienced loss, disappointment, trauma—you do know how I feel." It's a delicate balance we can learn to strike between usurping someone's experience with our own and knowing that in fact, suffering is suffering; and by a certain age, we all know what that is. We can connect, we can practice ahimsa—the cultivation of a gentle heart—by simply allowing ourselves to feel and be with this shared hurt. And we can get better with practice.

I'm not saying that you should just go out and tell everyone about your most private challenges. And I'm definitely not saying that if you did, everyone around you would act with courage and grace. I am suggesting that we might consider being more transparent, seeking support from others without fear of judgment and learning how we can offer a net of real support for people we care about. I do feel vulnerable through sharing my story, but if after reading it even one person feels more connected, if one person feels less alone, if one person is inspired to contemplate how to act directly from the heart, then it was worth sharing. If we can see that we perpetrate violence on ourselves and others in the simple act of insisting on our own separateness, if we understand that removing these barriers and accepting love and caring toward ourselves and from others will lead us to connection and grace, then we might be just that much more courageous in our love for ourselves and indeed for all beings everywhere.

When I finally returned from Costa Rica in April, the Seattle sun was starting to reemerge. My experience already felt like old news, and I was ready to step back into my familiar life in the Pacific Northwest. I looked different, but only because of my tan, and if I happened to have a big belly, it was from beer and guacamole. *Todo esta bien.*

I thank you God for this most amazing day, for the leaping greenly spirits of trees, and for the blue dream of sky and for everything which is natural, which is infinite, which is yes.

~ e.e.cummings

MOLLY LANNON KENNY

Be the Night Sky
Ishvara Pranidhana,
or the Yoga of Surrender

All know that the drop merges into the ocean, but few know the ocean merges into the drop. ~ Kabir

I think a lot about defining terms when I teach and when I talk about yoga and spirituality, especially when teaching or talking about terms like "God" or the idea and essence of surrender. Since one of the central tenets of the Yoga Sutras is Ishvara pranidhana — often translated as "surrender to God" — it feels important for me that I understand the use and context of these terms before I dive any further into agreement or rejection of this principle.

It seems that many people associate the word "God" with an image of an old man in the clouds who is looking down on us, ready to judge — and punish as necessary — our every move. Of course, there are other ways that people visualize or conceptualize God, but it brings up an important point for the discussion of the yogic tenet of "surrender to God." Who or what exactly, are we talking about when we are talking about "God?" For that matter, what do we mean when we use the word "surrender?" Or to go even further, what do we mean, exactly, by all of these terms we might reference in our yoga practice and studies -- love, compassion, suffering, mindfulness — but might never really examine?

This – defining terms - is a practice I am passionate about. For example, in a discussion group, some students and I were contemplating two of Patanjali's Yoga Sutras, heyam duhkham anagatam (2.16) and drastrdrsyayoh samyogah heyahetuh (2.17), which, in our *translation and commentary by Swami Satchidananda,* suggests that all pain is avoidable and that the cause of pain is the association or identification of the seer (atman, or soul) with the seen (prakriti, or material plane).

When I asked the students to give me their first impressions of these sutras, one of the overarching sentiments was that pain was a necessary part of growth and that it was, in a sense, something very precious to us. There was even a certain defensiveness of that idea and a resistance to what these sutras might suggest about our experience with pain or how to manage it.

I asked the students, before we went further in our discussion, to ask a pivotal question—what are we talking about, and what might the sutras and commentaries be talking about when they use the word "pain," or even "seer" or "seen," and furthermore, how would our definitions of these words influence our thoughts and conversations about them? In fact, pain is a necessary part of growth, and certainly an unavoidable part of life, but perhaps here what we are talking about is the difference between "pain" and how we react to that, and what we might call "suffering." A simple example I like to use is to think about something like insomnia. When we can't sleep, that's the pain. That's the unavoidable part. But when we toss and turn, and look incessantly at the clock and tell ourselves all kinds of stories about how the next day will be horrible because we couldn't sleep, that's the suffering. And that, thank God, is avoidable. God. Whoever, or whatever, that is. But I'm getting ahead of myself.

When I consider words and meanings in our practice and study, I believe we have to know exactly what we mean and how we are using the words to talk about whatever we are talking about, and we have to make sure that whomever we are talking with understands the same idea, the same definition. Otherwise, we end up arguing about words when we mean to be talking about concepts. This can be especially important in yoga philosophy, where texts are translated and commentaries are written on those texts that may vary widely in their interpretations. It matters less if one is more "correct" than another than to make sure that we are all talking about the same thing.

Especially, then, in discussing this idea that we might "surrender to God," I come back to the question of specifically who or what God is, and what exactly is being asked of me when I am offered the opportunity to surrender? When I think of the word "surrender" in general, I think of giving in, letting go, of relinquishing control. In the context of this topic as related to our spiritual life, I think of surrender also as a sense of releasing our often too tight hold on our various beliefs. Surrender, to me in this context, is a sense of faith, trust, and especially, choice.

In the yogic view, God is generally considered to be an amorphous, indescribable, all-pervasive force whose presence is the source of, and backdrop for, all creation and all manifestation. There is an important universal prayer that is often used in the Ramakrishna order that says this of our relationship with God:

Oh Lord, in my meditation I have attributed forms to Thee who are formless. O Thou Teacher of the world, by my hymns I have, as it were, contradicted that Thou are indescribable. By going on pilgrimage I have, as it were, denied Thy omnipresence. O Lord of the Universe, pray forgive me these three faults committed by me.

This prayer reminds us that out of necessity we often use symbols and forms to describe and conceive of a God who is in reality formless. This makes sense to me — how else can students, at least in the beginning, really feel a profound sense of connection to, and solace in, something they cannot even imagine?

One of my favorite teachers, Swami Vivekananda, suggests that there are at least two ways for us to conceive of and worship God in form as an intermediary step toward connection to formlessness: one is to see God in all other beings and show love and devotion to them as such and the other is to think of the most vast conception of nature we can bring to mind and use that as an analogy to the hugeness of God.

In my own practice and teachings, and in my observation, I have discovered that although it is hard for many of us, or at least consistently, to really see God in our fellow humans, with all of their messy complexity, most of us can quite easily feel the presence of the Divine in something truly awe-inspiring, like an endless mountain range, a night sky filled with constellations, or an ocean that seems to go on forever. These things fill us with a sense of wonder and a sense of our own tininess in comparison. And when we have these opportunities to see ourselves and our "issues" and insecurities, both big and small, that can take hold of and overwhelm us as truly insignificant in the vastness of this transcendent beauty, these very issues become smaller and more manageable, or perhaps, we may find, not really important at all. One way I think of this is by imagining my anger or frustration as a spoonful of poison. If I sip that poison as it is, I will become sick or even die. But if I were to dilute that spoonful of poison into an enormous, pristine glacial lake, then scoop out a handful to drink, the poison would have no effect.

In my years of teaching and talking to students about this notion, I have never found anyone, even people with very limited exposure to nature, who did not find that being in nature or conceiving of nature helped them to have an experience of essential "OK-ness," which is also a way to describe the fruits of our yoga practice.

In the West, we have a rich literary tradition of connecting God with nature. In the early 1800s, Ralph Waldo Emerson anonymously published an essay called "Nature," a seminal work for the emergence of American Transcendentalism, which was heavily influenced by Vedanta and Vedic literature — the common roots of our practice of yoga. Henry David Thoreau's experiences in "Walden" reflect this faith in nature as a reflection of Godliness itself, and he sought to express the deep sense of contentment and peace he found when surrendering himself to God as nature, or we might say more correctly, Nature as God.

This is one way for us to begin to understand the precept of Ishvara pranidhana, as "surrender to God," in a way that might truly make a difference in our everyday lives and provide us with a feeling of groundedness and infinite spaciousness at the same time. As we dive into the concept of surrender to God, we might give ourselves permission to begin with an image of God as whatever allows us to experience ourselves as divinely connected and divinely protected. Again thinking of the image of the vastness of a starry night sky, we might recall how tiny we really are, how tiny our pain, our arguments, our complaints, our grudges, our fears, when we compare them to, or better yet, drop them into, something that feels infinite and beautiful and perhaps even miraculous.

Remembering the task of defining what we are talking about, especially when we are considering ideas and beliefs that have been passed down orally for thousands of years, with myriad opportunities for interpretation and confusion, recall Patanjali's definition of yoga itself, yogash chitta vritti nirodhah, as well as its purpose, tada drashtuh svarupe avasthanam: Yoga is the stilling of the fluctuations of the mind. Then we rest in our own true nature.

I believe this — the quieting of the mind and the subsequent feeling of deep peace — is what we encounter when we immerse ourselves in the enormity of nature itself, and it is what Emerson, Thoreau, and others tried to illuminate in describing Nature as God. I believe that the very experience of taking in the profundity of the natural world causes our minds to spontaneously become still and awe-inspired in its true sense. We pause for a moment and surrender completely to this experience. In this state, we instantly connect with a sense of the Divine, of God, both within and without. It is in this place of surrender that we come to peace: Ishvara pranidhana.

As you move through this book, and in your own personal practice, consider using an image of nature's vastness in your meditations. Explore what it feels like to surrender yourself within that form, or we might even say formlessness — to perhaps experience giving in, letting go, and relinquishing control to something so much bigger than your everyday experience of yourself.

Consider the idea of surrender as a sense of releasing, a sense of faith and trust. Notice what it feels like to give yourself -- and especially your fears and worries -- over, by choice, to something much larger and more profound than the "you" with which you have become accustomed to identifying.

Take a moment to close your eyes and imagine the night sky in front of you. Take in its expanse, its sense of timelessness and infinite space. Now imagine that you are no longer looking at it, but are part of it. You are one of the stars, you are part of the cosmos — divinely connected, divinely protected. Find rest there. Ishvara pranidhana.

We are all in this together.

Ah, not to be cut off,
not through the slightest partition
shut out from the law of the stars.
The inner -- what is it?
if not the intensified sky,
hurled through with birds and deep
with the winds of homecoming.
~ Rainier Maria Rilke

Yoga and Change: The Power of Partnership

If you have come to help me, you are wasting your time. But if you have come because your liberation is bound up with mine, then let us work together. ~ Aboriginal Activists Group, Queensland

By July of 2000, I was done with my job as a clinician. Having worked for over six years as a speech-language pathologist at one of the country's largest HMOs, I felt burned out, turned off, and depleted. It wasn't that I didn't like the work — I did. In fact, I loved the opportunity to come into people's lives and help them with whatever life challenges brought them to my office. What I had difficulty with was the deficit model I felt was propagated by the conventional medical model I was a part of. It seemed to me that the overwhelming culture was one of hierarchy, "un"wellness, blame, and pity, mixed quite often with a healthy dose of irritation with the client. Of course, I know that this wasn't everyone, or not all the time, but in general, my experience with the clinical setting was one of high pressure, low return, and an unhealthy obsession with "outcome-driven" therapy. Now, I still am a clinician and, by training, also an empiricist. I know that we must have measurable goals and objectives in our work with others, especially if we are calling it therapy. I emphasize this strongly in my training of other clinicians and yogis. But I also know that when we focus only on the outcome, we miss important opportunities to celebrate process. It seems to me that this is a little like yoga itself. If we are only interested in getting into that handstand, having that ultimate experience of samadhi in meditation, or reaching enlightenment, we clearly miss some of the most sacred and valuable moments in our own evolution.

I will never forget one situation in my clinical practice in which I was seeing an older woman who was experiencing significant memory loss. We worked together for six months, and I provided her with strategies and practices for recalling names, tasks, and events. Every week we would meet and practice what we had learned and discovered together. We would talk about her grandchildren, her love of gardening and Bonsai, and her relationship with her spouse. We would use all of these conversations to practice the strategies we had settled on as aids to her cognition. She never missed a session, and she reported that the strategies seemed to help her — if not always in actually recalling the information that seemed lost in the packed files of her brain, then in her ability to manage her feelings regarding her memory loss.

One day, my supervisor called me into her office to review my caseload. When we got to this woman, my supervisor frowned. We had not, according to her, been making enough progress to justify continuing therapy. I described the changes I had seen and that the client had reported, and I told my boss how important the sessions were to my client. I was able to provide anecdotal and qualitative evidence of change, but in terms of quantifiable progress, we came up short. My supervisor advised me to discharge my client.

The next week when I saw this client, I told her the news. She began to cry; expressing the same sense of change she had seen in her relationship to herself, her memory loss, her family relationships, and above all, how our sessions were "the highlight of her week." As I sat with this older woman, with whom I had developed a caring and supportive relationship, and watched her weep, something inside of me shifted. My hands were tied. I had to discharge her — we were not meeting enough goals to warrant therapy in the eyes of the HMO. But I also decided then and there that there was something irreversibly broken in the system, and that I could no longer be a part of it. Our work together did matter. Our partnership had made a difference, and I truly believed that my "liberation was bound up with hers." As her suffering was alleviated, my sense of trust, wonder, and acceptance was strengthened. I did not feel like I was so much helping her as simply being with her, setting up the conditions for change, and providing feedback and encouragement on her path.

I left my clinical position shortly after that to develop my own method of yoga-based therapy, a framework that I call Integrated Movement Therapy, which I have now been practicing and teaching for over ten years. In my trainings, many of the students want to know, "What is the right pose for this condition?" or "What is the right breathing exercise for that?" We talk about those questions, and we seek their answers, but more than anything, what I tell my trainees is, "The yoga in this therapy is the yoga that is in YOU." It is in the way we look at people, the way we treat them, the way we find our own liberation to be bound up with theirs, rather than the typical hierarchical model of the smart doctor/therapist/teacher/parent who tells the client/student/ child what to do, who is frustrated when they don't do it, who blames them for their challenges, or who believes that whatever changes the client/student makes is a result of the teacher's or therapist's own brilliance. To me, this seems antithetical to the practice and teachings of yoga.

In my work and in my personal practice, I often think of this quote from the *Bhagavad Gita* (6.29): "The man equipped with yoga looks on all with an impartial eye, seeing Atman in all beings and all beings in Atman." In one of my favorite translations of the Bhagavad Gita[1], Mahatma Gandhi acknowledges how difficult it is for us to really see others with an impartial eye. Gandhi says, "The yogi is not one who sits down to practice breathing exercises. He is one who looks upon all with an equal eye, sees all creatures in himself. Such a one obtains moksha... It is not easy to see all creatures in ourselves...we must see them in ourselves by seeing them and oneself in God."

To me, the major difference here is in the internal shift we can make, using our own yoga practice, in looking at others and our role in relationship to them and positive changes they might make in their lives. If we can truly train ourselves to see Atman in all beings, we might naturally find ourselves in partnership with others, more inclined as therapists and teachers to follow our own dharma of setting up conditions for positive change, and less feeling the separation that comes with the belief that we are the "doers," that we are making the changes, or that we (or our clients) are to blame when the changes don't come fast enough, or are not the changes we had hoped for.

I still believe we must have goals and objectives, but we also must be open to the incredible healing that happens when we offer what humanistic psychologist Carl Rogers has so famously called "unconditional positive regard" to the people we work with. They, like us, are at once, only human and manifestations of the divine. As contemporary psychologist David G. Myers states, "This is an attitude of grace, an attitude that values us even knowing our failings. It is a profound relief to drop our pretenses, confess our worst feelings, and discover that we are still accepted."[2]

Sometimes I feel, even with all of my clinical background and my empirically inclined mind, that what I am really offering people is that experience of total love and acceptance — and that, in fact, is the very thing that heals them. I smile at the thought of calling up one of the many volunteer outreach programs where I teach yoga and offering an "experience of total love and acceptance," just because I know it is needed. I don't think I would get in anywhere, so instead I offer yoga. In some cases, to me, it is the same thing.

In fact, the other day, I was teaching a group of veterans at the Seattle VA's outpatient mental health clinic. At the end of class, I put my hands together, bowed my head and said, "Namaste." One of the vets said, "What was that about? What did you say?" I told him that namaste could be thought of as a catch-all term, kind of like aloha or shalom. He looked at me blankly. "Why did you bow?" he asked. I told him that sometimes people translate it to mean something like "the divine in me bows to the divine in you," so I bowed my head. He looked at me even more blankly, and with a hint of suspicion. I tried again, "It kind of just means, I see you, I really see you." At that, he brightened up, smiled and said, "Oh. Oh. OH! Yeah. Yeah! Well, thank you, I see you too."

References

1. Strohmeier J, Gandhi M, eds. The Bhagavad Gita According to Gandhi. Berkeley, CA: Berkeley Hill Books; 2000:97.

2. Myers D., Psychology: Eighth Edition in Modules, New York, NY: Worth Publishers, 2007. http://en.wikipedia.org/wiki/Unconditional_ positive_regard. Accessed August 1, 2011.

This article first appeared in the 2011 (No. 21) edition of The International Journal of Yoga Therapy and has been slightly modified. Reprinted with permission from the International Association of Yoga Therapists.

There's courage involved if you want to become truth. There is a broken - open place in a lover. Where are those qualities of bravery and sharp compassion in this group?

What's the use of old and frozen thought? I want a howling hurt. This is not a treasury where gold is stored; this is for copper.

We alchemists look for talent that can heat up and change. Lukewarm won't do.

Half-hearted holding back, well-enough getting by? Not here.

~ Rumi

The Still Point of Soul:
One Way of Thinking About Yoga
The Yoga Sutras of Patanjali

In thinking of what might exist beyond our experiences of each other and ourselves in a merely human way, I have reflected on several experiences I have had with other people that I believe have been windows into the spacious idea of Soul, or our divine connection to Source.

In this, I often think specifically about people who, through facing some huge hurdle, have expressed a new experience of themselves that tore down all of their ideas about who they were and what they believed was important to them. An example of this was told to me by one of my beloved yoga students, now a yoga teacher. He described his experience following a massive stroke in this way: "I found meaning in life after being so close to death. I found that the terror in death was lessened. It was giving up, surrendering over and over again to the higher power that made me humble and content. It's like the stroke was a new birthday. I am more comfortable and content than I was before the stroke."

So, what is this contentment, this ease and humility that this person found through his experience? What is the nature of his discovery that is somehow different from his prior experience of himself? One way we can look at this, through the lens of yoga, is by looking at the first three of Patanjali's Yoga Sutras.

The Yoga Sutras of Patanjali, the classical text of Raja Yoga–or the "yoga of practice" — is organized into four separate chapters, for a total of 196 short verses (sutra means "thread"), which describe and define a path to Self-realization. The Yoga Sutras can get pretty cerebral and esoteric at times, and sometimes the text seems more confusing than enlightening. But if we break it down little by little and, above all, understand the first three verses and link all subsequent verses back to those, we find that there is great wisdom and opportunity for exploration and contemplation, and perhaps for our own experience of stillness, or soul.

In diving into The Yoga Sutras, the first thing one should consider is the variation in translations and interpretations and the difficulty in finding the one, single, accurate translation. There are at least two reasons for this. The first is that our language does not always have the perfect or exact word or phrase that conveys the precise meaning or connotation of the Sanskrit word. Because of temporal distance between the use of Sanskrit and contemporary English, along with vast differences in culture and means of expression, it is often the case that there is not a single direct translation between a Sanskrit word and an English word. The second confounding factor is that many Sanskrit words have various meanings, some of them even seemingly pairs of opposites. The most correct meanings, then, are discerned from context within structurally complete prose or verse. The Yoga Sutras, as a text, is a composite of short aphorisms, often without the greater context needed to choose one singular, correct translation of a word. This can lead to great variability in translations and commentaries, all of them being in a sense correct, or, at least, faithful to the text itself.

Keeping this challenge in mind, let's explore those first three most-important verses and consider where we stand in our understanding and belief in their assertions, especially in relation to this idea of deep contentment through connection to something more than our self-imposed identities.

The very first sutra, or verse, *Atha yoga anushasam*, tells us something like, "Now we begin the exposition on yoga." While this may seem like a straightforward introductory sentence, I have often pondered the use of the word, "atha" or "now" in this sutra. In its placement as the first word in the text, it seems to have a special kind of power, and it has helped me immeasurably in relationships of all kinds, from situations with family, to my work in therapy as a client and as a therapist, to the various friends and intimate relationships I have had over the years.

When I think of this "now," this "atha" in Sanskrit, I think of it as a "now" that is auspicious and perfect. Now is the time to study yoga. Not "now" because it's time for your 6:00 pm gentle class, but now because everything has fallen into place for just this very moment. This is the time to study, this is the time to seek the teacher, and this is the time to ask those perfect, timely questions. This is the time to have this relationship, but not the time to have another. I think about how situations and interactions are not so much right or wrong in and of themselves, but that perhaps the timing was slightly off — or divinely on! This client left because it was not the right now. This therapist worked for me because it was the perfect now. This interpretation of atha inspires me to avoid the pendulum swing of taking credit for and feeling great about everything that seems to work for me while taking too much responsibility and feeling so terrible about things that don't seem to work as well; the egocentric viewpoint that somehow everything is about me, about my failures and my successes. That way of being in the world tends to move us further from a sense of stillness, the place that invites us to experience ourselves as greater than the sum of our ever-changing parts. But I can live and act from a place of ease and contentment when I offer myself the possibility that perhaps some external event, whether categorized as good or bad, was, in fact, just the quality of the now.

In my life and practice, I am continually redefining and refining my experience of now. In my own study of yoga, I often find myself in a cycle of questions and answers; the questions usually coming from the inherent challenges of life and the answers often coming from, or at least directly related to, yoga philosophy as I understand or interpret it. In a way, I am constantly starting afresh with my investigations, and each time around, my sense of faith in the teachings and in the practice is strengthened.

The second sutra, perhaps the most well known of all the sutras, goes on to answer the natural question that follows the first sutra: Now is the time to study yoga — what is yoga? The elegant and profound answer is *yogaś citta vṛtti nirodhaḥ*, which translates to something like, "Yoga is the stilling or restraint of the modifications of the mind stuff." I like to think of this sutra as referring to the settling of the various agitations of the mind, all of which deepen our sense of ego-identification when we get caught up in them. Stated another way, our minds are constantly in a state of movement and flux — happy thoughts, mundane thoughts, sad thoughts, anxious thoughts, those dark thoughts that we each have that continue to disturb our minds and hearts — and all of those thoughts create waves, ripples, and agitation that can keep us from seeing the grandness, the sweetness, the mystery of all that we are. I love the image of the ocean here, where we know what it's like to see the beautiful white sandy bottom through clear blue waters, and we know what it's like to see just murkiness when there is too much going on at the surface. Sometimes, if we are really getting tossed around, we forget that there even is a bottom of the ocean, and we might panic, feeling like there is only agitation and no solid ground, no still point. The second sutra tells us that yoga itself is the practice of settling all this thought, all of this "mind stuff" without having to suppress or express it. In other words, yoga is taking control of and modifying the conditioned patterns of the mind.

And what will happen if we do that?

Let me illustrate one possibility with an example of a person who I believe was experiencing her connection to her whole self, a moment which occurred when I was volunteering in our Samarya Center's end of life care, or Bedside Yoga, program. I remember walking into the woman's room to offer her this Bedside Yoga. She waved me in with a joyous smile and said,

"The doctor says I have only a few months to live, so I don't think I can do yoga right now, but come in, sit down, visit with me." Her spirit was bright; she laughed a lot and gave me tips on getting pregnant (I don't usually invite these!), and she talked about the beauty of her life, her friends, and her family. I asked her about dying, about leaving all of that which she so loved. Her face became clear and soft. She told me that while she was terribly sad to leave her life, she also knew that it was a part of the reality of being human, of living in a human body, and that she had accepted death and was not afraid; that she believed she would return to some state of being that was untouched by the ups and downs of our human experience. In those final days and weeks of her life, she embodied a spirit of contentment, ease, and light.

The third sutra describes this very experience: *tadā draṣṭuḥ svarupe 'vasthāna*, "Then the self abides in the Self," or "Then we realize our true nature." Our true nature, in yoga, is something like our Soul, or in Sanskrit, purusha. It is consciousness itself, that everlasting, perfect, divine part of ourselves that is not caught up in all of the external trappings and identities with which we become confused and that ultimately lead to more and more suffering. Our true nature is that of purusha, soul, or atman, another term for the authentic Self. Although the exact definition or use of these terms varies significantly in different translations, all of them describe in one way or another a transcendent state of lasting consciousness that is clothed or covered in a sheath of material nature—the bodies and lives we inhabit. Within this life, this material plane, we are given opportunities and challenges that invite us to question who we are, and who we might personally evolve into, with this unchanging, ever-perfect "soul" always residing at our center. The practice of yoga, say the Sutras, will allow us to steady and direct the mind, thereby allowing us to see a larger perspective. I like to think of this perspective as one in which we know our lives to be meaningful and ourselves to be connected—to other living things, to ourselves, to God-consciousness. It is a process of Self-actualization through living in the world and learning its lessons, ultimately for the greater good of all beings.

This is all so beautiful and poetic, and it sounds totally reasonable to me that if we were to be at the right point in our lives, with the right attitude and the right teacher, we might be able to still some of the thoughts that make us crazy and make our lives ever more difficult. And that if we did this, we might find a new and different sense of ourselves that was more at peace, more oriented toward contentment, compassion, forgiveness, and joy. But sometimes, when life seems too hard; when the teachings seem too "out there"; when I am the most irritated, sad, or confused; or when I see or experience someone or something I don't like, it seems impossible to steady the mind, to separate my small self from my larger Self, or even to believe that what seems so much like, well, "me," is actually just an illusion. Sometimes it feels like there's nothing else besides the me that I know, the me that is suffering and struggling. Sometimes, I just don't know what my true nature really is.

And then something reminds me, inspires me, and ignites in me the desire to practice, to become all of who I am, all of what and who I want to be, and all that I believe is possible. Is it my true nature? I don't know; but I do know that when this comes alive for me, and I experience myself dropping more deeply and easily into another part of myself, it is always the part of me that is, in fact, more at peace, more oriented toward contentment, compassion, forgiveness, and joy.

A few years ago, while teaching on our yoga teacher training, I was introduced to a new student who had traveled across the country to join us. Although it was not the very first thing I noticed about her, it was certainly obvious that something had happened to her that had impacted her body tremendously: she had one amputated arm and a clear imbalance in her gait. When I asked her about the accident that took her hand and changed her life, she didn't miss a beat in saying, "I can think of a hundred reasons why this might have happened to me, how it influenced my life, and what I have learned about myself and others." To me, this too is a reflection of Soul. This feels to me like a reflection of what we all have inside of us that for some people might be uncovered through trauma, others through aging (my 78-year-old aunt told me the other day, "We all get nicer as we get older"), others through being at the end of life, others through grace, and for others through practice, or, of course, any combination of those things.

All of these reminders that come from people and their experiences show me living reflections of what I think Patanjali means when he talks about Self, or soul. The practice of yoga is not the only way in which this experience of soul might happen. In my view, this is actually an experience of connection, an experience of transcendence, an experience of moving beyond what feels constrained and narrowly defined into something that feels spacious and wondrous. This experience of yoga — of connection — is not about "doing" yoga, it is about a particular orientation toward ourselves and our lives, and it can happen for any of us in many ways.

When I think of the three people I've described here, I know that they are still ordinary people, inhabiting their bodies and this world. But it feels to me that they have come closer to the still point; closer to freedom from the grip of ego, from the tenacious hold of some prison of identity. Ram Dass says, "Suffering brings us so close to God." I believe by this he means freedom from the self-centered viewpoint that so often keeps us in a place of fear — confined by our beliefs of what is right and wrong and how things should and shouldn't be. These people, these examples, for me, are reminders of now. We can learn these lessons of freedom through all kinds of means, and we can learn them simply through practice and dedication to yoga. We can learn to connect with that unchanging awareness now. We can manage our ego identification. We can reach that still point. Now. Now is the time to truly live our yoga. Then the self abides in the Self. And we are, finally, in harmony with that still point.

In the final analysis, the questions of why bad things happen to good people transmutes itself into some very different questions, no longer asking why something happened, but asking how we will respond, what we intend to do now that it happened.
~ Pierre Teilhard de Chardin

The Paths of Yoga ~
The Fall Line,
or "This is Why We Practice"

In Pandit Rajmani Tigunait's book *Touched by Fire: The Ongoing Journey of a Spiritual Seeker* he says: "It doesn't matter how we start our quest, what really matters is that we start, and through sustained study, self-realization, and methodical practice, we continue refining our understanding of the meaning and purpose of life."

My beloved Ram Dass says, "The spiritual journey is individual, highly personal. It can't be organized or regulated. It isn't true that everyone should follow one path. Listen to your own truth."

This, the idea that quest is truly individual, is one of the things I love most about yoga. It is one of the indicators to me that yoga is not a religion with just one way to achieve the goal, but a spiritual discipline with many different paths and practices. Because it is so varied in its approach, the practice of yoga offers a range of methods so that most anybody might find something that works as a guide and compass for life, for finding peace and contentment amid the inevitable challenges of simply being. It is quite lovely that we can find that sense of peace through many different avenues.

Yoga is often said to be both the means and the end. In other words, we practice the path of yoga to get to the state of yoga. Although practitioners usually think of the goal of yoga as something like "union with the Divine" or "union of body, mind, and spirit," I have also heard many other descriptions of the goals that add another level of subtlety or consideration. We might add to or refine the goals by also thinking of removing ignorance—the lack of awareness of ourselves as manifestations of the Divine—and as a result awakening to our real Self, which allows for the elimination of suffering and entrance into the highest states of consciousness.

We practice being in these states in order to dwell in them. We achieve self-realization through practicing self-realization. We rest in our own true nature by practicing resting there. We have an experience of shelter by practicing being sheltered. And, we attain the state of yoga, or union, through the paths of action, devotion, knowledge, and discipline. These can be considered to be the four main paths of yoga, and they are described in various texts, perhaps most importantly in the Bhagavad Gita.

Simply stated, the four paths are bhakti, or the yoga of devotion; karma, or the yoga of action; jnana, or the yoga of knowledge; and raja, or the yoga of practice. It is said in the Vedic literature that through any of these means, any of these paths, the payoff, or the "summit," will be the same: the attainment of yoga.

Bhakti Yoga is the yoga of devotion. In this path, the primary focus is on an outpouring of love and adoration for God through such practices as singing, worship, meditation, prayer, and ritual. Most of us have some familiarity with groups like the Hare Krishnas, who are bhaktas, and who are known to many through their joyous chanting of Krishna's name. We can also think of kirtan singers such as Jai Uttal or Krishna Das as bhaktas — people who commit their lives to devotion to and communion with the Divine through song and prayer. This path is described in the Gita as the most highly favored.

"And of all yogins, he who full of faith worships Me, with his inner self abiding in Me, him, I hold to be the most attuned (to me in Yoga)" - Bhagavad Gita 6.47

"Whoever offers Me with devotion a leaf, a flower, a fruit or a little water - that, so offered devotedly by the pure-minded, I accept" - Bhagavad Gita 9.26

Karma Yoga is the yoga of action, or service. It is through this path that one focuses on selfless service as a means of serving God, and by serving, knowing God. It is this as a primary practice, such as we might see in the lives of Mahatma

Gandhi, Mother Teresa, or Mata Amritanandamayi, (Amma), that the karma yogi finds fulfillment and contentment and begins to dissolve ego, for karma yoga is only karma yoga when we are not attached to the fruits of our efforts. We serve because we love to serve, because we see God in all beings, and we jump at the chance to serve and connect with God through serving and connecting with other living beings.

"Fixed in yoga, do thy work, O Winner of wealth (Arjuna), abandoning attachment, with an even mind in success and failure, for evenness of mind is called yoga." - Bhagavad Gita 2.47-8

Jnana Yoga is the yoga of knowledge. This is the yoga of nondual thought, or the exploration of who we are and what we are experiencing, from a standpoint of pursuit of absolute truth. It is the intention to see and understand oneself as pure consciousness, not separate from God, or any other thing, that inspires the jnana yogi. This knowledge is derived both from scripture and dedicated self-inquiry.

There is a famous story about a 20th century yoga master called Ramana Maharshi that is said to exemplify the path of the jnana yogi. Ramana Maharshi was born in 1879 in South India into a devout household. While Ramana Maharshi (then called Venkateswaram) was deeply interested in the deities and saints commonly referenced in his home and religious life, he was by all accounts, a typical young and early teenage boy. It is said that at the age of sixteen, he had an experience wherein he felt an overwhelming and inexplicable fear of imminent death. According to his history, in that moment, he did not panic, but instead laid down in his room with his body completely stiff and held his breath for as long as he could, asking himself over and over, "What am I if I am not this body?" It is believed that in this process, Ramana Maharshi gained full self-realization, or enlightenment, and lived out the rest of his life as a renunciate, inspiring thousands of people with his presence.

Our own self-realization is the greatest service we can render the world. ~ Ramana Maharshi

The Bhagavad Gita also references jnana yoga as a valid and important path.

"Those who see with eyes of knowledge the difference between the body and the knower of the body, and can also understand the process of liberation from bondage in material nature, attain to the supreme goal." (13.35)

"When a man puts away all the desires of his mind, O Partha [Arjuna], and when his spirit is content in itself, then is he called stable in intelligence" - Bhagavad Gita 2.55

Finally, we have Raja Yoga, the yoga of practice. This is the yoga we are more familiar with in the West, the yoga of Patanjali's Yoga Sutras, in which we reach the state of yoga through systematic techniques, including asana (poses), pranayama (breath practices), and dhyana (meditation). Our culture is very well suited to this path — it is laid out for us, step-wise and methodical. When I think about my own entrée into yoga practice, it was through Pattabhi Jois's Ashtanga Yoga, famously physical and systematic, and I often heard people quoting him: "Do your practice, all is coming." In other words, the dedication to practice itself will yield the fruits of the practice: the attainment of the state of yoga. The Gita references this path in the verse, "For him who has conquered the mind, the mind is the best of friends; but for one who has failed to do so, his mind will remain the greatest enemy" - Bhagavad Gita 6.6

In many ways, I have found the adage. "Do your practice, all is coming," to be true. Through my own Ashtanga yoga practice and without any specific training toward what might be considered the fruits of my practice, I did find myself changing. Others noticed the changes in me and encouraged me on my path, they too benefiting from my efforts as I became more self-assured, less reactive, and more forgiving. As I felt and saw these changes in myself, I knew I wanted more. I also knew that this yoga journey would become my spiritual compass for the rest of my life. However, over time I began to become more of a student of the place yoga had led me to, a feeling of divine presence, a place experienced, more so than intellectualized, rather than a student solely of the specific teachings of yoga itself.

This is, for me, where it has become really interesting and sometimes confusing. As I fell in love with yoga and, over time, saw how it transformed not only my life but the lives of thousands of others that I have had the honor of teaching and connecting with through the practice of yoga, I have become completely convinced of its almost magical powers to change lives and reduce suffering.

In my own personal journey, I have never had a consistent teacher, a guru, or a dedicated place and time to study scripture, text, and history with a loving and knowledgeable guide. I have never had just one particular path that I can point to as being the path that led me to my experience of yoga. I have only had my determination, my community, and myself. When I reflect on my journey and the journey of The Samarya Center for Humankind (ness), - the yoga school I founded in 2001 - it feels like we have followed all of the paths of yoga in some way or another, through devotion, service, self-inquiry, and practice. I have felt and seen myself and countless students heal and radically change for the better, with more ease and less suffering in their lives as a result of being a part of our yoga community. Yet, for me, the question persists: What is our path? What is my path? Is it one of these four paths, all of these, none of these?

Here is what I know. When things get really hard, we can rely on our practice. We can seek the fall line, the path of natural descent to ground, to what is stable and unchanging and safe in the face of challenge and confusion. We do that through practice, through devotion, through service, through community, through meditation, through love and dedication.

Through practice, we find that state where there is stability and transcendence, the state where we can say, "I am not confusion, I am not chaos, I am neither my shortcomings nor my accomplishments. I am awareness itself, I am love and pure consciousness." Is that state only the result of our practice, our study, of yoga? And if it is, and I'm certain our practice contributed, even if it doesn't count for it exclusively, how exactly did we arrive there? Which path? And could we get there without a scholarly knowledge of yoga? I don't know the answer in words, but I experience it. I feel the experience of yoga. I feel the awakening to my real Self, the elimination of suffering, and sometimes even entrance into the highest states of consciousness.

I love yoga. I love all of its paths. And I will always study yoga, and learn all I can, as long as it will help me help myself and others to be more steady, more connected, and more clear. But I don't think I have to study the texts just to experience it. We are already here. We are benefiting from our practice now, whatever that is. So what is our path? What is our fall line — our path of natural descent to our own grounding? Where is that place for each of us where we move from the place of more resistance to less?

I think that answer can only be individual, personal. We feel the fruits of our practice, we rely on our practice, we know we are descending safely to that still point within us that brings us freedom and ease. And yet, our paths may be different from one another, and they may even be different within ourselves at different times in our lives. For now, my personal mantra is the very first yoga advice I ever learned, "Do your practice, all is coming." We are indeed, all in this together.

Purnam ~ Wholeness, or an Exploration of Philandering and High School Angst

May I have your attention please?
May I have your attention please?
Will the real Slim Shady please stand up?
I repeat, will the real Slim Shady please stand up?
We're gonna have a problem here.
~Eminem – The Real Slim Shady 2000, Interscope records

I remember being in high school and trying desperately to fit in. It always seemed like I wasn't quite enough of any one thing to really be a part of a particular group or clique. I was a really good student, but not the best. I was always exercising and running, but I wasn't really athletic. I loved drama and being in plays and shows, but that was "uncool," so I quit. I loved partying in New York City with my friends, but I had an earlier curfew, and I never really liked staying out until the sun came up, like they did. I was kind of into the Grateful Dead, but didn't cut it as a Deadhead; I liked the Minutemen, but wasn't punk enough to be punk; I loved the Talking Heads but wasn't artsy enough to be swept up with the art kids. My family had money, but we weren't the mega-rich kids who had their own BMWs at 16. I was Catholic, but didn't go to Catholic school. I even remember wishing I was black, Italian, or Jewish, as so many of the people in our suburb were, because it seemed like each of those cultures had their own language, their own words, their own customs. If I was any one of those, I thought, I would fit in just by virtue of being a part of that culture. They would have to accept me. But I wasn't. I wasn't even a WASP, as we used to say, in my eyes at least then a culture based only on being rich, white, and a member of Bradford Bath and Tennis Club. But that pesky "P" for Protestant excluded me even from that. Come to think of it, the only real qualification I had for that moniker was the "w" for white.

What I remember most from high school was the feeling of being uncomfortable in my own skin and exhausted by trying to inhabit the skin of someone else. Someone real. Someone who belonged. Someone who had all the correct markers to be a bona fide part of the group. As I would later see, this tendency would make itself evident any time I stretched outside of my comfort zone. This desire for inclusion would continue to play out throughout my lifetime, and clearly throughout my process of diving into yoga. Just as in the early years of my yoga exploration when I so desperately wanted to be legitimized, in high school I was ruled by my desire to fit in. I wanted to be part of a group. Little matter, really, what group that actually was. I remember this too: my very best friend, Gina, never seemed to even try to fit in. She hung out with her older brother, listened to punk rock music, was a pretty good student and captain of the JV lacrosse team. But she was definitely not "cool" as we would have defined it then. She wasn't preppy, or particularly punky. She never tried to go to the cool kids' parties, and when she went to NYC to hang out, it was to watch bands, shop at the best vintage stores, and hang out with her brother's friends, not to go to the Mudd Club to try to get people to buy her drinks. I don't think Gina ever, as I did at 15 and 16 years old, pushed her "pretty" friend to the front of the line at a club to skulk in behind her, hopefully unnoticed in her plainness, as I did. And as it turns out, Gina was, and still is, the coolest of them all.

I remember being nine years old and standing in front of the mirror with Gina. She looked at both of us and said, "You know, you can just look at your face and say, 'Yeah, I have a big nose' (she thought hers was), 'so what?' That way, no one can ever make fun of you, because you already know what you are. It's not an insult, it's just a fact. It's just a part of you." I still remember that so clearly because (1) I couldn't believe anyone could ever say anything the least bit critical about me that I wouldn't take as an insult, especially when it came to external beauty, and (2) I couldn't believe that another person could just accept a part of themselves that other people might not like. In retrospect, it seems that our "job," as we saw it as teenagers (with the exception of Gina and others like her) was to hide anything about us that might show a weakness and to do anything and everything within our power to be accepted by others. Self-reflection, self-acceptance, and tending to the things that would actually bring me peace never occurred to me. Not at nine, not at fifteen, and not even in my twenties. You were just "in" or "out," "good" or "bad," "pretty" or "plain." And of course, these judgments were always made about the outside appearance. How you felt inside couldn't possibly matter, because no one could see that anyway. So I spent many years struggling, suffering, and feeling divided and excluded, while Gina, it seemed, was just herself and, although I couldn't imagine how, apparently content.

Gina and Molly

I've been thinking a lot about this idea of who we really are and what makes us both "good," whatever that means, and content. I've thought about this a lot over the years, but the inner dialogue was once again ignited in me because of a situation I encountered in Costa Rica.

Before settling in the little Tico town where we had made built a home, my husband Sasha and I decided to take a quick trip to visit some old friends who had bought property south of San José. We have been here many times and have gotten to know some of the other ex-pats in our friends' circle. One of those in particular had become sort of a friend in his own right, and Sasha and I knew both him and his longtime partner well. This friend was known to everyone in the town as one of the most generous, funny, gregarious, and helpful people who had settled in the town. He was well loved by everyone, and I had always found him to be a person of highest quality. However, on our first evening visiting, he leaned over to me, while his partner was just out of earshot, and intimated that he was having an affair with another man. Stunned, not just by what he was saying but also by his brashness, especially with his own partner in such close proximity, I didn't know what to say or how to respond. I let it go. A couple of days later, he showed up at a gathering with his new lover, while his partner had travelled to San José on business. Unfazed by his own lack of sensitivity or tact, he proceeded to get more and more drunk and more and more inappropriate with his lover. At one point, after a big shot of tequila, he looked directly at me and said, "Molly, I am the nicest guy you'll ever meet and the biggest asshole you'll ever meet." His boyfriend turned to me and started to giggle, then to ask me about my friend's partner, poking fun at him for being in the dark about this infidelity. I told the new guy that I didn't want to know anything about it, and I got up and left. I was disgusted and angry, and particularly so for feeling that I was now a part of the deceit. I decided that everything I had thought about my friend was wrong. He was not generous, funny, or helpful and, in fact, he was a big fake. And yet, in some ways, he actually was the "nicest guy." But how could both of those things be true? And just as important, what was I supposed to do with this knowledge?

This frustrating and painful situation led me to several reflections on yoga, wholeness, judgment, reality, and seeking contentment. I started to really contemplate the sense of being divided within ourselves and how that leads to our trying to create wholes, neat boxes, black and white, good or bad, to reduce our discomfort. I thought about how in the end all of that only serves to provoke more anxiety and confusion, and how in fact it takes us further away from contentment. Thinking back once again to high school, I remember how often we used the word "fake" when describing people we didn't like. As if being fake was the worst thing you could be. And at the same time, even then I remember thinking, well, a person can't really be "fake," because however they're being is a real part of them, even the fakeness. When I recall this sentiment now, I think about the various Hindu deities who show up in all kinds of forms to meet the particular situation at hand — is any one of those forms disingenuous or inauthentic? I'm not sure. They may be used for trickery or manipulation of some sort, but then again, in a sense our whole life is a series of manipulations, and certainly not always for some nefarious effect. The question for me then becomes not so much, Which one are you? but which of the many "ones" of you brings you the greatest feelings of contentment and ease, and which parts of you bring more shame, sadness, fear, or anxiety? And how do we begin, as Gina advised more than 36 years ago, to accept all parts of ourselves, and from that place begin to align ourselves towards more internal peace?

We all know people, in fact we all are people, who have many different parts. We might be the punk rocker who loves show tunes. The drama major who is also the star athlete. The alcoholic who is a wonderful schoolteacher. The super-nice person who has affairs. The helpful neighbor who is a child molester. The stand-up president who makes deals behind closed doors. It becomes confusing for us, both in our efforts to understand ourselves and when we make judgments about others — particularly when we have strong feelings for someone that are confounded by actions which seem so out of character, and specifically when those actions are hurtful to us or to others. Which of those aspects of personality is real and how do we decide not just how to judge our relationship with others, but how to be "ourselves?" Who is the real Slim Shady? Many "good" people do "bad" things and many "bad" people do "good" things. At what point does any one way of being, one single act, one aspect of our personality, one great talent, or one major limitation come to define us above all else?

I don't know the answer to that. What I do know is that, as spiritual seekers, we must find ways to integrate all the different parts of ourselves, and as we do so, the pendulum will have a much more narrow swing between seemingly conflicting parts of us. What I also know is that we must make choices about what we can reasonably tolerate in another and how to extricate ourselves and create distance from those people and relationships that feel completely out of tune with our own sense of contentment, and certainly from those that are harmful to us.

Toward the end of the Bhagavad Gita, Krishna finally reveals himself to Arjuna. Before doing so, he warns Arjuna, this could get ugly, are you sure you want to see it? When Arjuna confirms that he is ready to fully see Krishna, Krishna unveils himself and shows himself to be everything possible. He even says, "Of deceivers, I am the dice play," *(Bhagavad Gita: A New Translation – Stephen Mitchell, Harmony Publications, 2002)*. In another commentary on the same text, by Mahatma Gandhi, he explains this line by telling us, "God exists not only in what is good in the world, but also in what is evil." *(The*

Bhagavad Gita According to Ghandi, North Atlantic Books, 2010)
What Krishna seems to be saying to Arjuna is that God is the potential for every kind of action. So are we then to simply accept whatever a person does, however they act, whoever they are, whoever they harm, in the name of the omnipresence of God? No—in fact, according to the Gita, quite the opposite. It is our dedication to Self-realization, or God-realization, that spurs us to cultivate those qualities in us that bring us the deepest sense of contentment. Krishna explains to Arjuna that we exist as both God-consciousness itself and as the mortal vehicles we inhabit.

Here is how I see it: We have all of these different potentials, but we also know which of those bring us closer to a feeling of clear seeing and calm abiding and which of those bring us to places of greater discomfort and unease. As we develop our ability to be less identified with ourselves as human beings, we become more identified with who we are as manifestations of God. We naturally move toward an understanding of ourselves as flawed and limited and at the exact same time, we give ourselves over even more deeply to our deepest sense of a Self that feels steady, content and joyous. This is the place of purnam—of wholeness, of integration.

I like to think about the metaphor of a garden. In our own internal gardens, we are the fertile soil and the potential for any kind of plant, or quality, to grow in that soil. And, like gardeners, we can pick and choose the inner "plants" that bring us the most beauty, the most medicine, the most food, the greatest sense of accomplishment, and the most joy. We might also consider what brings beauty to others and how we might tend our garden in service of our neighbors. We also have in us, as in any garden, plenty of weeds, plenty of "volunteers," plenty of unwanted flowers and plants that grow as long as we allow them to, as long as we cultivate them. What if, in the end, we didn't judge the seeds for their potential to grow, but we dedicated ourselves to cultivating the seeds that bring us more light, more beauty, and ignored or weeded out the ones that bring us darkness, those that are disagreeable to the health of our relationships and our life's focus? Could my friend still be a good person even with his infidelity? Of course he could. And yet, his cultivation of this more negative aspect of his personality causes harm, unease, and disconnection within himself and in his relationships to others. I truly believe that if he integrates these two aspects of himself, the one that is harmful will naturally fade away. The only way we can carry out acts of wickedness and still keep our sense of being good people is to disconnect from and compartmentalize the different parts of ourselves. When we work toward integration of and connection with our whole selves, we naturally lose the urge to cultivate the parts of us that cause harm. But so many people, so many of us, so much of the time, don't even know how disconnected we are.

When I think of myself back in high school, the overwhelming feeling I recall was one of discomfort in simply being myself. That was most likely because I felt, as do so many young people, that I had to choose any one aspect of myself and be that. I had to be the good girl, or the party girl, or the drama major, or the academic, but if any of those seemed at odds, I believed I had to reject one in order to be the other. I also felt like my sense of self, my sense of feeling connected — to myself or to others — had to do with receiving the approval of those others. Gina, in her teen wisdom, knew that she could accept all parts of herself and that her sense of being OK came from the inside. For me, it took a while longer, and now I finally (mostly) feel comfortable being myself, "weeds" and all. I have also radically changed in what I judge in myself to be those weeds. They are no longer the superficial weeds of not being "cool enough" or "pretty enough"; they are the truly destructive, universal weeds of jealousy, envy, and insecurity — to name a few. But I don't separate myself from those feelings because they hurt or because they serve me in some backhanded way. I allow myself to feel deeply connected to those parts of myself and ask the questions over and over, "How do I feel when I cultivate this part of myself? How do I feel when I let these aspects of my personality overwhelm the aspects of myself that give me and others more joy, more contentment, more peace?"

When I think of my philandering friend, or of people by whom I personally have been deeply hurt or traumatized, or of anyone who victimizes or is intentionally deceitful, I can only believe that they were simply never able to fully integrate their compulsion to harm and manipulate others into their own psyche, and that this is what allows their hurtful behavior to continue. I can't change other people, but I can pray for their awakening and for their realization that this internal division, this lack of wholeness, is only bringing them shame, fear, sadness, anger, guilt, and disgust. I can wish for their self-realization for their own peace and for the peace of those who are hurt in their dis-integrated tornado. And I can choose to keep my distance from such people, to keep myself safe. I can do what I can to simply keep my own mind at ease. I can also choose to dedicate myself more deeply to tending my own garden, for I am certainly not the poster child for integration. But I have my practice.

Our yoga practice invites us back to purnam, wholeness. It invites us to accept and embody all the parts of ourselves. Who is the real you, the real me, the real Slim Shady, the real Krishna? It's all of you, all of me, all of Eminem, all of Krishna in his many forms. And from the fearless place of recognizing all of these different aspects of ourselves and of others, we are able to choose the place of contentment, of wholeness. It's not always easy, but in the end, we will have a beautiful, diverse garden; a garden that brings us joy, contentment, and peace, and one for which there is no need to apologize for what appears in it. May I have your attention please? There's no problem here; just you, just me.

.

If there is one word you find coming out like a bomb from the Upanishads, bursting like a bombshell upon masses of ignorance, it is the word fearlessness. And the only religion that ought to be taught is the religion of fearlessness. ~ Swami Vivekananda

MOLLY LANNON KENNY

*A*cknowledge

Sit silently for just a moment and reflect on all the work you have done so far in the journey of your life. Remind yourself that the path is sometimes easy and sometimes difficult, and sometimes it may feel like you are taking two steps forward and one step back. Acknowledge your dedication and intention and that even when you aren't living up to your own ideals of your best self, you are still determined and you are still making changes. Remind yourself that we all have setbacks and we all have great moments of clarity and epiphany. Remember the knowledge that you have gained so far, even in your mistakes. This is hard work, and you are doing it. Take a moment to also recall how many others are working just as hard, and acknowledge their progress, their right to make mistakes and their heartfelt goal of personal transformation for a better world.

"Because strait is the gate, and narrow is the way which leadeth unto life, and few there be that find it." Matthew 7:14

Asteya ~ Non-Stealing or Recognizing the Rotten Root of Desire

Been caught stealing
once, when I was five
I enjoy stealing
It's just as simple as that.
Well it's just a simple fact.
When I want something,
I don't want to pay for it.
~ Jane's Addiction, Ritual de lo Habitual, Warner Brothers, 1990

My life is amazing and great. I have so many things, opportunities, friendships, and experiences, I can hardly imagine wanting more.

When I sit in meditation, it's easy for me to feel the abundance of my life and the endless opening of my heart, and from this, the exquisite overwhelming light of gratitude.

Just the other day, in fact, I was sitting on a seat of impressive volcanic rock, facing the ocean, my beautiful husband Sasha wading peacefully through the warm waters of the thermal pools behind me, surrounded by the lush green of the palms, and breathing in some of the cleanest air on the planet. I dropped quickly and deeply into a contented state of easeful meditation and was surprised to hear my timer sound off its soft harp sounds, signaling the end of my sit. I opened my eyes slowly, took in a few deep breaths, and got up to find Sasha, eager to share with him the insights that had come to me without my even trying. It felt like the best meditation of my life, and I couldn't wait to include him in my discoveries.

As I walked up off of the rocks and over to the pools, I noticed several people standing and watching the ocean with excitement. I assumed they were just reveling in the huge waves and crystal blue color, until Sasha came running up to me calling, "Did you see those whales?" "What whales?" I responded. Although I had been enjoying my meditation, it didn't seem possible that I could have zoned right out of prime whale watching. "Are you serious?" Sasha continued, pointing to a large rock about ten yards off shore. "There was a mother and a calf and they were playing and jumping right there! Everyone was screaming and taking pictures—I've never seen whales so close in my life." I couldn't believe that I had actually sat through all the excitement without noticing it. Suddenly my "great sit" felt like a total waste of time. I didn't want my "inner peace" and "insight" any more, not when it meant missing seeing whales up close and personal. I kept asking Sasha to describe exactly what he saw, as if somehow by hearing it enough I would experience it too. I walked into the warm pools, listening to everyone sharing their excitement, the water washing over me like the feeling of disappointment and wanting that pervaded my mood.

I had already been pondering this feeling of wanting. I had just spent several months in my little town in Mexico before heading off to Hawaii. I had been asked to translate into English an important meeting of an afterschool program in my Mexican hometown. A cell phone had been stolen, and there was ample evidence that a young girl who worked for the program had taken it. The American founder of the program wanted to talk to all of the workers together to discuss what to do, and she needed my help in being understood. I translated as faithfully as I could, then I asked the founder if I could add something myself. I turned to the girl, whose family I know well, and said to her, "If you took it, just say so. Everyone makes mistakes, everyone wants things they can't have, and every thirteen year old has made an error in judgment. No one thinks you are a bad person for taking the phone, they just think you made a mistake, and you can remedy it by telling the truth." My little friend stared at me with a poker face and simply shrugged her shoulders. She was not going to admit her guilt, and there was no way I could make her.

When the founder and I spoke afterward, I told her that I believed the girl had taken the phone, but that we should now just let it go. There was nothing else we could do and, if in fact the teen had taken the phone, she would have to work through a process of knowing the position she had put her family in and recognizing that the adults around her were willing to listen to her and forgive her, that they understood her want. I believed that lesson would last. As the founder and I went through our own process, I put forth a question of complicity. Were we, the relatively rich Americans who live in the town, not also a part of the situation? Could it be possible that causing others to see us with our cell phones, our trucks, and our iPods, iPhones, and laptops is part of what stirred the sense of wanting and temptation in this young girl? And that this sense of both desire and lack, a common human experience that can be so very strong in its grip, might actually lead someone to the act of stealing?

She has what we want, a life in Mexico, and we have what she wants, things and money.

I thought of this too, because I had recently had another powerful experience of wanting it all. A good friend of mine in my town had just told me she was pregnant. In a moment of ungrounded jealousy and longing, I was talking to my sister about my so-far-unrealized desire to have a child. I found myself telling her, "I just get so mad when I think about my friend; I mean, she doesn't even have a boyfriend, she has no job and no opportunity, and no network of support." In other words, she doesn't have any of the wonderful things that I have, therefore she should not have this gift, whereas I, having everything, should have more. Of course, I realized that what I likely was feeling was also an assertion that I was in a better place to support a child, but still, this deep sense of jealousy and desire was there, agitating my ability for clear thinking. My sister and I both laughed when we realized my reasoning. This longing seems to cloud any sense of rational thought.

And yet we do want it all. And when this desire becomes too much to hold, we act on it, doing and saying things that we know at some level are at worst wrong, and at best, ridiculous. We steal peace from ourselves through our hurtful words, thoughts, and actions, both in things we say and do that take from our own contentment or that take from the contentment of others. We steal from others by diminishing their own desires and dreams, and we steal from each other when we reach out and take what is not freely given. All of this, in my view, stems from a sense of longing, of desire, of wanting — a deeply human error of thought in which we believe ourselves to be essentially incomplete and that in gaining the object of our desire, we will feel a sense of fulfillment. We are so quick to judge one another when we are convinced that we would act differently (and better) than others would in some situation or another. I think that we act differently just because we don't have the exact object of desire or the exact conditioning that others do (not necessarily because we are morally superior). When I hear myself or others saying, "I can't believe that he would do X, Y, or Z," I just want to say, "Really? You really can't believe it?" How could we not believe it? How could we not believe that he would act out of his conditioning, his longing?

The truth is, we all share this deep sense of longing. What we have is never enough, and we become consumed with getting more, taking what's ours, adding to what we have, whether it is a material thing, an opportunity, a relationship, or a state of being. In a silly yet very real example, I'm still always blown away by the people at the hotels in Puerto Vallarta, who get up at 6 o'clock in the morning to save a spot on the beach, even when they know that they are going back to bed and may actually not make it to the beach until noon. At least they got their place! I suppose to them it might seem reasonable – they want to be sure that they have their beach chair and umbrella - but to me it seems entitled and unfair when others are left wandering the beach with no place to sit, while looking at all of those empty chairs, "saved" by beach towels and paperback books.

When we think of asteya, non-stealing, we might feel relieved that this one is easy. We don't steal, right? And that makes it easy to feel superior to those who do. But if we change our perspective on what we all have in common — that longing, that seemingly insatiable sense of desire — we might realize that we steal in subtle ways more often than we think we do, and that we are only one life experience away from acting out our longing and taking what we want. And we want it all.

We may practice the ethical precepts of yoga, the yamas and niyamas, and in so doing, steady and still the waters of our own erratic thought stream. But it works both ways. When Pattabhi Jois says "Yoga is 99% practice," what he means is that if we just "do" our practice of asana, pranayama, and meditation, we will spontaneously calm the turbulence of our mind. When the mind is still then, we may also disrupt the relentless pursuit of desire by finding contentment, abundance, and fullness from an inner source.

When we acknowledge this longing, we can attend to it and not push it away, deny, defend, or judge it. Maybe we will see that this longing has a rightful place and a gift for us as well; perhaps it is this same essential longing that moves us toward a desire for freedom, a desire for sweetness, a desire for a spiritual life, a desire to feel less separate. And maybe, when we commit to tenderness toward our own suffering, we will open to new possibilities and gifts. It is truly a gift to realize that from the perspective in which we already have enough, our satisfaction is not dependent on phones, children, whales, or anything else. Perhaps the grip of this longing can be released simply by our recognition of it and by our knowing that we do not need the object of our desire to feel contentment. It is as close as our ability to recognize and appreciate it.

About a week after my sit, where I thought that seeing whales was better than the gift of contentment through meditation, I found myself sitting again facing the ocean and listening to the sound of the huge crashing waves, the salty air fresh on my face. The waves were getting louder and louder, and I decided that I should partially open my eyes to make sure the peace of my meditation was not disturbed by being washed away by a rogue wave. I allowed my eyes to open slowly to half-mast—"shiva eyes."

Directly in front of me were three huge whales, close enough to swim to, jumping and playing in the surf. I looked around for Sasha, or anyone, to see if this was really real. I didn't see another soul, so in a moment of wanting to hold on, I took out my camera and held it up to my face. As soon as the camera was there, I could no longer see the whales with the same clarity and directness. I realized I was trading in the actual experience for the desire to "save" it. I put the camera down and just breathed in gratitude and astonishment. Right then, the biggest whale jumped up out of the water, and as it landed, one of the group let out a huge playful bellow.

In that moment, I understood. I really did have it all, and perhaps, in some divine play, the gift of the whales was not the source of my contentment, but rather perhaps, the reward for letting go.

My profession is to always find God in nature.

~ Henry David Thoreau

Brahmacharya ~ Moderation or The Art and Practice of Really Living

Todo con medida. That's what it says on the side of the big Corona beer trucks. Who knew that the makers of Corona beer, Mexico's second favorite cerveza, would have had anything in common with the ancient sages? *Todo con medida.* Everything in moderation. That ol' adage? We've heard it a million times, but why is it so important? Important enough, even, to show up as one of our treasured yogic precepts, one of the five yamas, or "restraints," as described by Patanjali in the first limb of yoga?

When I consider the phrase "everything in moderation," I can't help but think of the many depictions of the Buddha—a great proponent of the "middle way" of moderation. There is one particular image that I love—the reclining Buddha, in which he appears so relaxed, so laid back, and yet at the same time, so full of vitality and life. Sure, he might be reclining, but you just feel that if you said to him, "Hey, Buddha, let's go grab a beer," he might just jump right up and join you. OK, well, maybe not, but we have the image of the Buddha, or any really well-adjusted person, as at once relaxed and easy going and at the same time full of energy as needed. It's about harmonious living. Brahmacharya is the precept of moderation, continence, and, yes, celibacy.

Since most modern yogis are not strictly fundamentalists, the concept of brahmacharya has evolved with our Western yoga culture, so we could take (ostensibly) the deepest meaning of the precept, which is to enjoin practitioners to conserve their energy for spiritual practice and to direct their focus toward Self-realization, and try to apply it to our daily lives. Most of us are probably "householders," just plain old regular people who generally enjoy having sex when we can, or at least enjoy having the option to enjoy sex. So what does brahmacharya mean to us, here and now, and how can we apply it to our daily lives? Think of this: think of all the ways you squander energy. Think of all your rules, habits, addictions, pleasures, desires, rituals, and think of your relationship to them. There are so many beautiful material and non-material things to be enjoyed in this life and yet, as spiritual seekers, most of us also realize at some level that we have a limited amount of energy and focus, and we would like to allot a generous amount of whatever we have to our pursuit of connection to ourselves, to our spiritual life, to God, and to our own divinity. So how do we find that balance?

Here's a story. When my husband and I met, he had been spending a lot of time on the Nicoya Peninsula of Costa Rica and I had been spending as much on the coast of Nayarit, Mexico. Through a run of good fortune and timing, we ended up with a house in both places. Going from south of the border to even more south, we instantly became a part of that "cool" group of people who travel: worldly, carefree, and interesting. We enjoyed easy conversations revolving around who'd been where, what were the coolest places to go, and who had a great story. We started to dream and talk about all the other places we would go and check out. We spent time reading travel novels and "insider's" guidebooks. We even began to check the Internet for opportunities to buy land in other great places: the Puna district of Hawaii, the Darien Gap in Panama, the southern coast of Vietnam. We loved travel, and we loved being travelers.

But there was another side to it. We also had to work, and time, just like money, as it happens, is always limited. We began to stress and argue about when we were going to go where and how we were going to spend enough time in the places we already had built homes. And there was another, deeper level of dissatisfaction. We love to travel because we love to see the world from an insider's view, getting to know the land, the people, the culture, and the language of our various destinations. And yet, that's not what was happening.

We were flying in and out of places only long enough to discover the best beaches and to meet other international expats. On one occasion, we spent two full weeks in Costa Rica barely ever speaking any Spanish and never once eating in a soda, one of Costa Rica's ubiquitous local cafes. The collection of travel experiences had apparently become more important than the reasons we loved to travel in the first place. Let's face it: at some point a beautiful beach is just a beautiful beach, no matter where it is.

Then through a new set of circumstances – a story unto itself, with many of its own deep lessons of love and loss - we had to give up our house in Costa Rica. It was devastating at first. Our little tree house in the jungle represented a long-time dream of my husband's, and he had designed and helped to build the house. The joy I once had in watching him throw open the floor-to-ceiling doors and stand looking out at the trees and monkeys, pointing and dreaming and expanding seemed priceless. And yet, even then, there was a price. The more entrenched we became in the house and in the community, the more we needed to get back there to really make it ours. Even at the time, as I watched Sasha glow with delight and pride, I felt the unease of knowing that having this house in Costa Rica, in addition to our little home in Mexico, would add to our tension of making travel plans and would take away from our ability to plan simple trips to see family and friends, even here in the United States. So, when the house was suddenly not a part of our great travel odyssey, there also came just the slightest sense of relief. We left Costa Rica and spent the following three months at our home in Mexico, cultivating our insider's view, getting to know the land, the people, the culture, and the language. We began to open up again to travel for all the reasons we really loved it. Yes, we grieved the loss of our beloved spot in Costa Rica, yet at the same time we understood that we would now be able to focus our energy in this one spot, while still allowing ourselves the dream of travel.

What does this have to do with brahmacharya? Todo con medida. The desire to see as much of the world as possible was limiting our ability to direct and manage our energy toward the most important part of traveling for us. It's not that traveling the world, or the desire to travel the world, is bad, it's just that perhaps travel in excess scatters our energy and results in our missing out on really getting to know a land or a culture. How much can another constant traveler really tell you about another place? In my experience, not much. It is about staying put, focusing energy, learning the language, the customs, and getting invited to special events, family dinners, making real friends with the locals, and giving back to that community through direct involvement. Not simply sampling the local beverage, hanging out at the beach, and comparing stories with other travelers.

It is the same with any of our worldly pleasures. Most of them are not, in and of themselves, destructive or bad. It is our relationship to them that can get us in trouble. When we allow our energy to be dissipated, or even misguided, we don't have what we need for our spiritual pursuit. Even the habits and rituals that we regularly practice to increase our sense of harmonious living can become more important than the day-to-day examination of how those practices affect our energy. Consider something like running, or yoga, or, heck, even sex. I think we would agree that those things are not bad, and they may even help us to feel good, connected, healthy, strong, alive. And yet, it is easy to become so attached to them that we come to believe they are central to our wellbeing: "I can't go out with my friends in the evening because I am so committed to my 6:00 am Ashtanga practice. I don't take drugs; therefore I will suffer with this headache or this depression. I can't be at ease when visiting family, because I have to get my five-mile run in at all costs. I don't eat fish, meat, cheese, wheat, vegetables, or drink water with ice, or without ice, therefore I cannot fully enjoy the company of my hosts in this foreign land. I am so in love, or infatuated, with this new person that sex is more important than anything, including my job, my friends, my sleep, my alone-time to recharge."

The precept of brahmacharya can be understood as an invitation to be fully present in the moment with what we are doing and to continually reassess our energy reserves so that we can skillfully decide how to direct them. If we know that a spiritual life is important to us, how do we make sure to allot enough energy to our practice? Traditionally, one way to do this was by limiting or refraining from sex, in order to direct that powerful energy toward God consciousness, or Self-realization. We each have to make these practices relevant for ourselves and for our lives as we live them now. Maybe choosing not to engage in the sex act is not an option — perhaps your partner is not on board or you don't have a partner with whom to limit your sexual engagement. But what if it isn't really just about sex? Each one of us has at least one thing that we overindulge in, even "healthy" things, including our own self-imposed restrictions, and many of us fritter away our energy on needless things. Brahmacharya is for all of us; we simply have to commit to the knowledge that our energy is finite and that we must make the effort to manage it to get the most out of all of life's possibilities. In a way, it's about having our cake and eating it too — we just have to make sure that we are eating the cake and it's not eating us. We need to ask ourselves, who's in charge here? Sex, yoga, running, that beer, the next flight — or me and my discriminating wisdom, my viveka? I remember once listening to a talk by Robert Svoboda when he suggested this very manner of discernment. Ask yourself, he said, Am I serving these things or are they serving me?

Wake up. Be present. Make careful choices. Reassess. Be brave, open, and intelligent. As far as we know, we have just this one life in this body. Use it well. Commit to your practice, let your practice serve you, for real.

Todo con medida.

I have one life and one chance to make it count for something... My faith demands that I do whatever I can, wherever I am, whenever I can, for as long as I can with whatever I have to try to make a difference.

~ Jimmy Carter

MOLLY LANNON KENNY

Aparigraha - A Loose Grip

Ahhh, aparigraha. It is one of my favorite tenets, and one that has great power to help us develop bodhicitta, or an enlightened heart and mind. Aparigraha means "non-hoarding," "non-covetousness," or "lack of greed." We can also think of it as non-grasping or non-attachment. This is a concept found in most spiritual traditions, the idea of letting go, or loosening our grip on our "things," - everything from the old clothes that we hope to fit into again one day, to our identities, to our money, to our cherished ideas.

I remember thinking about this a lot during the presidential primaries of 2009. Seeing the candidates "flip-flop" on their platforms and statements is a fascinating, and sometimes very disturbing, study on what politicians will do to get the vote, how quickly they will give up one tightly held idea and move on to another. I think as observers we collectively find this distasteful and dishonest. But it is possible, certainly, that a person can gain new information or new insight and with that new perspective, change his or her position. You might remember that President Obama, for example, was originally against the individual mandate for health care insurance and, in fact, campaigned hard against Hillary Clinton on that specific point, among others. Later when asked in a CBS interview whether he believed individuals should be required to have health insurance, Obama replied, "I have come to that conclusion. During the campaign I was opposed to this idea because my general attitude was the reason people don't have health insurance is not because they don't want it, it's because they can't afford it. And if you make it affordable, then they'll come. I am now in favor of some sort of individual mandate as long as there's a hardship exemption."

Now, I don't want to say that I know, or even believe, the reasons why President Obama changed his mind, but I do know that there are times when a change of mind, a change of perspective, not only makes sense, but shows an ability to be both humble and flexible. Of course, it's a bit different when we are talking about elected officials whose opinions are going to shape policy, but there must be some middle ground where changing our minds, letting go of our tightly held beliefs, is the right thing to do in the face of maturation and new information or insight.

Shortly after I moved to Seattle in 1990, I joined an all-girl punk rock band called 66 Saints. The other two women in the band were both queer, and I was thrown right into the middle of my first real experience of standing up as an ally for close friends who had been targets of institutionalized marginalization. I took a strong stand for my friends in the best ways I knew how as a kid — marching in the Gay Pride Parade, voicing my support in radio and print interviews — and beginning to evolve my first real social justice mindset, passionately advocating for the rights of people I was actually very close to. I remember at this time hearing that Joan Jett was gay and my friends talking about how she "should come out" — that it was the only right thing to do. I was so ardent in my wanting to stand up for my band mates that I would say this too. "Joan Jett should come out! It is her duty and her obligation!" I really did believe that. Now, not so much. I don't think anyone has to "come out" or "stand up" or be identified for anything they don't want to be. I believe these decisions are the choice of the individual; there are many complicated factors to consider that only the individual can accurately gauge for his or her own life.

When I began my Ashtanga practice, I was totally into it. I was one of those people who thought that Ashtanga was the only "real" yoga practice and that everything else was for wusses. I would even say, "I can't imagine what a person would do when they laid out their mat if they didn't have a prescribed sequence, or something to aspire to." Um … I don't think that any more.

And when I first started going down to what would later become my home in Mexico, I had all kinds of ideas about how the ex-pat and tourist community should interact with the locals, what they owed them, and how they should relate to, employ, teach, or donate to the local community. (Red flag number one, right?) Each year, it seemed, I had a new idea, always based on some new information or some new insight. I learned about neocolonialism and let everyone know they should stop trying to force their language, culture, and ideas onto the locals. Then I learned about cultural relativism, and taught all my ex-pat friends how they were only able to view the Mexican community through the lens of their own experience. Then I learned more and more about service and "helping." I learned the famous quote, sometimes attributed to Lilla Watson, an activist with the Aboriginal Queensland Group in Australia. She herself, however, wanted the quote attributed to the whole group, as this sharing reflects the very spirit of the quote itself: "If you have come here to help me, you are wasting your time. If you have come because your liberation is bound up with mine, then let us work together," and I reconsidered all my ideas about helping and serving. Then I read Father Greg Boyle's book *Tattoos on the Heart* and decided that it's actually kinship, not service at all, that I strive for in my interactions. This one seems to sit, because it's the easiest, because it's the closest to how I actually feel, and because it is the one I believe ... today.

But who knows? Maybe I will change my mind again. If I do, it won't be because I am campaigning or currying favor with anyone but because it is what I actually believe, in a deep and passionate way.

Our deepest held beliefs come from a place of passion and, yes, they often come with a sense of righteousness. I believe strongly that we should continue to feel passionate, and to take stands, and to be vocal about what we believe. But aparigraha has an important part to play here. Even as we hold our beliefs, what would happen if we simultaneously held them with a loose grip, an understanding that this is the truth now, with the information, life experience, and spiritual maturation we have now? What would happen if we allowed others to change their minds as well, without belittling or discrediting them, and instead assumed that their change of mind and heart came from new passion, new truth?

I wish I could say that I won't ever tout a silly or even hurtful belief again. This is my hope, but I am human. What I believe I can do is to know that every idea, every opinion, every belief I have, is open to change. I believe I can practice a loose grip and, in doing so, allow my own ideas and the ideas of others to evolve and change. It is this mental flexibility, an attribute of aparigraha, that truly helps us to develop bodhicitta – a clear and discerning heart and mind, mental flexibility, sympathetic joy, and contentment, and invites us to follow the path of compassion.

Let's consciously foster individual transformation as a means to radical social change.

We are all in this together.

Molly & 66 Saints

If you realized how powerful your thoughts are, you would never think a negative thought.

~ Peace Pilgrim

Loga and Shaucha– or Cleaning up our Identities in the Laughing Shower

Shaucha is the first of the niyamas, or "observances," that relate to the practitioner's inner world, as described in Patanjali's Yoga Sutras. Within the context of the eight limbs of yoga, the niyamas are considered to be the second limb, following the yamas, or "restraints," that relate to the practitioner's external world, and preceding asana, practice of the physical poses.

The concept of shaucha refers to cleanliness, purity, and orderliness. We can think of it as how we keep our homes, how we take care of our bodies, and how we take care of our relationships. But shaucha also refers to how we direct our energies and how we create both structure and freedom by creating a sense of order around us and within us. To me, the trick with shaucha is figuring out how to create order that feeds and nourishes my whole being and not to impose a false sense of order or rigidly stick to the "way things should be," which limits my own growth and opportunities in life. Sometimes, to find this sense of order, we actually have to be willing to rock the boat a bit, which may seem at first that we are creating more chaos than order.

I had an interesting experience with my own rigidity, my own sense of structure getting in the way of an opportunity, when I got to try Loga, a style of laughing yoga, developed by Seattleite Andrew Whitver, who offers Loga for free in a local park. I met Andrew when I was planning for a fundraising event in that same park. I had been given his name by a mutual contact who thought we might work well together and that Andrew might be able to leverage some of his regular students to join in our event. As soon as Andrew and I spoke on the phone I knew this would be an important relationship and that we would become great friends. Andrew was thoughtful, generous, funny, and genuinely friendly. He was immediately supportive of my work and was enthusiastic about offering whatever he could to help me, and I was eager to meet him in person. He asked me come to Loga in the park to meet him and to see what it was all about before making a commitment to him for our event, just to make sure I knew what I was getting into. I had heard of Laughter Yoga, and so far I really liked Andrew, but I wasn't sure I actually wanted to try Loga. It's not really "me." I'm just not the type to go out to the park, meet up with a bunch of strangers, open myself up to them, follow the exercises (laughing chorus anyone? Perhaps a laughing shower?), and lovingly connect through a kind of odd process on a normal Sunday morning. I just don't do "that sort of thing." I usually am a person who is up for anything, happy to be goofy — and I love to laugh — but I am also a person who likes to be, and stay, in control. So when I'm asked to do something that invites me to give up that control, that sense of order, I bristle, get all awkward and standoffish, and generally keep myself on the periphery. I guess I could say that I don't like to have fun on demand. Even so, this was my opportunity to meet Andrew, and he had been so generous with me, it was the least I could do to show up.

Sunday in the park was no different. It wasn't hard to find the Loga group — they were the ones who were standing in a circle laughing and apparently genuinely enjoying themselves. I don't quite know what I had expected to find, but I was both surprised and pleased to see a group of normally dressed, normal-looking people, who just happened to be laughing heartily under the direction of their leader, Andrew. As I approached the group, that joyful, energetic, and somewhat mischievous-looking "laughing choreographer" said, "You must be Molly!" There was a moment right there and then when I thought, "I could just smile, say no, and keep walking. He has no idea who I am or what I look like, and this is a public park." And then came the very next thought, "I have to stay, and I have to make a conscious decision right now to let down my guard, be totally present and non-judgmental, be open to the experience, and then decide if I like it or not." I stayed, I smiled, I laughed, I was moved. So much so, in fact, that I ended up offering an experience of two minutes of non-stop pretend-turning-to-real laughter for a group of folks at the end-of-life care facility where I had been offering Bedside Yoga sessions for several years, and ultimately brought Andrew into the facility to offer Loga himself. When we were done, the patients in the end of life group expressed the same thing — that they felt lighter, more connected to themselves and to each other, and more at ease. I never would have known this experience if I had insisted on clinging to a sense of order in my own little world. When I opened myself up to the possibility that this was a self-imposed limitation, when I "rocked my own boat" a little, I had a deeply integrating experience. Something shifted in me that day in the park. Simply by consciously softening my own sense of structure and identity, I had created a new (inner) world order.

I have been thinking about this idea of clinging to a structured identity a lot, especially with regard to communication and to how much we muddy the waters of relationship and expression by holding on too tightly to our ideas of how we communicate — the confines of our own identity that insist "this is how I am." I am the passive one; I am the aggressive one; I am the one who is in control; I am the one who flies under the radar. In an effort to maintain internal order, we often end up creating more disconnection, confusion, and chaos. For example, we might be too forceful in our communications, or conversely, we might be less than honest because we don't want to hurt someone's feelings or make waves. We might be reactive because we only have a partial understanding of the situation (which we then cling to so we can avoid stepping outside of our comfort zone). In any of these examples, our conscious or unconscious tendency to keep our identity, our structure, may actually result, not in harmony like we had hoped, but in misunderstanding and discord.

Our self-imposed, identity-based idea of order in our communication styles in fact brings us less structure, less reliability, less freedom. We might consider ourselves to be clear communicators because we "tell it like it is," only to find out that sometimes people agree with us out of fear and, in fact, end up harboring resentments toward -- and misgivings about -- us. Perhaps we consider ourselves to be the type that "doesn't create problems, goes with the flow," only to discover that we have put ourselves and others in awkward positions because no one actually knows what is going on, and people are working on false assumptions of what is. We might react to a communication directed toward us without looking deeper into it, because we consider ourselves to be "trusting and forthright," only to find out that the person communicating is just as unclear as we are, and then we experience a communication. In fact, if we took the time to check more deeply into the exchange, patiently and without judgment, we might find out that we are actually on the same page.

So shaucha (cleanliness, order, purity), which at first seems so simple, might actually be a little deeper and trickier than we thought. Oh, yoga. Isn't that how it always is? But yes, yoga is a practice of awareness, of self-reflection, of undoing our most ingrained senses of ourselves so that we might open up to something more beautiful, more intricate, than anything we had ever imagined ourselves to be. Yoga is the gift of discovery of oneself as something divine, perfect, complex, and finally, free.

So, we can think of shaucha as an attending to a sense of order and purity, finding structure that helps us to live in a place of greater tranquility and freedom. But we might also use our discriminating awareness to check in, to make sure that what we see as order, the way we believe things must be, is actually serving, and not limiting, us. Our practice of shaucha must also allow for new possibilities for joy and freedom in our lives.

I think here of a simple image of a house that is so perfect, so clean, so organized, so precise, that, while pleasing to the person who has set up the home in this manner, is not actually welcoming or comfortable to anyone else. In a more evolved relationship with shaucha, we might check in to be sure that this so called "structure" is not actually limiting our deeper experience, our opportunities for growth and transformation, for wonder and surprise.

Perhaps we should, after all, consider "laughing house chores" and "laughing showers." We might just get the best of both worlds.

MOLLY LANNON KENNY

Our duty, as men and women, is to proceed as if limits to our ability did not exist. We are collaborators in creation.

~ Pierre Teilhard de Chardin

MOLLY LANNON KENNY

Ishvara Pranidhana ~ Surrender to God, part 1

I wanna spread the news
That if it feels this good getting used
Oh, you just keep on using me
Until you use me up.
~Bill Withers, 1972 Sussex Records

Like many others, for as long as I can remember I have felt a palpable sense of presence that one might call something like "divinity" or even "God." It is a feeling that ultimately defies words, and descriptions of what it feels like, at least for me, all seem inadequate to truly express this inner experience. When I was younger, this feeling would be evoked through certain songs and music, through experiences in nature, and through a deep empathy for others. I experienced this feeling as something wholly internal and private, but never really thought of it as "God" or God working through me or with me. It just felt like a deep, comforting spaciousness in which I felt like I was somehow safe and connected. In fact, as a much younger person, I most likely would have categorically denied it as the presence of God, because that name and image had been confined and compartmentalized to the judging, punitive father figure I had learned through my Catholic upbringing.

Even though I turned away from organized religion in my twenties and early thirties, I retained that sense of presence; but I still didn't think of it as being any kind of relationship in which I acted in the grace of this presence and it responded to my experiences and desires. In fact, I have often said, that only since I started The Samarya Center did I really and truly understand and believe in the presence of God in my life, or, stated differently, in a sense of a relationship between me — my actions, thoughts, and emotions — and this experience of what I now often call divinity.

Now, more than a decade later, I have seen again and again, in myself, in my work with The Samarya Center, in its community and students, and in The Samarya Center itself, that when we trust in God, or the Universe, or the supreme, or the Divine — whatever we might name it — we are more readily able to connect with an experience of being nurtured and supported; we are more able to find a state of peace or contentment even in the face of challenge. There is a divine mystery constantly unfolding that helps us to weather storms and increases our ability to offer goodness to a world so much in need. However, in truth, over time that pendulum swung so far in the opposite direction, I became so trusting in this mysterious presence, that I stopped working to attain it or worrying about it at all, both within The Samarya Center and within my own life.

Molly and her Dad, George J. Kenny

I have not always been so trusting. I was never the one to just "give it up to God" or even to leave it to chance. In fact, I have been quite the opposite. I have always been a person who has been fortunate enough to get many of the things I wanted, most of it through what I believed to be hard work and direct action. It never occurred to me that this too might be God's presence, but I have certainly been grateful that whatever spirit I was born with was one that had this great ability to get things done. It also never occurred to me that this ability might actually be a gift from God and that I could use it for something bigger than myself.

Although some of my recollections of the various ways I used my capacity for "getting things done" might seem self-congratulatory, I offer them as examples of just how innate and powerful this capacity is, as well as how I often misused this gift for selfish motives. My intention here, and always, is to describe my real life, my real thoughts, my real accomplishments and missteps, in the hope that it might inspire someone, including myself, to consider how we relate to our unique and precious gifts.

Here's a silly story: When I was in high school, like all the good upper-middle-class suburban kids those days, I loved, and occasionally followed, the Grateful Dead. On one of their tours, they were playing Madison Square Garden, close to my parent's home, but before I was able to get a ticket, the show sold out. At about fifteen years old, I decided that I didn't need to buy a ticket; I would just get on the guest list. So I found out where the band was staying, asked myself which band member might get the least attention from fans (I won't tell you which one I decided that was), and called him up from the hotel lobby. We chatted for about five minutes, and then he asked me if I was going to the show. I told him I didn't have a ticket and he asked me if I wanted to be on the guest list. Just like that.

Another musical story: Years later, when I was actually playing in bands, I decided I wanted my band to be in the annual and prestigious South by Southwest music conference. Knowing competition was stiff, I booked a flight to Austin, found out who the promoter was, got a lunch meeting with her, and talked my way into a Friday night slot. Later, a similar effort helped my band play at our beloved Seattle Bumbershoot festival.

And after that, without being a yoga teacher or having had any experience at all in business, I decided to open a wellness center based on yoga in the Central District of Seattle. This was perhaps the first time that I consciously decided that I could use my gift for action and getting results to actually help others, rather than for my own self-service. I decided to apply for nonprofit status, and through more perseverance and determination, was soon granted a 501(c)(3). Then it seemed like a good idea to create a teacher training so that I could share what I knew and believed in with others. I was used to this hard work, and I was used to it paying off. It was around this time that my inner compass began to shift slightly; my capacity for getting results seemed to be in some kind of relationship to my experience of "divinity" or "grace." I couldn't name it then, but I could feel this reciprocity emerging

The Samarya Center, the entity I had started as a place to offer an evolving therapy approach borne out of my clinical experience and my love of yoga, started to become a wonderful place of healing, community, and outreach. I had never planned it to be exactly that, but I began to feel that God was ever more present in my life when I offered my gift of fire to serve a greater good. Soon, all of these incredible people, dedicated to love, inclusion, and social justice started showing up. I had never thought of that as a possibility. Frankly, I didn't even know people like that before The Samarya Center came into being. More and more it seemed that I just had to trust and that whatever this universal and divine source was, its direction would guide me, all of us, into the future. I didn't have to do anything but trust. And trust I did.

Then all of a sudden, things changed. Just before one of our annual holiday parties, I received a phone call from our director of operations. We were in a very serious financial situation that demanded immediate action and a plan. We couldn't cover payroll, and the payroll company told us that if we couldn't come up with nine thousand dollars by the end of the day, they would start pulling people's paychecks from their accounts. I felt paralyzed, scared, and let down. I started to think about all of the good people in the world who worked so hard and couldn't make ends meet. I felt for all the upstanding and faithful people who were threatened by banks, by loan sharks, by bullies, to come up with money they simply didn't have. I felt the need for a new word for "paralyzed and betrayed." We were doing great things. We were changing the world. We were mending hearts and uplifting lives. Why weren't we being taken care of?

I thought about my yoga, my practice, and all of my beliefs, both old and new. I recalled the concept of Ishvara pranidhana that I had learned in my readings on yoga. This is the last of the niyamas, or "observances," and refers to surrender to God. The word Ishvara means something like "lord" or "supreme being," while pranidhana might be translated as "love," or "faith," or as "offering up."

Donna Farhi, a well-known and respected yoga scholar, says in her book *Yoga Mind, Body and Spirit* that the practice of Ishvara pranidhana requires that we take time to contemplate and be open to an intelligence larger than ourselves (ourselves being our small "I," or the personal ego) and that, "ultimately, Ishvara pranidhana means surrendering our personal will to this intelligence so that we can fulfill our destiny." I wanted to surrender to God; I thought I already had. But right now it was feeling like God didn't care about me or my work. What could be intelligent about squashing our good work under the crush of financial collapse?

I thought back to a rare night of watching television, seeing Barbara Walters interviewing Oprah Winfrey, when an idea came to me, an idea that could influence our current predicament. There was a balance that was off, and I needed to find a way back to that balance in order to move forward with our work. I thought of Oprah.

As much as Oprah is a part of our common cultural experience, I sometimes forget how amazing she is. Here is this person, from very harsh beginnings, who has become one of the most influential and richest people in the world. Not only is she wealthy, creative, and talented, she is also black and a larger woman, both qualities that tend to be universally maligned in our collective culture. And she uses her money and her status to help others less fortunate than herself. She's constantly thinking of ways she can do more. In this interview, Oprah referred to a previous interview she did with Barbara Walters, way back in the eighties, where she stated that she believed she was meant to do great things. She talked about the incredible backlash she received from the media and the community for making that statement. Who is this person saying she is so great? Why isn't she more humble? Who does she think she is? How can she say that God meant for her to do great things? What about the rest of us?

Oprah and Barbara didn't have to laugh at the irony of it all. Oprah clearly is great and she does great things. She told Barbara that she often thinks of the refrain from the Bill Withers song, "Use me until you use me up," and uses that very phrase in her prayers to God every day. Here is a person who recognizes her considerable gifts and the guidance she receives from God, and uses them to uplift others. She said that her faith in God guides and supports everything she does, but I think we could also agree that Oprah works really, really hard. In her efforts to bring about positive change for others, Oprah has both joy and humility, not to mention an ever-flowing stream of creativity and money.

See, that's the funny thing about Ishvara pranidhana. We can surrender to God, we can ask God to use us, but we have to do our part too. In yoga, it is the balance between tapas, svadhyaya and Ishvara pranidhana, collectively described by Patanjali as Kriya Yoga. We have to put in the effort, evaluate and assess the results of our efforts, and at some point let go of holding on to the results of our efforts. That's the surrender part. In the Bhagavad Gita, Arjuna is famously counseled to relinquish the fruits of his actions. In a commentary by Mahatma Gandhi that I love, he explains this paradox. It's not that we completely don't care whether our work bears fruit; we do want to see the benefits of our efforts as they are directed towards important change. It's just that our attachment is not about what we, specifically, individually, receive from our actions, or what that return might look like, or whether or not we are good or worthy people based on the results we yield.

That period of my life, when The Samarya Center was faced with so much turmoil and distress, a time of really struggling with the interplay of work and surrender, was also the period in which I began my journey toward parenthood. Over the year, I shared with my beloved community my struggles, my losses, and my own letting go. In that case, I believe that I did do the work, and I also let go. I didn't just leave it up to God, but I also didn't blame or think God wrong when my plans didn't turn out as I had wished. That year, as we do every year, our community discussed a "topic of the month," and we began the year with the topic of ahimsa, or non-violence. It seems fitting then that our final topic that year would be surrender to God, as if it had always been the plan to start with the intention, ahimsa, and end with the letting go. We have a longing, and that longing may remain as part of our call to action, and may even remain so if our work doesn't produce the desired result. But, hopefully, we trust too that there is some divine mystery about our reason for being, the path of our lives, and how we worked toward fulfilling our own purpose, using the unique gifts we each were given. We might trust that our gifts will truly serve in ways perhaps yet unimagined by us.

I think again about Oprah's words, quoting Bill Withers. "Use me until you use me up." To me, this really is what the dedication, attentiveness, or faith in God is really all about. We can allow ourselves to be the vessels for God's work, and as such we do the work as God perhaps intended for us to do. We claim our power, we channel our gifts without apology, we turn down the voices of the naysayers, and we attune more deeply to whatever we understand to be the presence of God in our lives, whatever we want to call it or however we experience it. We each have the capacity for that, and we certainly don't have to be great or famous to achieve this. We only have to open ourselves to our own purpose and strive to be the very best we can be at it. It is in this opening that we find fulfillment in our lives and fulfill our own dharma, our inherent life's purpose.

While I am particularly inspired when I see famous people using their platform of fame and money to help alleviate suffering, especially in a world where we so highly value the vapid and self-serving, particularly among the rich and famous, I also know that we can do this by being the best parent, the kindest person, the most dedicated learner, the most humble and inspiring teacher—whatever we feel truly is our life's work and calling. We use every gift we have, we let God "use us," and we offer that to contribute goodness to our fellow beings and to the world.

For my part, in response to our financial crisis, work definitely kicked back into the equation. As soon as I realized we needed some very creative thinking to keep our great center thriving, I started to brainstorm possibilities. In a moment, harkening back to my teenage years, I decided I would somehow meet Michael Franti, a yoga class music favorite, also a yogi and social activist himself, and tell him about our little gem in Seattle's Central District. I announced to my staff that I would meet him and get us on his radar. For the first time since my previous forays into the world of music and rock stardom, I wanted to meet such a person not for myself but because I truly believed that somehow meeting him might plant a seed that could help The Samarya Center and all the people it serves. So I wrote to several people, explored and used all my resources, including trust, and ended up meeting him. Next time you see Michael Franti, don't be surprised if you see him wearing our Samarya Center trademarked "unfold" T-shirt.

I have learned, again, that it's not just work, and it's not just trust, but it is the alchemy between the two that allows us to channel God's presence and to create the changes we wish to see in ourselves, in our communities, and in the world.

Molly and Michael Franti

Santosha ~ The Practice and Cultivation of Contentment

It isn't what you have or who you are or where you are or what you are doing that makes you happy or unhappy. It is what you think about it. ~ Dale Carnegie

For after all, the best thing one can do when it is raining is let it rain. ~ Henry Wadsworth Longfellow

Here's a little story I like to share about one of my nephews, which, to me, really brings home the idea of santosha, "contentment," as a practice. It is one that I have told many times to my yoga students, and one in which we find the sweetness in the reminder, "Let's just be here."

This was many years ago, when my nephew Shanikai was about three. My husband, Sasha, and I were visiting Shanikai and his mom on her beautiful land on Vashon Island, a rural island not far from Seattle. Shanikai grabbed Sasha's hand and said, "Uncle Sasha, do you want to see my fort?" Sasha, always game for just about anything, answered, "Of course!"

Shanikai pulled Sasha over to a tiny grove of trees and hunkered down into a little clearing, hardly any bigger than Shanikai himself, under some branches. Now, Sasha is about 6 foot 1, so getting himself down into that "fort" was much like turning himself into a piece of human origami. But Sasha made it happen. The two of them crouched under the leafy cover for several moments, Shanikai just looking wordlessly at Sasha with pleasure and satisfaction. After a little while Sasha, from his crumpled up position said, "Well, let's go find Aunt Molly and your mom now." Shanikai just looked at him and said, "No, let's just be here." Content. No other place to be, nowhere to get to, nothing in particular to say or do. Let's just be here.

This story to me illustrates quite clearly both our desire to move on to the next place — to be done with this experience, to find something to do that is different than what is happening now — and our ability to simply "be" and to be deeply content in this moment, where in fact, maybe nothing in particular is happening. It reminds me that it is quite human to be restless, to be searching, to be busy, to be uncomfortable, but that it is also within our human capacity to be content, quiet, and still, even in the midst of discomfort or turmoil. But this doesn't seem to be our default mode so much as something we have to cultivate. Imagine how different our daily lives, our thoughts, our relationships might be if we really cultivated that ability to find stillness and "OK-ness" in all of our experiences: the ones that bring us great joy, the ones we feel ambivalent about, and the ones that feel like a struggle. If we recall that yoga is a practice of the mind, a practice in which we calm the turbulence of our thoughts to realize ourselves as "soul," or stillness, then we might be even more dedicated to our practice and its fruits, we might turn our attention even more toward our own ability to quiet and steady the mind so we are not washed away by its turbulence.

This seems to me like a very worthwhile endeavor: to give ourselves a little respite and then to extend that gift to the people around us.

We are all in this together. Let's just be here.

Don't just do something, sit there. ~ Thich Nhat Hanh

MOLLY LANNON KENNY

*L*ove

What would it be like if we could learn to truly love ourselves and to find a deep love for everyone around us, no matter how challenging that might be? What would it be like to move through the world with the feeling that everyone loved you, too, because they could see beyond the outer manifestation of your being, your "vehicle," and connect with the eternal divine spark that is your true self? What would we practice, and how would we change, if we could understand that no "bad behavior" originates in a vacuum, and that each person is carrying out his or her own conditioning. What if we saw that everyone is a product of genes and of circumstance; of opportunities given, taken, and missed; of experiences and culture? What if we were able to imagine every person as a baby, before they became tainted or flawed or deeply wounded on the basis of circumstance and environment? What if we recalled that every single person wants the exact same things: to be loved, accepted, and happy? Take a moment to imagine this kind of transcendent love emanating from you toward all beings. Remember that we are connected simply by being human, and offer unconditional love both into the world, and back into your own being.

Anything human is mentionable, and anything mentionable is manageable. ~ Mister Rogers

Be kinder than necessary for everyone you meet is fighting some kind of battle. ~ Source unconfirmed

Ishvara Pranidhana: Surrender to God, part 2

"Molly, falling forward."   Years ago, The Samarya Center sponsored a *Circus Yoga Teacher Training* at our Center for Humankind(ness). One of the activities involved walking around the room and then suddenly calling out your name and a direction: falling forward, falling backward, or flying. The intention was that everyone in the room would catch you as you surrendered your body to the group. If you called out "flying," the group would actually pick you up and "fly" you around the room.

This activity resonates deeply with me as I consider the niyama of Ishvara pranidhana, or "surrender to God." The experience of surrender, of letting go, can sometimes feel like falling. It may be an experience that feels light and liberating, but it can also be an experience of fear or confusion as we move from a sense of the individual self to a connection with something larger, deeper, stronger.

Sometimes, when I return to the States from my home in Mexico, I feel myself in a spiritual crisis. When I am in Mexico, things move slowly; I have lots of time and not many responsibilities. I can offer myself directly to the community and connect with my friends and students with a sense of clarity and peace. My "job" there, such as it is, consists only of things I want to do and which give me an immediate sense of connection and value. When I come back to Seattle, my job seems enormous: directing, administrating, holding, working, moving, shaking, decision making, taking care of the center and all of its community... and it can be exhausting. I often feel overwhelmed and harried and, to be honest, I sometimes feel totally disconnected from the very community I helped to create and foster.

So I turn inward and ask God, "What am I doing? What am I supposed to be doing? Is this really what you want from me? Where am I making an impact?" Sometimes even when I talk to God, I feel so frantic that I forget to listen for the answers.

Ishvara pranidhana is about faith. And faith is about trust and listening to our inner voice, the voice of God-consciousness that exists within each one of us that, if we take the time and create enough space and quiet, we can actually hear.

When I listen, really listen, the voice becomes clear. An inner truth emerges that can be called my dharma, or life's purpose. To me, this means that we open up to, and courageously claim, all of the gifts we were born with and all the ways those gifts might be used to uplift ourselves and others. It seems to me, in a sense, that when we simply make a clear and accurate accounting of our gifts, a pattern begins to emerge that can serve as a compass for our life's direction. When we find our dharma, we can move through the world with a sense of internal guidance that allows us to stop questioning and analyzing all the details of our lives and to view ourselves from a greater perspective, one that makes more sense. It's like the difference between looking at a painting at such a close distance that we can't actually make out what the image is and stepping back to take in the whole picture. When I do this holistic accounting of what I have come to realize and accept as my greatest gifts—courage, open-mindedness, empathy and compassion, a desire to advocate on others' behalf, and the ability for clear communication—I arrive at the belief that my dharma is service. I know myself to be an instrument of God, with talents that allow me to serve the community and the world in a variety of ways. When I am in Mexico offering free yoga, therapy, or English classes, I am in service. When I am in Seattle directing The Samarya Center, I am in service. They are the same things done in different ways. I am following my dharma. I don't need to compare the experiences. When I contextualize this sense of being an instrument within the concept of Ishvara pranidhana, I allow myself to flow naturally with grace in total trust and faith in my purpose. I surrender myself to God as an instrument of service in this lifetime.

I can experience myself in this place of service with fear, resentment, and fatigue or I can drop in to a sense of surrender and feel this service as my natural place in the world. Surrender is hardest when we resist it, of course. Surrendering is by definition giving up or handing over something, and we in U.S. culture are not generally socialized to do that. But the experience of giving up can also be seen as an experience of releasing, a handing over of your resistance to things as they are, to a deep trust in the mystery and divine wonder of God's plan; an experience in which we don't have to "do" anything extra. We simply have to "be." We can also think of it as giving up a heavy load, which is an appealing thought for me.

I invite you to explore the ideas of surrender, dharma, and faith. How do they manifest in your life? What is your truth? What is your purpose? Where and how might you put down your load and rest in a deep sense of trust? According to yoga, some sense of God-consciousness is within all of us, so surrendering to this is a natural process. Accept and explore any feelings of resistance, and remember them so that you can clearly discern the difference between resistance and surrender.

Be not afraid of anything. You will do marvelous work. It is fear that is the great cause of misery in the world. It is fear that is the greatest of all superstitions. It is fear that is the cause of all our woes, and it is fearlessness that brings heaven even in a moment. Therefore, "arise, awake and stop not until the goal is reached.

~ Swami Vivekananda

Brahmacharya ~ An Invitation to the Divine, part 2

Don't dig so many shallow holes to find your well, dig one place and dig deep. ~ Buddhist saying

Sutra 1.32: The obstacles to yoga are overcome by a single sustained practice as a means to realize the truth of oneness.

Sutra 2.38: When walking in the awareness of the highest reality is firmly established, then a great strength, capacity, or vitality is acquired. ~Swami Satchidananada

After one of my early podcasts, a listener wrote to me and asked me for recommendations of books about yoga. I gave some recommendations, but I also reminded my students and listeners that in our practice and study, we also want to find the yoga in the hidden places — in the non-yoga books, in the non-yoga classes, in the everyday details and experiences of our lives, not just in books or teachings that are specifically "about yoga." This is how we actually live our practice, by seeing everything in our lives in the context of our spiritual framework, rather than limiting ourselves to the overt lessons that come to us through didactic teaching.

An example of this openness to understanding through experience occurred for me when I was thinking again about the topic of brahmacharya, often translated as celibacy or continence. It was an experience that for me had nothing, and everything, to do with yoga, dedication, and the real life practice of brahmacharya.

This extraordinary experience was in a meeting I had with a young Catholic priest one November while visiting my parents. Father Emilio is a priest from Colombia, just 28 years old when I met him who was relatively new at my parents' church in suburban New Jersey. Even before I met him, it seemed as if almost every time I spoke to my mom she would tell me something about Father Emilio: something he had said that was sweet or funny, his dropping in at her weekly coffee klatch with other women from the church, his moving sermons, his advocacy for the underdog, his courage in the face of the politics of his institution. It was clear that she held him in very high esteem, but also that he had touched her heart in some profound way. I was looking forward to meeting him, and I was delighted when my mom asked me if I would set an appointment with him. He was interested in reducing his Colombian accent and, by chance, I had studied accent reduction during my graduate program in speech pathology. Doing my due diligence before our meeting, I reviewed the 41 sounds of English, as well as a written paragraph that contained all 41 sounds, to assess his current accent and to develop a plan for reducing it.

The day of my meeting with Father Emilio, I was in a terrible mood. I had gotten into an argument with my father over something he had said and was upset with my mother for who knows what reason. When my mother and I pulled into the parking lot of the church, I was nearly in tears of frustration. I walked several steps in front of her and grumbled inwardly about not being in the mood for the meeting after all. When Father Emilio met us at the door of the rectory, I pulled up my in-bred politeness to priests and greeted him with customary warmth and grace. In an instant, I felt light and comfortable. In his presence, the cloud of my dark mood lifted like the aftermath of a late afternoon tropical storm—one moment a torrential downpour, and the very next moment a gleaming blue sky.

I sat down next to Father Emilio, set my accent-reduction paperwork aside, and let out a deep breath. It felt like all of whatever I had been irritated by before had simply dissolved in his presence. He immediately began to ask me about yoga and about my teaching, and he was genuinely interested in the expansive view of yoga and meditation that I presented to him.

I took out one of the papers I had brought and turned it over to the blank side. I drew one of the pictures I always draw when talking about yoga, a crude line drawing of the bottom of the ocean and the waves that crash and swirl and make that still point nearly impossible to see. Father Emilio followed along and asked questions about the experience of meditation, aligning them to his own similar experiences in contemplation and prayer. He started to talk about his background and experience as a priest and particularly about his deep desire to share the exquisiteness of his relationship with Jesus more closely with his parishioners. He shared several defining moments and thoughts that occurred during his evolution toward priesthood, each one drawing me in and making an indelible mark on my own heart and mind.

As I described my teaching of yoga to him, and especially my work with veterans and other marginalized populations, I explained that I had no desire to convert anyone, only to share the profound experience of peace and grace that I found through my own yoga practice, with the hope that someone else, particularly someone in pain, might find solace and respite from my sharing. He nodded his head emphatically. He described his own recent experience of coming into the room of a 48-year-old woman, a dear family friend of ours in fact, as she was in her very last days of living with cancer. He told me that as he walked into her room, wearing his robe and collar, he saw a look of distinct aversion and cautiousness on her face. He felt and acknowledged her wariness; he was not there, he said, to tell her anything about Jesus, or to get her to confess, or to "accept Jesus as her lord and savior" on her deathbed. He was there only, he continued, to be present with her; to perhaps, in stillness and simple being, provide some of the same sense of ease and comfort that he found in his relationship with Jesus. He wanted, he said, only to embody his own sense of and experience of Jesus, and in being just that, to allow her to spend some time outside of fear and loss, even as she was dying. This, he told me, was a gift she could readily accept.

I asked Father Emilio about that relationship with Christ, how he had found it and how he had cultivated it. His answer will also stay with me for a lifetime. Father Emilio talked about Jesus as a friend, and I was reminded of the Sufi mystics who refer to God as "the friend" and who seem to share a sort of ecstatic, and yet also very real, relationship with him. Father Emilio told me that growing up, he was not close to his father. Although he knew his father, he did not live with him and did not have the kind of relationship that he so longed for as a young boy. He lived in a village, and as is common in Latino culture, had a familial relationship with many of the elders in his village. In particular, he described a man from his town whom he had always respected and looked up to. This man, Father Emilio said, was so deeply kind, loving, and compassionate that he knew he wanted to be whatever this man was. It turned out the man was a priest, and Father Emilio, following his heart, went into the priesthood himself. He talked about his changing relationship with Jesus. How, for him, Jesus had begun as the unconditionally loving father figure that he so desired but who over time had evolved into a friend, the kind of friend who knows you and loves you no matter what and in whose presence you feel like everything will be -- and in fact already is -- "OK." Father Emilio's face lit up and he laughed a hearty laugh as he talked about his other friends, about women and dancing and clubbing, and about being a fully Latino young man, with the same love of music and beautiful women as many men, both Latino and not, seemed to have ingrained in them. "I still love to go out dancing when I go home. I try to tell my friends to still just call me Emilio, not 'Father,' and yet they see me as something different, and because of my relationship with Jesus, I realize that I am different." This commitment, the intensity and focus of this relationship, is exactly what does make Father Emilio different.

It's not just because he's a priest; it's because he truly cultivates and basks in his relationship with Jesus as a living expression of God. His choice of priesthood, and therefore the monastic vow of celibacy, is not a denial of life but an affirmation of it. For Father Emilio it seems, his vow reflects his true faith — that this singular focus, this love, this relationship, this commitment, provides a depth of being so worthwhile that the vow of celibacy is a joy, even when faced with the potential temptation of beautiful women, and a strong connection, still, to being "just Emilio," just a young man.

So how does this all relate to our yoga practice? For me, it is an opportunity to shed a different, perhaps more fundamental, light on brahmacharya — the practice of continence or celibacy, which is quite distinct from simply moderating and conserving any of our various energies in everyday life, as is it often described, even by me.

Brahmacharya can feel tricky to us as Westerners and householders. We don't want to think too much about celibacy, or really about anything that feels like suppression or restriction, and especially not of intimacy or sexual urges. At the same time, we want to be committed to our spiritual practice, and our practice of yoga clearly asks us to examine our relationship with celibacy. We don't want to skip it altogether, so it is natural that we might talk about it as the idea of moderation or management of our energy. At the same time, we also all know when an idea has been so watered down as to be almost irrelevant. We don't want to make this mistake with the practice of brahmacharya. We want to experience, as deeply as we can, the fruits of our practice, and we know we need discipline to really dive into all that our practice can offer. But what is "our practice?" and what are its fruits? And how will this practice of brahmacharya really affect or inform it?

First, we must remember, always, that yoga is a spiritual practice — both a means and an end. It is a way of life, a way of thinking, a way of being and acting, which brings us to self-realization, union with the Divine. Realizing this state allows us deep peace and contentment and helps us to shed our identification with our bodies, our minds and emotions, our egos. According to Patanjali, yoga is a stilling of the fluctuations of the mind. This stilling allows us to rest in our own true nature—our nature as unchanging awareness, our nature as completely continuous with the Divine. This is yoga. This is both our practice and its result. Aside from the bountiful fruits of this state of equipoise on the mental and spiritual levels, our practice often also bestows the fruits of good health, or at least more grace in dealing with poor health and health challenges, and a light and loving presence. These, on the most practical and visible level, while not exclusive to the practice of yoga, can be some of the indicators that our practice is working. Brahmacharya, continence, directly influences this state in several ways.

Before I jump right into discussing the monastic view of celibacy and how we as lay people might benefit from its teachings, let me digress for a moment to talk about the concept of vitality as it is discussed in Ayurveda, yoga's sister science, as it will also help us to understand the concept of brahmacharya. According to Ayurveda, one result of brahmacharya is increased vitality in the form of a substance called ojas. Ojas is considered to be a vital fluid that keeps us healthy, especially at the physical level, but which also influences our mental and emotional health. It is believed to be a pure, essential substance that nourishes the whole body. According to Ayurveda, ojas is collected from all the tissues in the body and directed to the heart, where it is distilled and distributed back throughout the body, encouraging and preserving optimal health. This "nectar" of ojas, a kind of perfect bodily fluid, is believed to bring about increased immunity, a pure heart and mind, and higher states of consciousness. But still, how does this relate to brahmacharya, you might ask? Well, according to Ayurveda, fluids associated with reproduction, and especially semen, are considered to be pure or near pure sources of ojas, a wellspring of vitality. We can imagine, then, that yogis would want to maintain and increase ojas—for its benefits on the physical level, but even more so for its ability to induce these higher states of consciousness; states in which practitioners easily see their own true nature, their continuity with God consciousness. A dedicated aspirant then would conceivably not want to squander this vital fluid, especially on the sex act, when the very same substance could be directed back into the body to reach those higher states of health and transcendence. The practice of brahmacharya becomes a practice that is literally life-giving, a life which becomes a dedication to spiritual inquiry and union with the Divine. One could imagine that a person practicing brahmacharya, with that quality of vitality and pure consciousness, might even be recognizable for his or her tender, impassioned presence. Isn't this what we want from our practice? And isn't this in fact the very indicator of the efficacy and value of our path?

In my view, one-pointed attention and direction toward the presence of God in our lives is a lot about simply keeping our focus. As yoga students, most of us share the desire for a certain kind of life, a spiritual life, and we want to realize the fruits of this desire: a life that is more filled with sweetness, love, kindness, and compassion. We want to expand endlessly into the mystery of the Divine; but we can only really do this by keeping ourselves on track, by conserving, increasing, and directing our energy through our focus. So, in a sense, we restrict our focus, we home in on the objective of our life, in order to expand fully into it. We reign ourselves in, we distill ourselves, in order to surrender to and merge with the astounding capacity of our own hearts, which are a true reflection of God. When we are distracted, when we search in too many places, when we divide our attention, we miss the core of our seeking. There is a saying, sometimes attributed to the Buddha, that in order for us to find the well of our own being, we must dig our holes deeper and deeper in one place, until we find what we seek. Similarly, Sutra 1.32 reminds us that in keeping our focus, we are ultimately liberated from the distractions that cause us suffering. There is something universal here, a call to deepen our conviction, to truly commit to our lives and especially to our relationship with the God that exists within the infinite breadth and depth of our own hearts. Do we need to practice celibacy to achieve this commitment? I don't think so. But I am quite sure that we only reach a state of pure awareness through a single focus, with a deep dedication and a desire to attain this ideal state. Just as celibacy is not easy, neither is the true commitment to spiritual life. And just as one might undertake a practice like celibacy as a total dedication to God-realization, we might consider how our own practice of total dedication, whatever it might be for each of us, gathers up our energy to reach for, and maybe attain, the same state.

In thinking about brahmacharya, and in thinking about my talk with Father Emilio, I decided to dig a bit deeper into the vow of celibacy for Catholic priests, as well as for others who have taken monastic vows, including various sects committed to a dedicated relationship with the Divine. Father Emilio seemed to have plenty of ojas — a vitality, a deep and light spirit that shone through everything he did and said. We never once talked about accent reduction; it seemed irrelevant to the real reason for our meeting. Father Emilio so clearly embodied a higher consciousness, and yet was so openly and honestly a "regular guy," that I wanted to know how his vow of celibacy specifically might contribute to who he is and who he represents in the world, both as a priest and as a model of someone deeply committed to his relationship with God—not just a commitment to the "rules" of his religion, but to the essence of his religion itself, Christ consciousness.

In my online research, one of my best finds was a treatise on celibacy that describes the vow and practice from its earliest, and perhaps most mystical, roots. In a beautiful paper presented at a 2006 conference by Brother Gregory Perron, OSB, the vow of celibacy is likened to the "desert of solitude" one seeks in order to merge completely with God. Drawing heavily from the works of Thomas Merton, Brother Gregory says, "We discover that our mystery and the mystery of God merge into one reality, which is the only reality." I feel the sense of deep peace in my relationship with the Divine that he is evoking when he continues, "We dedicate ourselves to a life of solitude because we believe that God lives in us and we in God—not precisely in the way that words seem to suggest (for words have no power to comprehend the reality) but in a way that makes words lose their shape, as it were, and become not thoughts, not things, but the unspeakable beating of a Heart within the heart of our own life." *(www.urbandharma.org)*

I see a close parallel here with Eastern philosophy, and Perron's description resonates with my own experience of time spent in silence, solitude, contemplation and prayer. In this contemplative place, I do not feel lonely or stifled by the rules and prescribed techniques that are often, in fact, no more than interpretations of God's desires. Instead, it really does feel like I am gathering up ojas, gathering up some essential life force that seems to nourish and feed every cell in my body. It seems to me that this sense of aliveness is what we experience as the Divine presence in others and is what I saw—no, felt—right away in Father Emilio. The Divine presence in him was so distilled, so concentrated, that I sensed it instantly, even through the veil of my mind's machinations, and within this divine presence my bad mood was dissolved in a moment.

Brother Gregory continues, "Celibacy, if it is to have any real meaning for us as monks, has to be understood as being most truly rooted in and, hence, an expression of our solitude, our love, our awareness of what it means to be wholly human and thus fully alive." Another way to translate brahmacharya is something like "walking with God" or "prayerful conduct." The sense of love and awareness expressed by Brother Gregory seems very in-line with the simple suggestion of walking with God or prayerful conduct, a state in which one really does feel "fully alive" as a human.

With Father Emilio, I immediately felt this sense of being fully alive through my own relationship with God, magnified by the relationship with Jesus that Emilio himself described. In this safe and open space, I felt supported to express my own experience of being an outsider, even, or perhaps especially, within the yoga community of which I was a part. There remained a part of me that was wary, cautious, even insecure about what I knew about yoga and my right to be practicing, let alone teaching, it. In hearing this, Father Emilio gave me a broad smile, and a mischievous sparkle flashed from his deep brown eyes. "You know," he said, "I remember that man in my village and the reason I wanted to be a priest. It was to be that loving presence, that compassionate guide, that open heart, for myself and for others who were suffering. In some ways, the fact that I am actually a Catholic priest also seems incidental. When I see priests now who seem to say, 'Respect me, I am a priest; I am wearing this collar, I am wearing this robe, I have the final word and I know the final truth.'" -- Father Emilio became increasingly impassioned at the thought of this posturing of other priests and continued, -- "I just want to say, 'Fuck you, go to hell.'" I swear, that is exactly what this young priest said to me. Of course, I was rather taken aback, and a bit amused, by a priest cursing like that, but just as quickly as the words came out, Emilio's intensity once again relaxed and the kind smile returned to soften his face. My attention to Father's bold colorful language faded back into a softer watercolor of texture and light, in which I knew again that I was truly in the presence of the Divine. I feel and see that same inflated sense of importance in the yoga world, and I see and feel it in myself. In relating to many prominent yoga teachers, I often find myself disheartened and somewhat lost when I see or hear about the posturing, the exclusiveness, the one-upping that goes on: Who knows yoga the best? Who has studied it the longest? Who can quote the Sutras? Who can interpret the Gita? All of this, all too often, seems to come at the expense of the deepest and most important gifts of yoga—the experience of contentment and faith in the oneness with God.

My conversation with Father Emilio moved me deeply, and I became more interested in, and aware of, the ways in which I move both toward and away from those experiences of contentment and faith. During that same trip I noticed something disturbing about myself. I had seen it peripherally for some time, but on that trip specifically, as I taught at multiple locations around the East Coast and met many passionate and devoted yoga students, this aspect of myself became so clear and was so disturbing that I finally had to acknowledge it to myself and tend to it right away. Here's what I saw: when I did my work, and acted from my heart and my own lifelong desire to connect and share myself with others, I felt steady and uplifted. But when I "networked," when I learned more about other teachers and organizations and what they were doing and when I talked about my own yoga teaching and service, I felt insecure and anxious. In other words, when I connected directly with divine presence, when I focused my heart and mind on that relationship, and asked for that presence to guide my words and my work, I felt at peace. When I attempted to connect with that same desire to somehow prove or legitimize my relationship with God through any kind of intermediary, whether it be self-aggrandizing or self-flagellation, competing for attention or acknowledgment, or even sometimes through trying to use and teach the principles or practices of yoga, I felt uneasy and unfulfilled. When the focus shifted, I lost my way.

In other words, as Father Emilio had seen and experienced, there was a big difference between the experience of connecting with the Divine directly and the experience of using the trappings of that connection—the priest's collar, the yoga mat at the front of the class—to prove how connected we are. Those things are not, in the end, important. What is it that we truly seek? And how do we find that?

Again, it goes back to where we place our focus. Yoga is what I have focused on; yoga is the home that contextualizes my sense of divine presence and my longing for an ever-deepening relationship with it. I have also come to believe that faith is a belief system that one inherently questions. I realized that, in some ways, it didn't matter so much what I believed, in terms of the framework, only that I believed in, focused on, something—a construct that gave me that very sense of certainty in a life of uncertainty, a grounding that held my sense of myself as loving presence. A way of walking with God.

For me, this means two important and perhaps seemingly contradictory things. "Don't dig so many shallow holes looking for the well. Dig one and dig deep." Choose the primary focus, the primary home for your spiritual life. Don't dilute it with a hundred different ideas and little bits of constructs from here and there. This will never serve you well when things get really hard. That doesn't mean you shouldn't explore, be inspired, seek to deepen and broaden your faith by learning about other faiths and finding varied sources of inspiration. But don't do it at the expense of finding a faith that you can really commit to, one that enables you to create and cultivate and honor a relationship that strengthens and serves you over time, in all of the challenges you will inevitably face in your lifetime.

Which brings me to the second caution: don't let the construct you choose become the enemy of the reason you chose it. In other words, when you find something that touches you deeply and invites you into prayerful conduct or your own experience of walking with God, stay focused on that and not on the rituals and trappings that can confine the experience. Don't become so fixated on yoga -- or Catholicism, or Buddhism -- as the means that you become more interested in preaching and defending the idea, its rules and its practices, than in the relationship with the Divine it is affording you.

We might not end up practicing celibacy or choosing the practice of brahmacharya as a primary means to our relationship with the Divine. But, when we see the depth of relationship that can flourish in this "desert of solitude," this building of ojas, this loving presence that we too can embody, we might more readily consider the practice of brahmacharya as worthy of exploration. We might see celibacy, or other acts of total dedication and focus, as a means to an end, moving us to deeper stillness and insight.

Perhaps we take the time just to be still, to be in solitude, to quiet our thoughts. We might take the time to notice how we feel when we are focused on our heart, on our relationship with divine presence. We might notice how we act and how we respond to life from this focus. We might explore what happens within when we become distracted by the trappings of yoga, by competition or expectation; we may notice that something changes and we become more uneasy and anxious. We might become attuned to people we meet who seem to have this abundance of ojas, people in whose presence we feel light and steady. We might notice when those same qualities emanate from us and ask ourselves — does this have anything to do with stillness, with solitude, with a trust in a deep personal relationship with the Divine?

If the answer is yes, which it surely will be, we might reconsider what brahmacharya could mean, for us, to simply stay focused on loving presence when we are with others, especially those who are suffering, and on the expansion of our hearts and minds. The practice of brahmacharya might even ask us to pull back from the distraction of external practices, even of the techniques of yoga, and to trust and immerse ourselves fully in an unconditional kinship with God.

Don't mistake the technique for the goal.

Never doubt that a small group of thoughtful, committed citizens can change the world; indeed, it's the only thing that ever has.

~ Margaret Mead

A Call to Love,
a Celebration of Life ~
Insights and Updates from Mexico,
Winter 2013

The last several months in Seattle were intense and chaotic. I worried if The Samarya Center would make its fundraising goal, I panicked when the permits for the build-out of our new center were going to take longer than expected, I arranged our last community forums, our annual holiday party, and our final satsang - a beautiful puja in which a priest joined us and let us in a blessing and honoring of our space. I was very happy on Christmas Day to head to my house in Mexico for a much needed break.

It has, for the most part, been lovely here - connecting with friends, teaching yoga and meditation to friends from the community, sleeping, reading and swimming.

But it has too, of course, offered its own unique challenges and insights.

As I write this today, I'm lying in bed with the chills, trying to get my energy together to get to the local clinic to be checked for Dengue fever. But that's nothing compared to everything else that has happened in my short time away from Seattle.

We arrived in Mexico to a beautiful day and spent the day at the beach with friends. While in the water, we witnessed an accident of two jet skis colliding, two people being thrown off the jet skis, a woman screaming hysterically, and a child being pulled out of the water. The papers showed the next day that she had died in the accident.

This experience created such a depth of darkness within me, or I should say, revealed that darkness, and I had a hard time shaking it for days. I felt moments of extreme anxiety and near panic attacks, and a sense that anything that could go wrong would. I grasped at my practice and felt little relief.

What a shadow of darkness, and not even mine. I have been holding and churning this experience. I have been writing it all down, like I don't want to forget those experiences, because even though they are so ugly and scary, they are there. They awaken me, which is good. I am feeling spacious. In fact, paradoxically, this horrible scene will always remind me of the darkness that is present within us, just beneath the surface, alongside the light and our simultaneous imperative to learn and practice metta - loving kindness.

In the meanwhile, with this experience always finding someplace in my mind, life goes on.

I am feeling much better, even with the chills and headache of what could be a cold, what could be the flu, or what could be dengue.

I'm here alone. Sasha left last Saturday to check on the relocation project for Samarya. The permits are in, he is talking to the contractors, and it looks like we should be able to begin work within the next couple of weeks.

Here on my own, I am in the midst of a "remodel" so to speak, in an old, crumbling cement house in super rural town in Mexico -- meaning I let a group of guys in around 9 every morning and they literally throw cement at literally every wall. I have no stove, no hot water, and what used to be some semblance of a living room and kitchen -- scrappy and quaint but fully functional, and even able to be made "cute" with some candles and flowers -- is now just a big open room, with hand made wet, stinky concrete walls with single light bulbs poking out of them from a riot of electrical wires. It's an odd time, and yet in some way, very grounding.

The other day I caught myself as I said to one of the workers, "Que manera de vivir!" As the words came out of my mouth, it occurred to me that I was complaining about the "desmadre" – the chaos - of my life, when in fact, my life is amazing. Yes, I don't feel so well. Yes, I haven't had a hot shower in days. Yes, I have no stove and nothing to cook on and nowhere to sit. Yes,

I saw and experienced something really hard. But I am here. And I have the luxury to be here, and to pay someone to throw cement at my walls, and to write from bed on a Macbook Air, and to talk and think and write about tragedy.

As I fell asleep last night, chilled and hungry, I had an incredibly liberating thought. "I don't need anything."

I realized that life itself is the gift, and our ability to be strong and spacious for ourselves and others is the only thing that matters.

Food is good, and I missed it last night when I went to bed hungry. But I knew, for the most part, I could do without it, and that in fact, I bet I will never experience a true hunger, one that I don't know when it will be appeased, not just a hunger of inconvenience.

Hot showers are good, but I don't need them. A comfortable place to live is great, but not necessary. I began to think of our work together as the Samarya community - how it might be to feel anxious, frustrated, uninformed. "Que manera de vivir!" What a way to live! With our anxiety about when our yoga school will open, where we will have our yoga class, will it have the right props and the best teachers? Indeed, what a way to live. Life is good, and hard.

Life is funny and confusing and so weird. I guess we just have to roll with it. For me, I just want to be kinder and kinder and kinder, because that is the only thing that matters. For me, that is encouraged and directed by a profound sense of devotion. But a devotion to something that I really have no idea what it is.

Some kind of God. Some kind of Love.

I look forward to our continued unfolding together – our shared journey of teaching and learning and growing. I look forward to the next phase of The Samarya Center for Humankind (ness) and of my own personal spiritual journey, and know that even these experiences I'm having in Mexico, in a sense testing me on multiple levels, will bring to bear in the new incarnation.

Thank you for your love, your dedication and your patience. Celebrate life. "Need" less. Practice slowing down and being in the moment. Practice love.

We are all in this together.

According to Vedanta, there are only two symptoms of enlightenment, just two indications that a transformation is taking place within you toward a higher consciousness. The first symptom is that you stop worrying. Things don't bother you anymore. You become light-hearted and full of joy. The second symptom is that you encounter more and more meaningful coincidences in your life, more and more synchronicities. And this accelerates to the point where you actually experience the miraculous. ~ Deepak Chopra

MOLLY LANNON KENNY

A Love Song to Devotion

Dedication devotion
Turning all the night time into the day
And after all the violence and double talk
There's just a song in all the trouble and the strife
You do the walk, you do the walk of life
~ Dire Straits, 1985, Brothers in Arms, Vertigo Records

There are so many things that I love about my life in Mexico. There are the obvious ones like the beach, the language, the people, the guacamole and the culture that supports and celebrates social interaction over productivity, just to name a few that come to me right away.

And then there are the less obvious gifts of my life in small town Mexico, gifts that reveal themselves to me again and again, and yet each time feel like a revelation and a relief. These are things like the spaciousness of my thoughts and the profound depths of my hearts stirrings. My sense of ease and creativity. The way my days roll languidly out of bed and in their sleepy way suggest one or two activities, as if that is all we could possibly fit in. Maybe a trip to the beach and a stop to visit friends. Maybe an errand to the seamstress and teaching one yoga class. Maybe a swim and a bike ride. Anything more than just one or two instantly seems too much.

Even beyond that, there is another gift that continually arises and offers itself to me, indeed, perhaps the most precious gift to my dedicated spiritual life: the gift of knowing that whatever life we are living, believing it to be THE life, OUR life, is in fact only an illusion, and we could have a very different life with different people and different routines, even a different language. And in this other life, we also have very different experiences and opportunities - new ways of being afraid, new ways of trusting, new ways of being let down, new ways of creating friendships, even new ways of conducting those

181

friendships. We get to be reminded that the "we" we think of as being "us," as evidenced by our habitual lives - "we" eat this food, and go to this yoga class, and have this partner - is in fact no more than the two dimensional construct we have created over time, with the complicity of our families, our partners, our jobs. The "me" as I know it is called into question, because the construct is so radically different. It's as if I thought I was "me" because I wore the standard northwest fare of jeans, boots and a knock off Northface jacket. Because I drink microbrew beer. Because I rooted for the Seahawks. But when suddenly those things are not a part of my day, or my life (although I did watch the Superbowl with some northern friends!), I get to discover, again, that the real "me" is not actually dependent on any of those things, and in fact, exists outside of any particular identity.

Ralph Waldo Emerson wrote in his powerful essay, The Oversoul, "A man is the façade of a temple wherein all wisdom and good abide. What we commonly call man, the eating, drinking, planting, counting man, does not, as we know him, represent himself, but misrepresents himself."

We have misrepresented ourselves to ourselves for so long that we easily forget that we are not the "eating, drinking, counting, planting" façade that we have created over our lifetime. And if we are not that, then, what are we?

This very question has been presented to us as one of the ways to liberate our own souls. If we can begin to disentangle ourselves from our firmly entrenched identities, we might begin to open to the possibility of another identity, one as a manifestation of divine presence, an egoless sense of unchanging awareness that unites us, not just with God consciousness, but with each other in the deepest sense of shared humanity through the presence of the divine.

For me, this is another precious gift my life here affords me. Without the tenacious grip of a single identity, and with time and space, and curiously long days, my mind and heart have plenty of time to simply dwell in this question, and its possible resolution. Who am I? Who is God? How are we connected? Why am I here? What can I offer? How can I be uplifted? What gives me courage and sustenance? How can I uplift others? How can I be the most real, the most useful?

I get to choose, easily, a life of measured and concentrated focus on my relationship with God, and to tend to and cultivate that relationship with the same (and perhaps even more) care and joy that I offer to the friends and support who are in my life in their human form.

For me, this cultivation of relationship comes, very much, in the form of acts of devotion. I start my days very differently here in Mexico. I wake up daily around eight and walk out to my yoga studio. I sweep the floor, turn on the fans and clean the altar. Then I might go for a bike ride to collect wildflowers - hibiscus, bougainvillea, ginger - which I toss into the basket of my clunky no speed bike. I return home and, starting from the front of my house, empty all the water bowls, large and small, that are filled with yesterday's offerings of flowers. I spread the old flowers out around the studio for even in their process of decay they are still offering forth their bursts of color, their affirmations of life and beauty. I clean all the water bowls, then refill them one by one with fresh water. I carefully take the flowers from my basket and clean and trim them, then arrange them into the various water bowls, or around the neck of Kwan-Yin, or over the framed picture of Swami Vivekananda, or into the hands of Buddha, along with the beautiful tiny copper folding mirror with the picture of Jesus, beatific and kind, on the front. Of all the things on my altar, I may just love that tiny mirror the best. It's Jesus. Then, I open it, and it's me. I close it and it is Jesus again, serene, ever watchful. Sometimes I hold it throughout my meditation and periodically open my eyes to look at it. It's Jesus. Then it's me. But I digress....

My mornings in Mexico begin with acts of devotion, and these acts of devotion fill me with a sense of divine protection and courage. Things happen in Mexico that could of course happen anywhere, but they feel different when they happen here. Serious illness, arguments with loved ones, feelings of exclusion, loss, rejection. These too have more space, so they are not only more easily absorbed into a rarified sea of thought and heart, they also have the tendency at first to linger a bit longer, to feel a bit more jagged and isolating. Without the distraction of internet and traffic and work and deadlines and decisions, I seem to feel everything more.

Sometimes even just as the measurable daytime seems to defy the constraints of minutes and hours, the metaphoric nights can seem also seem darker and longer. My own tendencies for sadness and feeling overwhelmed by suffering - both my own and universal - seem to expand here in perfect relationship to the general fluidity of time and space. Here in Mexico, I welcome this sadness because even as I know it will sting, I know too that I will be able to place it at my altar, I will be able to gather it in flowers, I will be able to cleanse it in fresh water, I will be able to transform it through acts of devotion, I will be able to cash in, as it were, on my practice of dedication. The nighttime turns to day. The tears turn into a song. I open the tiny mirror held reverently in my folded hands. Jesus. Me.

I'm alive. I am doing the walk of life. Personally, I feel infinitely more confident in it when I believe that I am accompanied by a divine presence I may never be able to fully describe or define. This is the gift of giving up our one single identity. This is the gift of questioning, of creating relationship to something greater than whatever we imagine ourselves to be. This is the gift of devotion. This is the reward for a heart and mind concentrated on divine love.

Let us create a community that allows one another to be fluid in their identity, one that is all inclusive, that asks more questions than it answers, that offers a place of solace, safety and welcoming for all people as reflections of that same divine presence. Let us bring flowers, care for our altar, explore prayer and contemplation in the myriad ways until every single person has something that fits for them, that makes them feel their own personal "night times" will soon burst into daylight and song. Let us be patient and faithful and trusting. Let's do the walk of life. Together. With dedication and yes, devotion.

We are all in this together.

MOLLY LANNON KENNY

Pray in any way, for the Lord hears even the footfall of an ant.

~ Sri Ramakrishna

Angelina 12/26/2013

Our arrival in Puerto Vallarta was standard – the same trip we had made hundreds of times before - except that we were traveling with the family of some good friends: mom, dad and two little girls, age 6 and 8. We waited with them excitedly at the luggage carousel, passed through the red light/green light system of customs and made our way out to the highway to catch a cab. The girls were troopers – each carrying a piece of luggage as we traipsed the dusty road under the hot sun. Negotiating two cabs to get to our hotel, we took a momentary leave of our guests and discussed how things might be different having friends with little kids with us and what we could do to ensure they had a great trip.

Settled into our respective rooms at our hotel, we were anxious to enjoy the last hours of sun -- seemingly a million miles away from the cold and gray weather we had left behind in the Pacific Northwest on this Christmas Day. We spent an evening as we had a hundred times before -- playing in the waves, drinking a beer, and settling into our vacation. I loved watching Sasha share his beloved "Playa de los Muertos" with his friends, giddy with the excitement of sharing a place we both love so much.

The next day, December 26, was another bluebird day. We ran some errands in the morning, anxious to return to the beach and play in the waves with our guests, especially given that our six year old guest had told me that the one thing she wanted to do was to swim out beyond the break to where the water was calm. I was very much looking forward to making that simple wish come true.

As is our usual ritual, I ran directly into the water, while Sasha planted himself under a palapa to read. This time however, instead of swimming alone, I got to swim with my two young friends and their parents. It was a day like any other – people splashing and laughing, boats cruising both fast and slow and tourists and beach workers doing their dance of commerce and conviviality.

In the water, my little friends practiced swimming, floating alone for the count of ten, watching the parasailers fly above us, and learning to gauge the waves to decide which ones to go over and which ones to swim under. At one point, my friend Lisa, the girls' mom, was looking out at the water nearby and suddenly said, "Did those two jet skis just crash?" I looked up and looked around, not yet cognizant of the fact that this would be a strange question --she saw what she saw -- they either did or didn't crash. In fact, it wasn't a question of reality, but a question of incredulousness and shock. Her face was wooden -- "They flew like, ten feet in the air." At that same moment, up on the beach, Sasha would later tell us that he heard a crash louder than anything he had ever heard before, and also saw the passengers thrown off their jet skis. All around us, for the most part, people continued to play and swim, just a few starting to orient their gaze to the place about a fifty yards away where a small cluster of boats was forming. Someone nearby said, "I hope they have insurance."

At just that instant, I heard a scream like no other I have ever known. In all my time at the beach, I have heard many people shouting, even yelling for help when they are in over their heads, but this one was different. This was a guttural cry of absolute anguish and panic. Time seemed to slow down, and we vacillated between acting like everything was normal for the sake of the girls, and not being able to take our eyes off the scene that was unfolding in front of us. People began to run toward the scene, boats pushed out as fast as possible, and a frenzy of horror and confusion overtook the usual calm of the beach.

"What's happening?" asked my little friend. "Are they OK?" "Yes," I answered. "I'm sure they're ok, they just had an accident – see, people are there going to help them." But what I could actually see was very different than what I was saying.

The first boat to get to the scene was on its way back, and I watched as they lifted a tiny frame out of the boat – "My god," I said quietly to my friend, "It's a little kid." I could see the child's arms and legs hanging lifelessly from the embrace of the person carrying her, and one of the others from the accident walking onto the beach with heavy, deliberate steps, her head down in total shock. "Oh my god," I repeated, "That person is dead."

We continued to downplay and distract for the sake of the children we were with, but at some point, I could no longer stand the tension between pretending and the reality of what I knew had just happened in front of us. I said, "I have to talk to Sasha," and ran out of the water to him, as if simply by connecting with him, this would all somehow not be true. I ran to where Sasha was sitting alone. "Sasha," I whispered, "someone just died there." "I know," he replied quietly. But by now the beach was buzzing with talk of the accident, what people had seen, what was happening now, with questions about the age of the little girl and why she was on the boat, with talk of waivers and culpability. I couldn't stand that either, and quickly returned to the water. The absolute unreality, and simultaneous total, horrific reality, of the scene had me completely ungrounded. I sought the ocean waves to wash this away, make it not be true. Once in the water again, I realized that the very place that had for so long been my total respite, a place I could always go to feel totally at peace, had turned to a place of darkness and anguish. Time seemed to move in some new, suspended dimension. We pretended, we swam, we finally left the water to drink a beer, or to build a sand castle or to otherwise carry on as if nothing had happened. While we talked about mundane things, I, and everyone else, knew that our minds were completely distracted and filled with the horror of what we had witnessed. I heard someone come by and say the little girl was unresponsive; someone else said she was breathing. I prayed and prayed for her recovery – perhaps she was not killed after all. I repeated to myself over and over, "Please God, let her be ok."

That evening we checked the news for a report but saw nothing. We showered, ate dinner, watched TV – everything business as usual, except for the incessant question in our minds and empty, sick feelings in our bellies. We slept fitfully.

The next morning arrived – not as a beautiful sunny vacation day, but with giant dark clouds in the sky and on again off again downpours. I woke up early and went to get coffee, feeling in a daze. Everything just went on. People bought coffee, and talked about the weather. I checked the internet at the coffee shop but couldn't find any news. No one was talking about the accident. I guess, in fact, if they weren't there, that they didn't know about it at all. As if it had never happened. As if the trajectory of these lives had not been irreversibly changed in an instant. The rain poured down from the dark sky.

We decided to leave as quickly as possible. I asked everyone I saw, quietly, "Do you know what happened to that little girl?" At first, no one seemed to know. My friend, Ana, who runs the front desk at our hotel said, "Molly, tu tienes que pensar en algo diferente. A ti, te encanta la playa, no tienes que guardar esta imagen en tu mente." But I couldn't think of anything else, and I couldn't find my love for the beach – indeed that image pervaded my every thought. Lisa asking if the jetskis had crashed. The anquished scream. The little arms and legs dangling, as if someone was carrying a tiny sleeping body into the house to tuck her safely into bed. The woman with her life jacket half opened, walking numbly out of the water.

As our friends packed up the last of their stuff, I sat in the lobby searching the internet for news. I felt compelled to know her name, and what had happened. I couldn't let it go. I didn't want it to be true, and I didn't want it to just disappear as if the world had not just completely shattered for this family. Just before we left, I ran back up to my room, and again asked the cleaner – "Have you heard anything about that little girl?" "Si," she responded in a hushed voice, "ella se murió." "How do you know that?" I asked. "It's in the paper," she said. For some reason I felt desperate to see for myself. "Which paper?" I asked. The cleaner gave me the names of two daily papers from Puerto Vallarta, and a shared look of overwhelming sadness at the death of a child and the life of the mother and cousin who were with her in the accident. I left the room quietly, sick and distracted.

Everyone finally together in the lobby, we got two cabs to the nearest bus stop to make our way up to our house. The younger of the two girls we had with us asked if she could ride in the cab with Sasha and me. She cuddled under my arm, tried to put on her seatbelt, and when at first she couldn't fasten it said to me with great authority, "It's OK. We don't have to wear seatbelts in Mexico." I laughed, and helped her to buckle in. But my laugh was uneasy – it was more the ironic recognition of this suspension of reality - nothing bad can happen when we are on vacation. All bets are off, and we are invincible. Except that we're not.

We arrived at the bus stop with its usual chaos. The rain had mostly stopped, but the day was gray and heavy and sad. In my mind, every person at that bus stop was deeply depressed, although of course I knew that most of them were probably perfectly content. Their lives had not changed between yesterday and today. Go shopping, go to work, tend children, make plans. Everything normal. Everything fine. While we waited, I walked to a newsstand to check the papers. The man at the stand asked me which paper I was looking for, and I asked him if he had heard news of the accident. "Si." He motioned to a paper in front of him – the front page was filled with images of the beach and the huge headline: Se mató una niña de 7 años. My eyes ran over the subheading, confirming what we had seen. Three people in an accident – a mother, her child and a cousin. The child had died. I wanted to buy the paper, to keep it and read it more closely. I closed my eyes and turned away from the stand. I didn't have any money on me anyway, and I also believed that Sasha would find it obsessive and unhealthy of me to buy the paper. For what? I didn't know what I wanted or why I thought I needed it, but the pull was as strong as any ocean wave, drawing me out into a sea of isolation and unknown depths.

I walked back to the bus stop where the bus was just arriving. We got on with all of our luggage, and squeezed in among all the people going on with their lives. I waited for about a half hour before telling Sasha what I had read. "You have to stop thinking about it, Molly." "Ok," I said. "I will." But I knew I wouldn't and couldn't. I just stopped talking about it. We sat silently the rest of the rainy ride to our home an hour north. The girls slept. The bus sputtered. The rain started again. Puerto Vallarta became a world away. A world where life went on, people played and swam and rented jetskis with their family. On vacation.

Finally arrived at our little cement and brick home, Sasha and I sat outside on the patio. Sasha began to talk about the various things we needed to do with the house and the yard. Suddenly, as he was talking, I felt a grip and pulsation in my solar plexus and my mind began to close in in a way I had never before experienced. The scene had created such a depth of darkness within me, or I should say, revealed that darkness, and I didn't know what to do with it. I honestly thought it could be a place that, if I let myself go there, I might never return. I knew I was completely alone. I began to cry. "Sasha, please stop talking about those details. I feel like I am losing my mind. I can't stop thinking about what happened." I remember saying, "I want it to be, like, five days from now, when I won't feel this way anymore," while knowing intensely that it would never be five days, or five years or five lifetimes, that would allow the pain of this experience to subside for this family. For that mother. For that cousin. For everyone who knew that little girl. Angeline.

Over the next several days, I continued to experience moments of extreme anxiety and near panic attacks, and a sense that anything that could go wrong would. I became afraid to eat salad in case it would make me sick, or to have workers in my house in case my house would fall down, or to ride in a truck in case it would crash. I would wake up in the night with the image of the little girl being pulled from the water, and more intense images - projected - of her mom and the reality of the rest of her life and how she could go on. I created unhelpful images in my mind of the mom lying in her bed, never stopping her crying, wanting to die too. I imagined her being given valium and her finding only fragmented sleep. I imagined the blame, the anger, the overwhelming reality of it all. I imagined the young cousin, and her playing out the scene over and over in her mind, as I did in mine, even without being there. I grasped at my practice and felt little relief. I looked every day - almost obsessively - for news of the family, to know who this girl was, who these people were, and my mind continually leaned towards thoughts of all the people suffering everywhere. An overwhelming shadow of darkness, and not even mine.

It has been intense.

Finally one day during meditation, I opened my eyes and looked at my altar and saw the face of Swami Vivekananda looking back at me. In an instant, I knew I had to pull out of this thing, and that altogether in our lives we have to constantly find our inner resources, not just for ourselves, but to keep a strength and hold a faith that there may be peace and some kind of healing for others.

I realized how tenuous our grip is on all we think is secure -- our lives, our families, our friendships, our bodies, and above all our mental stability. I knew, again, that we have to work always at strengthening our mind, even if we think it is already sound - only God knows how we might actually be tested.

I knew too, that I had to be that person. I had to continually develop my own inner strength. I had to keep my mind and heart infinitely open – for all the people with whom who I might come into contact, but never know what they are carrying, or what their inner life is –- for all the people who, even as they chit chat, or have a tequila, or share a laugh –- even while seemingly participating in the daily doings of life-- are at the same time bearing an inner load that is so heavy and so dark and that they keep constantly at bay -- just barely. Images coming and going -- what appears to be reality on the outside is a facade to the person who is experiencing the images and the trauma on the inside. An inner world that may never be revealed to us, but that is always there.

I knew that I would have to write about this experience to integrate it. But why? How? Not because "everything happens for a reason." Not because "there is a lesson to be learned from everything," not because "God has a plan." To me, these are the very statements we use that allow us to effectively distance ourselves from the reality of a pain so intense it is almost unbearable. They have a tendency to close down the expression of pain, of fear and suffering in their tidy effort to appease.

No, I knew I would write for myself. To remember some of the observations I made about myself, and people in general, and about life as we think we know it. I would write to remind myself why I practice, indeed to intensify my practice -- to be able to bear and hold all of this pain and suffering. I would write to be strong, and to be soft. I would write to open and honor the expression of pain in all its dimensions, and in an attempt to bring us closer together through our shared experiences. I would write what I saw, and what I felt.

May my observations offer some light in the deep shadows of grief, and perhaps ignite in all of us yet another reason to practice kindness.

If you judge people, you have no time to love them.
~*Mother Teresa*

People want, desperately, to connect. We want to know that our life has meaning, and that our actions and our thoughts matter. We feel a deep connection to others in their joy and in their suffering and seek to share in both experiences. At the same time, it seems that, when things are really hard, and they are not ours, we feel conflicted. We run down the beach to see what is happening, to know that this is real, to maybe do something. We want to connect. But perhaps we also run towards the pain to remind ourselves, indeed assure ourselves, that it is not ours. We begin to assign blame and culpability, we reduce the situation to a handful of facts and trivialities, "I hope they have insurance..." and compare our own beliefs and actions to those of another to assure ourselves that we would not do that, we are not like that, so that, of course, whatever it is would never happen to us. The pain is too intense so we disconnect through judgment and comparison.

This does no one any good. Perhaps when we notice ourselves disconnecting in this way, we can remind ourselves that it doesn't matter how or why. It matters only that someone is in unbearable pain, and it is our job only to open our hearts and offer whatever grace we can. The world needs this much more than it needs our evaluation and separation.

Compassion is not a relationship between the healer and the wounded. It's a relationship between equals. Only when we know our own darkness well can we be present with the darkness of others. Compassion becomes real when we recognize our shared humanity.
~ *Pema Chodron*

People live through horrible things. We have to begin to understand and acknowledge that we may never know the depth of trauma, heart break, fear and isolation people have experienced or are currently experiencing in their lives. What would it take for us to offer kindness to all beings, at all times, with the assumption that whatever is happening now, kindness and care can only help.

As Thich Nhat Hanh says, "When another person makes you suffer, it is because he suffers deeply within himself, and his suffering is spilling over. He does not need punishment; he needs help. That's the message he is sending."

Think of how many times we have been less than patient, less than thoughtful, less than forgiving, because we didn't like the way a person was acting, or what they were saying, or not saying. Think how rarely we take the time to consider where a person might be coming from, what they might be going through. How would our actions change if we reminded ourselves that everyone is carrying a heavy burden, and considered our most important job in this life to be simply taking care of each other?

Nothing in the world is permanent, and we're foolish when we ask anything to last, but surely we're still more foolish not to take delight in it while we have it. If change is of the essence of existence one would have thought it only sensible to make it the premise of our philosophy.
~ W. Somerset Maugham

Nothing is what it seems, nothing lasts forever. Our life is one way, and then it is another. In an instant everything can change, including our mental state. We know all too well that when we have an uncomfortable experience, even a common cold, we can feel like we will never be well again. In the same way, when we are feeling good, we don't often stop to reflect on how wonderful it feels to be free from sickness or suffering. In fact, all of life -- our physical and mental health, our emotions, our relationships -- are in a constant state of flux. How can we more deeply appreciate all we have now, while strengthening our systems – physical, emotional, spiritual and relational – so that we are best equipped to navigate the inevitable changing tides of our circumstances? And how can we be with others, as a beacon and a steward, through their own

It is possible to become discouraged about the injustice we see everywhere. But God did not promise us that the world would be humane and just. He gives us the gift of life and allows us to choose the way we will use our limited time on earth. It is an awesome opportunity. ~ Cesar Chavez

It is sometimes difficult to acknowledge that, in fact, suffering of this magnitude happens everywhere all the time, both on large scales – of communities and of nations – as well as on individual scales. In either case, we seem to have a hardwiring for something called "compassion down regulation," a largely adaptive aspect of our cognition that helps us to not become overwhelmed when we perceive the suffering of others to threaten our own resources. While this response can be helpful in combatting experiences such as "compassion fatigue," it is important for us to be aware of this tendency when we do want to stay present, without feeling like we are falling apart ourselves. This is something I help my students with often, and especially on our pilgrimages to India. How can we at once keep our hearts open and not pretend that the suffering is not occurring, while not becoming so absorbed in the suffering that we become ineffectual? This is, indeed, an awesome opportunity for our own spiritual reflection and growth.

I believe that we learn by practice. Whether it means to learn to dance by practicing dancing or to learn to live by practicing living, the principles are the same. In each, it is the performance of a dedicated precise set of acts, physical or intellectual, from which comes shape of achievement, a sense of one's being, a satisfaction of spirit. One becomes, in some area, an athlete of

God. Practice means to perform, over and over again in the face of all obstacles, some act of vision, of faith, of desire. Practice is a means of inviting the perfection desired.
~ Martha Graham

While I was going through this inner experience, I would go out to my meditation room daily and try to sit, or practice asana, or pray. And I would find, again and again, that it felt like my practice wasn't working, that my practice itself seemed inadequate and even trivial for what I was experiencing. The attempts at practice felt contrived, and I felt like a fraud myself, simply for trying to "do" my practice in the midst of these intense emotions. I have since talked to many students who have shared the same experience, especially when it seemed like their practice would serve them the most – students going through cancer treatment, the death of a family member, a devastating break-up.

What was revealed to me through this experience, and what seems to have resonated with students, is the thought that perhaps during those dark nights it is not the time to "do" your practice, it is the time to "be" your practice – the time to reap the benefit that your dedication to practice has given you. In these times, if it feels like your practice isn't working, consider letting go of what you think your practice should be, and become deeply open to receiving its fruits - perhaps moments of relief, moments of strength and forbearance, even moments of peace and joy.

One ought to hold on to one's heart; for if one lets it go, one soon loses control of the head too.
~ Friedrich Nietzsche

While I have worked with people experiencing PTSD for over a decade and a half, it was only through this experience that I felt I had some true sense of the thoughts and sensations that pervade the mind and body in this condition.

If I didn't fully understand it prior, I now knew that the experience of PTSD is real, tenacious and visceral – anxiety, panic attacks, fear -- and it is all around us. I felt for all the people who are showing their symptoms and for all those who are not. For every person who is sitting, laughing, sharing a beer, or a sunset, and yet, just under the surface is the sickly feeling of coming undone. Words, small talk, images – all become potential sources of aggravation and unraveling. How can I, how can we all, become ever more patient and attuned to the hidden traumas of others and to the accompanying discomfort? How can we more deeply understand and offer care to this condition through own deep deep practice of empathy and openness to the inner experiences of another?

Is there an answer to the question of why bad things happen to good people?...The response would be... to forgive the world for not being perfect, to forgive God for not making a better world, to reach out to the people around us, and to go on living despite it all... no longer asking why something happened, but asking how we will respond, what we intend to do now that it has happened. ~ Harold S. Kushner

Love, unselfconscious, unrestrained and imaginative, is the only answer. Let our practice be one of perfecting our capacity to love completely.

Finally, in these experiences we often hear, "nothing can prepare you for something like that." And of course, in a sense that's true. But I believe we can prepare ourselves in general for the inevitable suffering that comes with life itself. We can prepare ourselves for the sensations, we can learn to breathe, we can practice directing our minds, we can practice open and kind heartedness, and we can prepare ourselves to receive the suffering of others.

I don't have any answers. I don't have any neat truisms to sum up this experience. I have questions and observations, and a sense that sharing these might open anyone who reads them up to a more expansive reality. May you find something within these words that resonates, uplifts, and simply allows.

She Responded
The birds' favorite songs
You do not hear,
For their most flamboyant music takes place
When their wings are stretched
Above the trees
And they are smoking the opium
Of pure freedom.
It is healthy for the prisoner
To have faith
That one day he will again move about
Wherever he wants,
Feel the wondrous grit of life–
Less structured,
Find all wounds, debts stamped canceled,
Paid.
I once asked a bird,
"How is it that you fly in this gravity
of darkness?"
She responded,
"Love lifts
Me."
~ Hafiz

Svadhyaya ~
Stillness and Movement,
Courage and Change

We are shaped by our thoughts. We become what we think.
~The Buddha

A few years back, I attended a five-day yoga workshop in Arizona. When I signed up for the training, I was very excited about it, but following a series of personal challenges I was less than enthusiastic when the time actually came. When I landed in Arizona, I was feeling stressed, lonely, and physically and emotionally drained. When I arrived at my hotel, I thought more about lounging by the pool than showing up at the workshop in downtown Tempe.

On the very first day of the workshop, I started to become anxious about the content and the process of the training. I didn't really want to do partner exercises, I didn't want to do group sharing, and I was having a hard time feeling articulate or even interested. When I did do a bit of group and partner processing, I felt misunderstood and frustrated. I was ready to leave the workshop, initially staying only because I had already paid for it. But then I made a deal with myself to try and fulfill the yogic concept of tapas, or determination and perseverance - I would stay and I would keep a positive attitude. I would sit up front by the teacher and focus on his teachings, and I would be kind and generous with myself when I felt myself becoming separate. I decided that was my tapas, to keep recommitting, to keep showing up, and to keep learning. I was proud of my super-yogic ability to turn my bad attitude around. I even exchanged some pleasantries with the person sitting next to me. I began to relax and soak in the teaching. After all, that's what I had come for.

It was a typical American yoga workshop set-up. Everyone had their mats on the floor, sitting on blankets or with back-jacks, intermittently stretching their legs or moving around to adjust their position. The teacher stood in front of us and lectured. On this particular morning, I had pulled up all of my emotional and physical reserves and had sat down in front and slightly to the right of the teacher. I was feeling fragile but determined.

As the teacher began to speak, I became engrossed in the teachings and was starting to feel a deeper sense of peace and belonging than I had on any of the previous days. I kept my eyes on the teacher as I stretched my legs out in front of me, hoping to get some relief from the ache that was creeping into my knees from sitting cross-legged for so long. Suddenly, the woman to my right tapped me on the shoulder. "How unusual," I thought, "she's trying to get my attention right in the middle of the lecture." I leaned over to her, still trying to stay focused on the teacher. She whispered, "In our tradition..." Before she had said any more, I thought, "Oh, she just wants to share a thought she's having about her practice," and although I wished she hadn't interrupted the teacher to tell me, I leaned in to listen to what she had to say. "In our tradition, we don't point our feet toward the teacher, so you may want to cover your feet." BAM! I came right out of every tiny bit of peace I had mustered and went careening into defensiveness, irritation, judgment, anger, and vindication. I just looked at her and said, "No thanks," then stretched my legs out even further. In that moment, I was instantly back in the fifth grade, but I didn't care. She was not going to tell me what to do! My mind reeled with all the possible retorts I wanted to give: "In my tradition, we mind our own business. In my tradition, we prioritize non-harming over schooling a total stranger. In my tradition, we don't interrupt our teacher to try to tell another student what to do," and on and on. And, trust me, those are only the PG comebacks that whirled like unhinged dervishes through my head. I couldn't focus. I kept thinking about the woman and her comment. I felt like I was oozing anger, and I felt like I was going to cry. Move my feet? Then she'll think I'm doing it because she told me to. Don't move my feet? Then the teacher will think I am disrespecting him, or someone else will reprimand me again.

I managed to make it through the lecture, but carried my anger and insecurity through the asana practice and on into lunch. I thought of even more and better comebacks. When we came back from lunch, I managed not to look at the offender. When she tried to engage me, I just ignored her. While I smiled and acted friendly with others, I made sure she knew that we were not friends. It felt really good — wait — no it didn't. But at least I was sticking up for myself. Sort of? I felt infused with reactive, even hostile energy. It didn't feel good; it didn't even feel like it was mine any more, but I didn't know how to make it stop. It almost felt as if I had been hijacked by some alien intruder who was infinitely petty, reactive, and unforgiving.

I had been thinking about tapas, Patanjali's precept of determination, to keep myself focused on the teacher, but now I needed something else to help me out of this mind-mire I found myself in. Now, I needed the precept that follows tapas: svadhyaya, or self-inquiry, which in many ways is the foundation for all of the other yamas and niyamas. We can't know how to act with ahimsa, non-violence, without inquiring into the nature of our actions. We can't find santosha, contentment, without questioning what brings us discontentment. It is only through seeing ourselves clearly and honestly that we are able to practice satya, truthfulness. It is only through observing our greed and clinging that we are able to practice aparigraha, non-grasping. Truly knowing and acknowledging our deepest selves, the good, the bad, and the ugly, is the only way to create real and lasting change in ourselves, in our relationships, in our communities, and in our world. Even practicing tapas requires self-study. We might have the fire and perseverance to create change, but without svadhyaya we might easily neglect to see our own part in creating conflict, both internal and external.

It is important to note that svadhyaya is not just about the awareness of how we show up in the world. Although it is important and useful to practice svadhyaya as the ability to know our part in a conflict, or to accept our faults, or to celebrate our strengths and put them to good use, it is also about inquiring into our own true nature, or God realization. Yet another aspect of self-study is the study of the scriptures and spiritual texts to gain insight and reflection into ourselves as part of the Divine cosmology. Svadhyaya is indeed the deep acknowledgment of the oneness of our own soul with all that is. With the practice of svadhyaya, we begin to dissolve the illusion of separateness that is at the root of all suffering. As we become more grounded in this practice, we are able to find God presence in everything – in ourselves, in our families, in our communities. We are able to see God in the natural world, and in the person standing in front of us at any moment.

But how could I find God in that woman, in that moment, where I felt I had been diminished and shamed by her? How could I even find the mental clarity that would allow me to soften or dissolve this wall I had built up between us?

I had been thinking a lot about awareness and particularly self-awareness at all of its many levels. I had been noticing how often I held on to an idea, or a grudge, or an insecurity, simply by choosing to not be self-aware and by choosing to deny or defend the very actions that caused me pain and suffering. I could see that it was my own limited view of myself, and indeed of my own mind, that was creating this inner turmoil. I knew that I needed to find a way back to stillness.

In the teachings of meditation, the image of a still lake is often offered for the quality of mind we are trying to cultivate through the practice. I have heard, and used, this image on many occasions. Meditation is certainly one of the practices that can help us to develop svadhyaya. We might say that emotions, thoughts, reactions are all things that keep us swirling in confusion or illusion—these are like the ripples and waves on the lake. As we cultivate stillness, we develop the capacity to see the "bottom of the lake," or the still point in ourselves, the awareness in us that is objective, non-judgmental, and reflective. In yoga, this is considered to be our true nature — one of stillness and equanimity.

During a recent morning meditation, the image of a lake came to me spontaneously. This time, I saw the lake that I actually know the best—the lake where my family has a summer house and where I spent all of my summers growing up. This lake is of the On Golden Pond variety; quiet, remote, and peaceful. I saw myself, my mind, as that lake; but in that image, I didn't see just stillness. I also saw the activity on the lake, which more often than not consists of things like loons and kayaks. I thought about how the kayaks, like our thoughts, come into our vision in a quiet and stealthy way. They slip through the water and then they're gone, moving swiftly and almost silently. Sometimes thoughts are like that. They seem to come out of nowhere and then they disappear. If we wait long enough, we will surely see the kayaks—like our thoughts— come back around. So the lake remains very still, even though it has movement and activity.

Then I thought of the loons. They are quiet and stealthy too, but they move very differently than the kayaks. They just emerge up out of the lake then sit, as if they've always been there. Sometimes they are silent, sometimes they call out, and sometimes their calls are answered. The calls can be loud and have a sense of urgency or they can be haunting and isolated. Similarly, our thoughts may barely disturb the surface of the mind but can feel pervasive and lingering, even in their quietness. Other times, our thoughts seem to be calling out, having long conversations of their own, which we do not understand at all but feel compelled to listen to. Then another image of the loon on the lake came to me. It was of how the loon suddenly becomes aware of some disturbance, perhaps from our presence or from something beneath the surface, and dives out of sight. If we had not seen it go under, we would never have known it was there. But we did see it, and we do know it had been there. And in fact, if we know there are loons in a lake, then we can guess that sometimes they are under the surface, even if we don't happen to see them. I suddenly understood: thoughts are like that too. They too go under the surface and live a whole other life in the murky unseen depths. It is this aspect of thought, of consciousness, of self-awareness that, if uncovered, might offer us an even deeper understanding of ourselves and what drives us. And yet, because they are not immediately apparent, we can deny them. We can pretend we don't know they exist. Or we can just forget that they do. But we can never know the whole lake without having some understanding of what is under the surface, even when the lake is still. Similarly, we cannot truly know ourselves without committing to curiosity, courage, and excavating the deepest parts of our own psyche. It's scary going there, but if we want to truly foster real individual change, ultimately leading to social change, we really have no choice.

Back in Tempe, the teacher didn't seem to mind my feet facing towards him. In fact, he was very vocal about his support for The Samarya Center, so much so in fact that several people came up to me asking about this amazing organization that their teacher kept championing. My "arch-enemy" looked at me with sweet, loving, and persistent eyes, and asked me, "What does your organization do?" Well, I was stuck. I couldn't just not answer her. So I took a breath and then started to tell her about all of the things The Samarya Center does and stands for. She engaged me and surprised me by telling me that the organization for which she worked, a company that makes yoga jewelry, had offered us support in the past for our fundraisers, and she asked if I would like her to suggest us as a recipient of their donor program. In fact, she told me that she had sample jewelry in her car and would be happy to send some back with me. I sat there, humbled, embarrassed, and confused. I really was mad that she had "schooled me," but she was a sweet and beautiful woman offering love and generosity. What to do? I took a deep breath. And then told her what had happened in my head. I told her that I was feeling insecure and that in my fragile state, I had been brought back to childhood fears of doing wrong, being the outsider, not being included, being shamed. She told me that she had been working with trying to stand up for herself, overcoming the "loud voice" of her father that "always overpowered" her. That she wanted to practice this by telling me something that was important to her, but that she didn't know how. When she finally mustered her courage and spoke her truth, she immediately wished she hadn't and felt conflicted about the situation and how it had turned out. We talked about how we could each handle the same thing in the future and she – incredibly- asked for my advice. I told her I thought she should definitely continue to speak her truth, but that her svadhyaya in such situations might be to first consider where her impulse was coming from, and what its impact might be on the other person, and then to speak from her own experience rather than reprimanding a peer for "breaking the rules." She told me that she understood how I felt in the workshop — she knew what it felt like to feel like an outsider too — and that my svadhyaya was also helpful for her as I owned my own craziness in the situation and acknowledged, without self-judgment, all the under-the-surface emotions driving a disproportionate reaction.

Right after that, our teacher asked us to lie down for a Yoga Nidra practice. We both settled in to a comfortable position and covered up with blankets. As we lay there, ready for the practice to begin, I opened my eyes and turned to her and said quietly, "I'm so glad we talked." She responded without missing a beat, "I was just thinking that same thing." We closed our eyes and were led peacefully off into meditation. Minds still as lakes. Loons and all.

The only reason we don't open our hearts and minds to other people is that they trigger confusion in us that we don't feel brave enough or sane enough to deal with. To the degree that we look clearly and compassionately at ourselves, we feel confident and fearless about looking into someone else's eyes.

~ Pema Chödrön

Patience Toward the Unsolved
and Practicing Tapas

Be patient toward all that is unsolved in your heart. And try to love the questions themselves. ~ Rainer Maria Rilke

The Samarya Center's mission is to foster individual change as a means to radical social transformation. In other words, we believe that it is only through each one of us fundamentally changing our comfortable constructs of self and other—by courageously examining our own beliefs and biases, by acknowledging that each one of us has a part in maintaining or deconstructing conventional paradigms that perpetuate separateness—that real social change will ever truly occur and be sustained. And we also know that individual change is not easy. It takes the desire and dedication of each one of us to make the change happen.

One spring, upon returning from a Samarya yoga teacher training, I was sharing with my husband the great appreciation, satisfaction, and humility I felt for being part of creating an experience that allows people to be open, spacious, and compassionate with themselves and their many stories of trauma and suffering. He was struck by the stories, and he commented, "Wow, a lot of people in a lot of pain end up on your trainings." I thought about that for a moment then responded, "A lot of people are in a lot of pain. The experience of the training just allows each student to share their own experiences, both heartbreaking and joyous, in the pursuit of self-knowledge and enlightenment. I think that when any of us feels that we are affirmed, whole and correct just as we are, we are more able to share our challenges and fears with vulnerability, and through this process we move toward a sweeter life."

In the past ten years, my faculty and I have trained well over two hundred students in our yoga teacher training, and literally thousands more students have come through our doors and, by their own accounts, have found the simple experience of being a part of our community to be truly transformative. But the work has to go beyond the initial feeling of hopefulness and that glimpse of encouragement and acknowledgement. Indeed, healing ourselves, healing our deep wounds, revealing our traumas and grief, our deepest secrets, and our greatest sources of shame, requires effort and determination; it is a tapas that takes a lifetime. It is a continuous return to practice; a brave, unfiltered look into ourselves; an unearthing of our fears and limitations; and an acceptance of healing as a process of integration rather than exorcism. We cannot go to a therapist for a couple of sessions and call it "good"; we cannot go to our twice a week evening yoga class and expect that to do the trick. True healing is a long-term, lifelong process that requires fire, determination, and steadfastness.

In many ways, our American culture is suited to this kind of hard work. We like to get the job done, to pull ourselves up by the bootstraps, to get on with it. During the time I was facing the loss of my pregnancy, I reached out to a friend to tell her of the heartbreak I was experiencing, and she, with the best of intentions, advised me to "go for a run, sweat it out, work it out." And in fact, that is what I had planned to do, without consciously knowing it. As soon as I found out that my pregnancy would not progress, I decided to move on, join the gym, get back in shape, organize a workshop, write a newsletter, and meet with the adoption counselor. In our adoption interview, we were asked, "How are you dealing with your recent loss?" I came back right away with a sort of "Oh that? We've processed that already. I mean, that's my work, I know how to do that." I had already done that work. I had talked about it ad infinitum, I had rationalized my choices, and I had used the experience to learn something. So, it all seemed OK. Until it didn't.

During teacher training one morning, we were practicing the challenging and illuminating Naikan (meaning "inside looking") meditation, developed by a Japanese Buddhist. We asked ourselves silently, "What have I given; what have I received; what troubles or difficulties have I caused?" Later, in discussion, one student shared her experience of the meditation, saying, "That meditation was hard! I didn't want to ask myself those questions, and I found myself getting angry, even angry at you, thinking, why does she keep asking those questions over and over?" The student continued, "Finally, I just decided to stay with it and just work through the questions, but that still didn't work. I wanted to just tackle them and answer them, but I couldn't. So I finally decided to just be with the questions. That's when I felt the deepest peace."

It seems we are hardwired to reaction and response; when we have or hear a question, we instinctively search for the answer. But sometimes this active seeking limits our ability to simply be present to whatever the deeper, internal response might be, in whatever form this answer might manifest. If we return to the second of Patanjali's sutras, Yogascittavritti nirodah, or "Yoga is the stilling of the fluctuations of the mindstuff," and the third sutra, Tada drashtuh svarupe avasthanam, "Then we know our true nature," we might consider that all this seeking, all this "work," may be simply creating more waves on the surface of our minds, making it increasingly difficult to find the stillness of our own true nature, where the most important answers, and the deepest healing, reside. In the field of spiritual direction, there is a concept referred to as "holding the question," in which questions are purposely left open and spacious, the "answer" lying in the very act of posing the question. When we do not try to find a response, a way to tie up all the loose ends in a neat package, the necessary response will be revealed to us from within. But holding this space is hard work, it is tapas, because it is not what we are conditioned to do. Stopping and stilling and just "be-ing" is not what we normally think of as taking action and yet, perhaps, the dedication to quiet and space requires the greatest amount of discipline.

The concept of the work of stillness, of both action and inaction, is found throughout the Bhagavad Gita. In Chapter 6, Krishna advises Arjuna, "For the man who seeks to scale the heights of yoga, action is said to be the means. For the same man, when he has scaled those heights, repose is said to be the means." In other words, there is the work, or tapas, of our yoga in action, but there is also necessary work in repose, in rest. (Stephen Mitchell, The Bhagavad Gita – a new translation, Harmony Press)

This is one way for us to think of healing, as the capacity for us to be with both action and with stillness, to ask and to hold questions without trying to answer them. Of course, this happens in many different ways. It's about allowing the questions to be without seeking answers, it's about allowing answers to come from a deeper place, and it's about the discernment required to know when to act and when not to act. Sometimes it's about moving toward, and sometimes it's about moving away from, our process of healing and finding a comfortable, peaceful balance in the places in between.

While on teacher training, I had two opportunities to walk a labyrinth with my students. On the second round, I had a profound experience. I happened to be the last person to enter the labyrinth, a triple spiral, and as such at times was very far away from the rest of the group. For the first time ever in this fairly familiar endeavor, I had very strong feelings about my relative (and changing) positions within the labyrinth and to the group. When I was on the outer most circles within the spiral, with the rest of the group seemingly miles away, I found myself feeling anxious and isolated; when I joined the group in the center circles, I felt cramped, crowded, and uncomfortable. I found that when I was somewhere in between, where I could feel connected to the group without feeling restricted, I felt safe, relaxed, and present. This is an easy metaphor for the process of healing. The labyrinth itself is a physical structure that has an entry point and an exit point, and there is only one direction to get from one to the other, albeit through many twists and turns — much like the process of healing. And like the process of healing, there are times when we feel like we are moving in the right direction, times when we feel like we are moving away from our process, times when we feel like there is too much space and isolation, and times when we feel like we are too constricted, doing "too much work." But the process continues to move toward the goal, and it is our practice of tapas that urges us to move on and move through, even when that "action" means resting in space, in stillness.

I remember watching with joyful anticipation the 2010 rescue of the miners who had been trapped deep below the earth's surface in Chile. Without knowing these people at all, many of us around the world collectively prayed for their safe return and cheered in tearful ecstasy as we saw them each emerge from the depths of darkness that had been their home for over two months. I couldn't help but think of this same process of action and inaction for them, their families, their rescuers, and all of us, as we waited with guarded optimism for them to resurface. Yes, they and their rescuers needed to work hard to preserve their lives. At the same time, it seems that the hardest work for the miners may have been the waiting itself. Although we can certainly never know exactly how these men reacted in the mine, we can imagine that it required great discipline and restraint to simply be, to simply wait, rather than expend energy and emotion spinning out in the face of immeasurable fear and despair. After some point, there was nothing to do but to wait and pray and be. The two efforts combined, the hard work of problem solving and the hard work of just being, resulted in the best possible outcome — all thirty-three miners brought safely back home. We all celebrated their triumphant return, crying in relief for the wellbeing of people most of us have never met.

Imagine a world in which we collectively encouraged in one another a steadfast commitment to healing—for ourselves, for our families, for our communities, and for our planet. Imagine that as a culture we acknowledged and honored both kinds of work, the kind that requires a disciplined return to the mat, the therapist's chair, the Thanksgiving table with family, the process of determined self-inquiry and action, and the kind that requires patience, stillness, and space. Imagine what it would be like to sit quietly with a suffering friend and to trust that the healing was being facilitated, not by our pearls of wisdom and advice to "run it out," but by the space of simply being with the process. Imagine if we all trusted that we could and would heal but that it would require time, patience, and effort and that we could afford one another that time and, as if in the labyrinth, that as long as we stayed committed to the process, there could only be one result, one outcome, that of healing. Finally, imagine if we assumed that everyone had their own personal dark, lonely, and often terrifying depths, and—as we did for the thirty-three miners in Chile—we held vigil, trusting in the process, praying for their safe emergence from those depths, back to light and life. Imagine if we celebrated every return to joy, peace, and stillness. Could you imagine saying to one of those miners, "Geez, are you still down there?" or "Stop processing your situation in that way—it doesn't make sense to me," or "If you really want to get out, try harder," or "Stop trying so hard?" That would be crazy and we know it. There was a process, and only those miners and God knew what it could or would be in any moment. Imagine then, that we could look at our own process of healing, or the process of healing in our communities and in our planet, with the same determination, the same discernment, the same patience, and the same optimism. It would take practice, it would take will and determination, but more than anything, it would take a full understanding of tapas, the work of doing and the work of simply being.

We are all in this together.

God to enfold me,
God to surround me,
God in my speaking,
God in my thinking.
God in my sleeping,
God in my waking,
God in my watching,
God in my hoping.
God in my life,
God in my lips,
God in my soul,
God in my heart.
God in my sufficing,
God in my slumber,
God in mine ever-living soul,
God in mine eternity.

~ Ancient Celtic oral traditions - Carmina Gadelica

Shaucha — Hey! Watch Your Language.

Shaucha (pronounced "sh-ouch-a") is the yogic principle of cleanliness, orderliness, and purity. In the studio, simple practices such as folding your mats and blankets properly, taking time to make sure tossed paper lands in the trash, and throwing away used paper cups are all simple ways to honor this practice and your community. But, of course, it's not so simple. You knew that.

These days, I've been thinking a lot about the language we use and how clarity, or lack thereof, in our language can become such an important pivot point for our own growth, self-inquiry, and discernment. I think about this often and especially when I talk with students about Samarya yoga and what makes it unique. For me, one thing that recurs in our conversations is our use of language and the thought and care that goes into everything we say, from the way we offer variations in class, to the way we describe bodies, to the language we use to talk about ourselves. This last one has been particularly interesting to me as I work with more and more people interested in yoga as a tool for social change and social justice.

In this conversation, one of the things that comes up a lot is the question of prejudice, particularly racism, and our part in maintaining a nationwide culture of institutionalized oppression. We talk about the dynamic tension that comes with holding the opposing thoughts of "I am a good person" and "I am racist," for example. It is hard for many of us to reconcile these two thoughts, and so we choose just one to hold on to. I think we all know which one. And yet, we live in a fundamentally racist society. We grow up with racism, and other forms of prejudice, and oppression at all levels of our culture. These are messages that we receive and pass on in the subtlest of ways. And yet, we are often alarmed and even offended when someone calls us racist. That is not true! I am a good, nice person.

I have been pushing this conversation for a couple of years now and have made some interesting observations and discoveries. Several years ago, I created a website, called Diversity in Yoga, in order to address some of these issues. My hope for that platform was that we could have a real conversation about biases, conditioning, inclusion and exclusion. While the site itself never got any traction, I still stand by the mission, which I have included here (slightly modified):

I have been a yoga student and teacher for well over ten years, but I have been a white girl from Jersey my whole life. My identity as a yoga teacher is only one part of my total life experience and evolution, although it is now my professional identity and one with which I feel both a deep connection and a dynamic tension.

In this "yoga identity," I often feel like an uneasy outsider, sort of Groucho Marx-ish, as in his famous joke, "I don't want to belong to any club that would accept me as a member." The reason I feel this way, when I do, is that I see my yoga practice, and the practices that I share as a teacher, as a grand opportunity to explore myself and my own biases. It is through my sharing and stories and relationship with others that I get to see the ways in which my thinking, my responding, my reacting, my upbringing all affect people around me in ways that can sometimes be uplifting but also in ways that can be hurtful. I become frustrated when I see others who are deeply involved in yoga not taking this same opportunity. We have the chance as a community of spiritual practitioners to really start to heal wounds and create lasting social change—and I don't always see that happening. This is when I feel disconnected from or disillusioned by other yoga practitioners, especially those in positions to ignite and steward these changes.

The beginning of my own practice of yoga was an accidental meeting of a physical discipline that was the "prefect workout" and my soul's deep and inborn desire to feel, seek, and cultivate true kinship with people on the margins. In yoga, I have found both a place for my soul to thrive and a medium through which I can teach out to, meet, and connect with people I might not normally get to be with. This experience has given me much to think about; but perhaps most of all, it has given me an opportunity to really face head-on the ways in which we continue to hurt each other and divide ourselves, through race, class, size, ability, and gender, just to name a few. The hurt continues because of many complex but removable obstacles.

I recently shared some yoga with a group of folks who were part of the social service system. I asked them, "When you think of yoga and who practices it, who do you picture?" The answer was the same that I've heard a thousand times and the answer I'm sure that you guessed: white people, rich people, skinny people. One woman pantomimed her response by pursing her lips, looking down her nose, and bobbing her head in the universal charade for "hoity-toity." I got it.

This is the perception that many people have about yoga and those who practice it, especially those who feel excluded by them. But yoga is not a practice cornered by the white straight non-disabled upper middle class, even if it is most often affiliated with, and sometimes even co-opted by, them in our culture.

By "them" what I mean is me. I am a white woman who feels comfortable in most yoga classes, at least on the levels of class and race. I may not hang out with a lot of the people I see and meet who practice yoga, but it isn't because I feel socially, culturally, racially, or economically inferior to or oppressed by them at a societal and institutional level.

There is a much deeper issue here. It is the issue of diversity in who practices yoga, yes, but at a far more profound and personally transformative level it is the issue of using our yoga, our practice, to have challenging conversations about exclusion.

If blaming, attacking, patronizing, minimizing, defending, posturing, and intolerance worked to actually create the change we seek, we wouldn't still be having this conversation at all. But it's not working. However, as yoga practitioners we are committed to a practice that also offers us guidelines of how to treat one another, how to hang in there, and how to let go.

I am up for that conversation. Over the past decade or so, I have taught yoga to literally thousands of people from, and in, very diverse circumstances. But this conversation is not just about me. It is about the simple and consistent observation I have made within that time about the issue of diversity in yoga, a spiritual practice evolved from a place where everyone was "of color." A practice that inherently doesn't recognize skin color, or size, or ability, or class, or gender— in fact, a practice that, for some, essentially denies the physical body and circumstance as being anything more than illusion.

Following is a discussion about what I have observed, in two parts.

Part 1: When people within the yoga community are asked about diversity and inclusion, or seek to promote it, it is almost invariably within the context of "outreach" and "underserved populations" and very rarely about the simple integration of mainstream yoga classes, including yoga teachers of diverse ethnic and social backgrounds. At the larger organizational levels, the issue of diversity, if touched on at all, is relegated to a response of something like, "Check out this organization that is doing outreach, or serving underserved populations." I have been knocking on this door for literally years with the same response.

Although it is of course good to focus on outreach and service as a means of acknowledging a desire to share yoga with more people who might benefit from it, it can also be very problematic. There are a few questions that need to be deeply contemplated and addressed that would strengthen our collective capacity and perhaps redefine our intentions to share our practice.

- what level of cultural competency — the ability to appreciate and positively relate to people with belief systems and practices that are (sometimes very) different than our own — do the folks who are reaching out to these "underserved" people have?

- why aren't we actually talking about increasing diversity within the existing yoga communities? Yes, I mean in the yoga studios and yoga teacher trainings! Do we really need to go to the margins to find, for example, middle- and high-income people of color who may want to participate in yoga, but who feel excluded or uncomfortable participating in mainstream classes and training programs?

- why aren't we as a community working harder to get a more diverse cohort of yoga teachers?

- why aren't we using our positions as spiritual guides and mentors, or our dedication to our practice at any level, to address huge source of suffering in our own culture — racism, homophobia, fear of people with disabilities, and on and on. One might argue that people coming from a truly yogic perspective should be the very ones starting and hanging in for these conversations.

In fact, what if the question wasn't even "Why aren't we seeing more diverse engagement within the yoga community?" but "Why aren't we using our practice to open our hearts and minds and to change the way we think and act to address all types of exclusion and oppression — regardless of where or how it is happening?"

Part 2: People cannot talk about this stuff! What I have observed, repeatedly, is that "non-target" or "agent" groups —

or differently stated, people with the most power and privilege in our society — are too afraid of the cognitive dissonance that is engendered by the statements "I am progressive and open minded" and "I am prejudiced" (for example), so one of those two statements has to go underground. You know which one, because you are smart. "Target" groups, groups that have historically been marginalized and oppressed, often can't talk about it because there is so much anger, hurt, and blame that it very often comes out as aggressive and attacking, which only shuts down the conversation and reinforces the idea of "other" and increases distance, disconnection, alienation, and confirmation of bias on both sides.

Then it all starts over, and we stand in the same place we started. Is that really the best we can do?

It's crazy. We can (and must!) talk about this stuff. So finally, one day on a walk, it hit me: DIY. Do it yourself. Start the conversation. DIY. Diversity in Yoga.

The DIY ethic comes from the punk rock vernacular. We need to be punk rock about this! What I mean by that is, let's do it another way. What we are doing now, by and large, is not working. Step outside the box. Be courageous, be expansive, open your mind! Let's share experiences, open the conversation, and start to make real change.

I'll go first. I can share a perspective, and a personal experience, that helped me to see my own part in the dynamic of racism, power, privilege and unexamined thoughts. Here it is:

There is one particular part of the conversation on racism that I have been thinking of lately. Maybe part of the problem is that the language doesn't exactly fit. Or we don't have the exact language to describe where we are, where we came from, and where we are going. So we resist language that feels "off," and without a better alternative, the conversation, even the self-inquiry, comes to a screeching halt. Let me offer a couple of examples from my own experience. I do not think I am racist.

Or, at least, I don't believe I am "a" racist. Does this tiny modification between "racist" and "a racist" matter? I think it just might. But let's go backward a little.

I was raised in a very racially integrated town, in fact one of the most racially diverse cities in America, with a legacy of desegregation and a national diversity index (an algorithm that is used to measure biodiversity of all types) of 248, with the national average being 100. Montclair, New Jersey, itself is in fact a nationally recognized study in racial diversity. When our town pushed itself toward desegregation in 1978, my parents put me on a bus to attend school across town, in the "black neighborhood," despite the fact that there was a middle school right up the street from my family home, which was just one street up from where the neighborhoods seemed to skew one way or another. I continued in Montclair's very diverse public schools through high school. I grew up with friends of all ethnic and racial backgrounds but particularly with an integration of what we then just called, "black" and "white." At home, I was a part of very open-minded and socially conscious family that itself became quite racially diverse as my brothers and sisters married, creating a next generation of Kennys who span the color spectrum. So, really, there is no way I could be a racist ... right?

But then, just very recently, this happened: I was at my parent's house, in Montclair, and decided to go running. I didn't have a reflective vest, so my dad lent me a bike light; I clipped it to the back of my jacket and set out to run a familiar route in my hometown. As I ran through the park, I saw a group of kids sitting on a bench. Now, one thing that can get me kind of anxious is a group of teenagers together. I know what my teenage friends and I were like, and we could be pretty mouthy and obnoxious. Sure enough, as I ran past, one of the kids called out, "She's wearing a bike light!" The others laughed. I kept running. The next kid called out, "Hey! Are you a bike?" I kept running, more laughter. Then, as I passed, another voice:

"Bitch!" My whole being contracted. I felt rage and reaction flooding my arms and legs and belly. My mind started to go crazy. "I should go back there and get in those kids' faces. I will get right up on them and mad dog them down, scare the crap out of them, let them know not to mess with me." I kept running, my mind kept retaliating. "I wish I knew martial arts. I'd go back there and kick some ass, or at least scare them." Then it occurred to me how crazy I was being, how much that single word had gotten this huge reaction out of me, how my friend Tristan, a real martial artist, heck, a real yogi, wouldn't even be bothered by some dumb obnoxious kids. Then this occurred to me, seemingly out of the blue: if it had been a group of black kids, it wouldn't even have crossed my mind that I would go back and get in their face. Why? I didn't know. I guessed I was scared of black kids, but not white kids. Why? I had no idea. I have never been a target by any black person, ever. I have never felt threatened by a black person. I have never had the sense that a black person was being aggressive toward me. I have family — family! — who are black. I ran all the way home, frustrated, sad, and angry — at myself, at the kids, and at the culture and society that had influenced and infiltrated me like a disease, without my knowing, and certainly without my permission. OK. So, my reaction was proof that I am racist, because this discrimination occurred in my mind. Or am I? I think this is where the conversation gets either interesting or impossible, depending on how you look at it and how committed we are to talking through it. Clearly, I am racially biased. Even in spite of both my most externalized and my deepest — and I thought, internalized — beliefs. Even in spite of all of my work, and my friends, and my upbringing (now this seems called into question too). This bias is in me, it's like an accent that I can work to get rid of, but is always there, lingering and ready to come out, just the same way as my Jersey accent really comes through when I talk with friends from

Jersey. It's lying there, dormant, just waiting for an opportunity to come alive.

So, what's this all about? Is it easier for me to say I am racially biased than to say I am racist or even prejudiced? Yes. Marginally. Is it easier for me to say, and does it also ring more true, than for me to say, I am a racist? Yes, absolutely. Why? Well, I think for a couple of reasons. First, my yoga practice reminds me that to say I am anything is to identify with that thing as if it defines me. Being racist does not define me. That I know without a doubt. But also because being biased seems more like something that is a filter that has been created inside me from my conditioning, from being privileged, and white, and from being from a culture that is at its core racially biased. I don't feel as much like it is something I am actively doing or being. It seems almost inescapable; and yet, I also know that it is not. However, the only way I might get closer to "losing my accent," is to become aware that it is there, and not to feel so horrible or guilty or ashamed that I refuse to recognize it. I have to be able to see when it comes out, even in the subtlest ways, to ever be able to change it. Saying that I do not have this bias only keeps me in the cycle of perpetuating this huge source of hurt, suffering and division in our culture.

One of my students recently sent me a video of a TED talk by the prominent DJ Jay Smooth entitled, "How I Learned to Stop Worrying and Love Discussing Race." It is a great talk, in which Smooth talks about how we might be able to hear from others that we are being racist or offensive in some way in the same manner we might be able to hear that we have food stuck in our teeth. That it shouldn't be something we feel ashamed about, or need to deny or defend, but something we might actually thank someone for giving us the heads-up about. I loved the video and posted it on the DIY site. Then I kept thinking about it. I thought about how Smooth kept portraying the white folks as being too sensitive, even when a person of color felt hurt or uncomfortable in some way and just wanted to tell their white friends how they were feeling. Then I kept thinking about how on the DIY site I say the same thing, and I say (although I didn't really think of it this way at the time) that the "target" groups are often too aggressive in their presentation, which shuts the conversation down. Who's right? Both of us. Who is racially biased? Both of us. Who is racist? I believe, neither one of us.

This conversation always opens up a huge can of worms. But I am willing to do it. I am willing to take the risk, because I think the conversation has to continue to move forward. But I also believe that the conversation will only move forward if we are all willing to check our language and the way it confines, construes, defines, and scares us and perpetuates, repeats, and creates identities that people will never accept. Maybe the question is not whether we should be having the conversation, but rather can we find words and descriptions and subtleties that allow people to move a little into places they might feel uncomfortable, instead of pushing them into places they will never inhabit and never claim and which will only serve to shut the conversation down. Maybe we are not this or that. Maybe we are something somewhere in the middle, and that's the place we could meet ourselves and each other. Saucha. Purity, cleanliness, orderliness. Maybe we can find more order in our language, a more clear and pure-hearted way to talk to each other with the nuance and complexity that is inherent in the topic. Maybe we can use our practice to create the conversation and to soften the rigid ideas that make us repeatedly turn away from each other. I don't know. That's just me. I'm an agitator. I'm an optimist. I am a human being.

Out beyond ideas of wrongdoing and rightdoing, there is a field. I'll meet you there. When the soul lies down in that grass, the world is too full to talk about.

Ideas, language, even the phrase "each other" doesn't make any sense. ~ Mevlana Jelaluddin Rumi - 13th century Sufi mystic

We're all in this together.

My beloved child, break your heart no longer.
Each time you judge yourself, you break your own heart.
You stop feeding on the love, which is the wellspring of your vitality.
The time has come. Your time. To live. To celebrate,
and to see the goodness that you are.
Do not fight the dark. Just turn on the light.
Let go, and breathe into the goodness that you are.

~Swami Kripalu

MOLLY LANNON KENNY

Yoga: Embodiment without Body

I first met Drew through one of my yoga students at The Samarya Center. She had learned about him from her neighbor, who happened to be Drew's aunt. In their conversations, Drew's aunt told my student that her nephew, an Army captain, had been shot by a sniper during his second tour in Iraq. He had been flown home to face his new life with no ability to move his body or feel any sensation below the neck. While telling Drew's story to my student, his aunt mentioned that he was open to and ready for an alternative to the medical management he was receiving at the VA Hospital. Drew was having panic attacks that were slowing his progress by interfering with some of his therapies. My student thought of me and in a leap of faith gave Drew's aunt my number. Within a week, I had begun a ten-week journey with Drew, bringing yoga to his bedside.

Although in my clinical work I had been in many hospital rooms with people in very challenging and often very bleak situations, I remember being taken aback the first time I entered Drew's room. He was lying on his bed, unclothed except for a small towel covering his hips and pelvis. He was surrounded by machines and people — family, doctors, and mental health workers — and appeared so small in comparison to all of them. Although his body had already atrophied significantly, his face was clear and bright, and when he invited me into his room, his voice was strong. I entered somewhat timidly. Even with so many people in the room, the room was mostly quiet, with some talking among family and professionals and the constant rhythm of the ventilator that kept Drew breathing, punctuated periodically with little beeps and lights from the various other machines that fed into one another like some kind of Seussian contraption.

I was never afraid that I would not be able to help Drew; I just didn't know exactly how I would. Although I had worked with many people in extremely difficult places in their lives, including people with progressive neurological diseases, people dying from AIDS, and parents who had lost their babies to sudden illness, I had never worked with anyone who was not able to be "in" their body, to feel any sensations, at all. This new situation challenged much of what I had come to rely on in my work: an ability to use the body as a gateway, a way to enter through the gross physical body into the more subtle aspects of a person's total experience, including emotions and energy.

Tara Brach, PhD, writes in her book *Radical Acceptance*, "Bringing Radical Acceptance into our lives starts at this most basic level - becoming aware of the sensations that are continually taking place in our physical being...We experience our lives through our bodies whether we are aware of it or not."

As a longtime yoga practitioner, teacher, and therapist, I would have normally agreed wholeheartedly with that passage. For example, a person who might not want to talk about the circumstances of a sad event at the beginning of a session, after some movement, is often quite willing. I used to be fond of saying, "The mind and the mouth lie, the breath and the body don't." People say they are feeling one way, but in fact are feeling another. If we are able to tune in to the messages of a person's body and the breath, we will usually be able to read the feelings behind the words. "We experience our lives through our bodies whether we are aware of it or not."

This had indeed always been my modus operandi for using yoga and movement as a part of my therapeutic approach. However, when I read Tara Brach's book for the first time, I had already started working with Drew and I wondered, if he could not experience his life through his body, how then was he to bring "radical acceptance" into his life? Indeed, how was he to experience his life now?

Drew could not be in touch with his body. Drew could not breathe volitionally. If I could not work with the body, and I could not work with breath, what could I work with? Where did I begin? I realized that I now had an opportunity to look at yoga and my therapeutic approach—Integrated Movement Therapy (IMT)—through a new lens: one in which the body and the breath were secondary, and the mind and heart were primary.

IMT is based in the yogic view of health, healing, and connection to a divine spirit. Yoga is a process of undoing our sense of separateness and a coming home to connection with God, with ourselves, with each other, with our shared sense of suffering and joy. In this place, in this coming home, there is a deep sense of wellbeing. That is yoga. Now was the time to really explore this idea of connection as the primary focus of my therapy.

We began by talking. I told Drew that I saw him as a man, a spark of life, and not as his injury. I told him that I knew I could help him if he guided me by honestly telling me what he was feeling, and what he was hoping to feel, in each of our sessions. Within just a few sessions, we dropped into a comfortable rhythm together. We began with attention to the breath, using the rhythmic whooshing sound of the ventilator as a point of focus. Drew could not control his breath, but he could become one with it instead of regarding it as a threatening outsider. Next, we began to practice rotations of consciousness, a process of guiding Drew to awareness of different areas of his body that he could no longer feel, but could still perceive.

Drew and I talked and joked about lots of things: yoga philosophy, family, his condition; but most importantly, the space was always open for Drew to talk about his life and his death. During our sixth session, Drew told me that he had asked to be removed from his ventilator and that he wanted to practice one specific meditation until the day came on which he would finally leave his broken body.

This meditation involved a process of rarifying the physical, energetic, and mental-emotional bodies until all that remained in awareness was a tiny spark of light representing consciousness itself, infinite freedom. We referred to this experience as becoming a firefly. After our sessions, Drew's wife would ask him what we had done together. Drew would answer, with his wry smile, "I left my body; I became a firefly." Soon she also wanted to participate in the meditation.

On more than one occasion, Drew's ventilator released a small air leak, which resulted in an alarm going off and a flood of medical personnel racing into the room. Drew and his wife would simply ask me to wait; we would keep the meditation music on and silently wait for the situation to be resolved. As soon as the respiratory therapists and nurses left, we would simply pick up where we left off and continue in this state of spaciousness and fearlessness. When in these meditations, we were in the ultimate state of radical acceptance, one in which there was nothing to let go of and nothing to hold on to. When we relinquished our connection to the body and its sensations, we were most able to connect directly to spirit.

In our last session together, Drew entered the meditation deeply. As I was preparing to leave, I placed my hands on his head and thanked him for the honor of being with him through this experience. He opened his eyes and said, "Goodbye." He told me that he didn't know what it was that brought us together, but that he had benefited greatly from our sessions and was not afraid to die. He told me he would see me around, "But not too soon." I asked him if I could embrace him and he laughed and said yes. The last word Drew said to me was peace.

Drew died peacefully on September 7, 2007, and, I like to believe, in full awareness of himself as both form and consciousness.

We experience our lives through myriad avenues of connection and sensation. These include our bodies and minds and eyes and energies and thoughts and things far beyond our understanding. To fully experience life, we must develop our ability to become aware of ourselves, on as many different levels and as deeply as we possibly can. Life shifts its shape and forms new energies to travel the avenues we present it with. It is through this process that we are able to fully embody our own experience, to fully practice and, perhaps to attain, yoga.

The next Buddha will not take the form of an individual. The next Buddha may take the form of a community; a community practicing understanding and loving kindness, a community practicing mindful living. This may be the most important thing we can do for the survival of the Earth.

~ Thich Nhat Hanh

MOLLY LANNON KENNY

*F*orgive

Be still for some moments to simply reflect on the power of forgiveness. Remind yourself that everyone makes mistakes, both huge and tiny, and that even when we are doing our very best we sometimes hurt people, including ourselves. Send a thought of forgiveness to all of the people around you who are working diligently on themselves, seeking real personal transformation, and who, even in this effort, continue to make mistakes, to say or do the wrong thing. Recognize how it feels to screw up and how it feels to be forgiven.

Reflections On Coming Home

Often when I return from my home in Mexico to my home in Seattle, I have a mixture of feelings: I'm happy to be home but I'm also missing the sun and lazy days of my life in Mexico, wondering what I am actually doing in my "real" life, working so hard, when I could be there living simply and unencumbered by the demands of running The Samarya Center. I find that I can easily become overwhelmed by our culture of consumerism and self-judgment, our inability to find true and lasting peace amidst all of our "things," by our collective (un)consciousness, our sense of entitlement and lack of appreciation for our incredible abundance.

And then these words from Swami Kripalvanandji find their way into my mind, "My beloved child, break your heart no longer. Each time you judge yourself, you break your own heart."

I remember that it is because of this very culture that I was born into that I am able to offer what I can to my friends in Mexico, to my students, and to myself. I remember that it is often the challenges of our lives that inspire us to make change and offer goodness to a world in need. Again and again, wherever you go, there you are; and I come home, I am home, in my own heart. Life anywhere affords us the opportunity, whether we take it or not, to reflect, to discriminate, to wake up. We are each offered a path, and it is our job to make the best of it and to do whatever we can through our path to make the world a better place. Why would I break my own heart through malaise and self-judgment when I was given this great opportunity to make change happen?

What a miracle this life is! Each of us with the opportunity to do our part, each of us with the capacity to long for a better world, the collective potential of all of us working together to help alleviate suffering everywhere. Let's not sit in judgment of ourselves or of others. Let's stop breaking our own hearts. We are here, now, together, beautiful, flawed, perfect, limitless, confused, clear, human. We are all in this together. Thank you for being here with me.

A life without love is of no account. Don't ask yourself what kind of love you should seek, spiritual or material, divine or mundane, eastern or western...divisions only lead to more divisions. Love has no labels, no definitions. It is what it is, pure and simple. Love is the water of life.

~ Shams of Tabriz

MOLLY LANNON KENNY

Prana, life force, and forgiveness ~
The Unexpected Power of the Prana Vayus

The weak can never forgive. Forgiveness is the attribute of the strong.
~ Gandhi

I like to think of my home as always being open to family. I imagine it being a place where my brothers and sisters and all their kids always feel welcome, safe, and valued and where they can just be themselves in all of the joy, complexity, and chaos that family so often brings. In reality, my family is very far flung and I can go for months without even speaking to some of them. Sometimes, then, I can also romanticize the reunion and picture a scenario that runs quite a bit more smoothly than is actually likely to happen.

This was the case a couple of years ago when one of my brothers came to visit, on fairly short notice, bringing his three kids with him who ranged in age from five years old to their late twenties. I had not seen this brother since my wedding four years previously. We have ebbed and flowed in our closeness, often being disconnected by different views and relationships with the rest of the family. I was elated that he was finally making it out to Seattle, by way of the Rainbow Gathering, and that I was going to meet his five-year-old daughter, my niece, for the first time. It turned out that our visit was wonderful. On one particular evening, we sat on my bed and spent hours talking. I asked him what had prompted what felt to me like a change of heart in his relationship to the rest of the family. That simple question opened the floodgates for a deluge of stories, emotions, and meticulously painted pictures to flow from his unique perspective. At times, I found myself wanting to jump in, to hurry past some of the details I thought were extraneous, or to question a side of the story, or to justify some action. But I didn't. I just listened, with my heart and ears and mind open. This was a story that needed to be told, a perspective that needed to be heard, and a heart that longed for connection. I felt humbled and honored to hold that space for my brother, a space that ultimately was contained in a story of forgiveness. When we hugged that night before bed, I felt the power of forgiveness pass through and between us. Forgiveness, I believe, has the power to heal all wounds.

Marianne Williamson has said, "The practice of forgiveness is our most important contribution to the healing of the world." I believe she is right. And yet, the practice of forgiveness is just that—a practice. We have all been in situations where we have found it difficult, even seemingly impossible, to forgive.

I have a very large, extended, multiracial, multinational, multidimensional family, a family that I sometimes refer to as a "tribe." Like a tribe, we are connected for life and, it seems to me, that we tend to live by an unspoken code wherein we know, no matter how distant or frustrated or angry or removed we become, due to whatever life circumstances, that we will ultimately be supported by, welcomed (back) into, and protected by the tribe. In fact, when looking up the word "tribe" to find out what some common elements might be in the different definitions and if my family shared them, I kept coming across these elements, expressed in slightly different ways: a common focus, fairness and trust, open communication and acceptance of one another, complementary strengths, generosity of heart, and forgiveness.

It was interesting to me to see the word "forgiveness" as one of the common elements. Indeed, my brother and I had just been talking about the power and challenges of forgiveness, its capacity for total healing, and its often-elusive nature. In fact, the absence of forgiveness can destroy the feeling and function of the tribe and the feeling and function of connectedness in general. But forgiveness isn't easy. It's not for the faint of heart or the shaky ego. It requires great strength and inner determination, primarily the determination to live a life of contentment and ease. Even culturally, we don't necessarily value forgiveness. People who forgive may be confused with people who give up or give in. People who hold on to grievances may feel and be perceived as one who "doesn't let anyone mess with them."

My family, in general, is a family of talkers. Many of us, including the younger generation, share quite freely with one another, often sharing perspectives and opinions, hurts and injustices, feelings of gratitude, and feelings of connection, as well as feelings of disconnection. It wasn't just my brother and I who ended up talking about the power and complexity of forgiveness that summer. Somehow it managed to come up in all the various constellations of family that came to visit, whether it was in relation to parents, siblings, friends, school mates, culture, or self. I began to feel that forgiveness was the key word of the summer. Summer 2011: The Forgiveness Tour. The teenagers in the family talked about different situations with their own families and friends, and expressed not only the need for forgiveness but also the capacity to forgive. Even Vika, my five-year-old niece, one day leaned forward from her car seat in the back of the car and expressed a wrong she had committed. She said, "I'm guilty"—unusual words coming from the mouth of such a little person, but expressing that basic human need for forgiveness. In another conversation, one of my nieces said to me, "People make all kinds of mistakes, but in some way, in that moment, they thought they were doing the right thing." Yet another teenaged niece, after a perceived injustice perpetrated on her Facebook page by a "best friend," said, "No matter how good a friend someone is, they're going to hurt you every once in awhile and you must forgive them for that."

In my family life, there have been many, many opportunities for forgiveness—of myself, of my parents, of my brothers and sisters, of my life circumstances and experiences. The opportunities become immeasurable when I include forgiveness of and by my closest circle of friends—my chosen "family," my secondary tribe in the absence of my family of origin.

Thinking of these countless opportunities for forgiveness, I wish I could say they had all been taken, but sadly, and inevitably, they were not. The gift, I suppose, in this, is to be able to see in plain view the difference between forgiving and holding on.

In an email conversation with one of my nieces, she asked me, "Here's a question. Is there ever a time where you shouldn't forgive someone? Sometimes for me especially it is really hard to forgive people...especially family. And even if I forgive them, it still lingers in the back of my mind when I'm with them."

My response was simply to say, "Are there times when we shouldn't forgive? Not if we want to be at peace. But it's really, really hard, right? Sometimes the thing the person did is so huge that it seems unforgivable."

I think this is a common question when considering forgiveness. Are there instances in which we are justified in never forgiving someone? This depends on what we consider forgiveness to be, and what we hope for our own lives and sense of peace and freedom.

In my looking around for thoughts and quotes on forgiveness, I came across this powerful list from R. T. Kendall, the Christian writer and author of the book *Total Forgiveness*.

Total forgiveness is not:
1. Approval of what they did.
2. Excusing what they did.
3. Justifying what they did.
4. Pardoning what they did.
5. Reconciliation.
6. Denying what they did.
7. Blindness to what happened.
8. Forgetting.

9. Refusing to take the wrong seriously.
10. Pretending we are not hurt.

Total forgiveness is:
1. Being aware of what someone has done and still forgiving them.
2. Choosing to keep no record of wrongs.
3. Refusing to punish.
4. Not telling what they did.
5. Being Merciful.
6. Graciousness.
7. An inner condition — total forgiveness must take place in the heart or it is worthless.
8. The absence of bitterness.
9. Forgiving God — all bitterness is ultimately traceable to a resentment of God.
10. Forgiving ourselves.

This list is so beautiful to me, such a precious accounting of the qualities of the truly open heart. And yet, it also seems almost unreachable in its expansiveness. How do we get there? How can we be gracious and merciful when we feel hurt, let down, betrayed? How do we relinquish bitterness when we have righteous anger, oftentimes rooted so deeply through our earliest experiences with family? I think again about my brother, his epiphany and ultimately his freedom, when he was able to forgive our family. It's not that there is so much to forgive in our family specifically -- or I should say, I guess not too much more than any other family -- it's just that families are complicated and challenging, and forgiveness is complicated and challenging, and it seems that where there is family, there is opportunity for forgiveness. Families, it seems, are full of opportunities to practice forgiveness.

But how do we practice forgiveness? What practices will help us? It has to be a focus. It has to be a desire. It has to be a dedicated practice that emanates directly from our hearts, where the healing occurs because of our own choice to be different, to live in contentment and not anger, to steady the fluctuations of our mind and to find rest and refuge in the heart. Forgiveness requires depth, courage, and strength. Mahatma Gandhi said, "The weak can never forgive. Forgiveness is the attribute of the strong." But how do we get there? Surely a spiritual practice in some form is required, but what might we use specifically from the practices and principles of yoga that would give us some direction, something substantive to work with?

In thinking about this, the prana vayus come to mind as one possible focus. The vayus are described in the yoga tradition as movements, or functions, of prana, or life force. There are generally considered to be five prana vayus, each with different and specific physical, physiological, and psycho-emotional attributes associated with it. They each govern different areas of the body, and through the innate intelligence of prana, the vayus seek to find balance. Harmony between the vayus invites maximum health and wellbeing on all levels.

In a workshop with one of my teachers, Yogarupa Rod Stryker, I was especially touched by his description of specific psycho-spiritual attributes related to each of the prana vayus and found myself thinking about them over and over with regard to my life and my own wellbeing. I kept thinking about one in particular, apana vayu, which my teacher described as necessary for surrender, for letting go, and for forgiveness. As I began to think about them more in this way, I started to consider how all of the prana vayus might support, encourage, and allow for forgiveness in their own way. Forgiveness, as I said earlier, is not an easy thing to achieve. We all know that. So can we build up our capacity for forgiveness through our yoga practice? I believe we can, and I believe the prana vayus could be a key element.

Since I started by talking about apana, let me tell more about this one and move on from there.

Apana is a downward- and outward-moving force, the force of elimination at all levels. It is located at the pelvic floor and is related to all of the physical eliminating in our bodies. Apana is also the force behind surrender, acceptance, and letting go, including the ability to eliminate negative thoughts and feelings. Hence, a healthy apana prana vayu is the cornerstone of forgiveness.

Prana (which refers to both the umbrella term prana and the specific term for this vayu) is located in the heart and the head. It is an inward-moving force with the main function of energizing and revitalizing. I remember Scott Blossom often talking about "packing in the prana," asking us to think of packing prana into every cell of the body for maximum vitality. I think of this now, specifically for prana vayu. This prana rules the inhale breath and is responsible for screening and filtering sensory information. We know we are depleted of prana vayu when we feel that we just "can't take any more in." With regard to forgiveness, we might intuit that a feeling of fullness of life force, a feeling of strength and vitality, and a feeling of being able to filter our emotions and what comes in through our senses might prepare us for the hard work of forgiving.

Udana is located in the throat and is an upward-moving force. It is related to the enthusiasm and inspiration to grow and evolve. When udana is strong, we feel motivated to grow and change physically, mentally, and spiritually. Upana rules the exhale breath, as it is the upward expression, the release, of the diaphragm that produces the exhale. The exhale breath is the breath of speech and verbal expression. Healthy udana allows us to communicate clearly and to express our longing for change and growth. We can think of this desire and inspiration to evolve as a necessary component of forgiveness — true forgiveness can feel like a big exhalation, a great sense of relief when we evolve from what we are to what we are becoming, a letting go and moving on.

Vyana is the distributing and integrating force. It is centered in the heart and moves outward in all directions. Physiologically, vyana is the force of circulation and expansion. Emotionally, vyana is related to our ability to be responsive and adaptable. It invites us to stretch ourselves, to become light, to be amenable to changes in our environment. Clearly, forgiveness requires heart-centeredness, but it also is the gift of forgiveness that allows us to have a feeling of freedom and lightness and to adapt our hearts and minds to a new way of thinking about ourselves and about each other. When we can see both ourselves and others in a more expansive light, we are more easily able to forgive.

Finally, there is samana, the balancing, or equalizing, force. This vayu is centered in the abdomen and is related to digestion and assimilation on both the physical and mental levels. Samana's power to balance our bodies and minds is related to homeostasis, the body's tendency to seek and maintain a condition of equilibrium within its internal environment, even when faced with external changes. We can imagine that forgiveness would have to come from this balanced state, but would also encourage it. We can maintain a sense of peace within ourselves and with our environment when we are willing to let go and be unaffected by things outside of ourselves, including our real and perceived hurts and wounds.

It might be helpful to remind ourselves just how difficult forgiveness is, perhaps how little practice we have had with it, and how culturally under-celebrated it is. My niece said to me, after reading RT Kendall's list of total forgiveness, "When you forgive someone, should you let them know that you have not forgotten what they have done?" Another great and important question from a thirteen year old, and one I think many of us share. Again, my response comes from my practice,

"Forgiveness is inside you. It doesn't even matter if the other person knows or doesn't. I think you (we) should process our very real hurt and then choose to move on with our own lives and find our own happiness. If the hurt is not too much to bear, we can look at how we might understand the other person's actions and realize that maybe, just maybe, we would have done the same thing in the same situation. Or we could think about how a person made a horrible judgment at one time, but is still a good person. But if the hurt is too strong, or the situation is dangerous, then we can forgive a person but not have them in our lives at all. That is important too."

My beloved niece responded, "I really get what you're saying, especially because I have a real hard time forgiving people."

I think we all have a "real hard time forgiving people," but we can practice and get better. We can start by forgiving smaller things and work up to bigger ones. In the end, forgiveness is for ourselves. If we go back to one of the most basic definitions of yoga, "Yoga is the stilling of the fluctuations of the mind," we can see that an inability, or an unwillingness, to forgive is a serious fluctuation and distraction of the mind. It becomes a source of held anger and resentment, and it muddies the waters of our heart, mind, and consciousness. If our goal in yoga is to "rest in our own true nature," then this holding on becomes an impediment to that resting and an impediment to that sense of freedom and contentment that yoga describes as our birthright.

Yoga is a practice. Forgiveness is a practice. Yoga is freedom and forgiveness, too, is freedom. Mark Twain said, "Forgiveness is the fragrance that the violet sheds on the heel that has crushed it." In other words, forgiveness is a gift we can give to the person who caused the hurt, but it is also a gift that we can give to ourselves in our pursuit of yoga -- a deep sense of freedom and peace. The prana vayus can be a powerful tool for us to cultivate our capacity for forgiveness, and forgiveness can be a powerful tool for us to cultivate the prana vayus.

Consider the influence of the prana vayus on your practice, on your life, and on your greater pursuit of yoga. What a relief to simply rest in your own true nature, one with the great capacity to forgive.

We are all in this together.

People are more than the worst thing they have ever done in their lives ~ Helen Prejean

MOLLY LANNON KENNY

Lessons from the Bhagavad Gita ~ or Swimming in the Big Surf

When another person makes you suffer, it is because he suffers deeply within himself, and his suffering is spilling over. He does not need punishment; he needs help. That is the message he is sending.
~ Thich Nhat Han

The wave forgets the truth that it is ocean, thinking itself to be the grand shape that it has temporarily taken. For a while, it takes on the rupa (form) of wave. Finally, it remembers its true rupa (form) of ocean. The two coexist, though one is true, and the other, though beautiful, is only relatively true. So too, we humans forget our true nature, but, through yoga, can remember. ~ Swami Jnaneshwara

The man equipped with yoga looks on all with an impartial eye, seeing Atman in all beings and all beings in Atman. ~ Bhagavad Gita 6.29

I love the Big Island of Hawaii. I love the smell of night-blooming jasmine, the sound of coqui frogs, the lilt of "jah-waiian" music, the exquisite taste of the mangoes, passion fruit, and soursop. More than anything, though, I love being in the middle of the Pacific Ocean, the constant presence of the sea, and the reminder that we are such small and inconsequential beings in the scheme of things. The ocean and its waves provide countless metaphors and opportunities for learning; our relative tininess begs us not to take ourselves so seriously, to expand our ideas of right and wrong, and to lean into the big unknown. The ocean for me, a strong swimmer, is also a constant dare, a seductive companion that is always asking me to trust myself and to test my own courage, strength, and wit.

When on the Big Island, my husband Sasha and I like to go to a particular beach, known for its crystal clear waters, its black sand, its friendly herd of spinner dolphins, and its strong surf. We both enjoy the delight of watching the rhythm of the waves, the cautious and thoughtful entry of other swimmers, and the intrepid run into the surf, diving under at just the right moment, allowing ourselves to be tossed around, then coming up for air with a sense of triumph and exhilaration. Sometimes though, the surf is not as friendly, not as forgiving and we find ourselves in a place that tests our confidence and endurance.

I have the great good fortune of having carved a life that includes occasional trips to this beach, coupled with teaching yoga retreats at a beautiful nonprofit retreat center just minutes away. My life also includes constant opportunities to test myself, to test my understanding of yoga and the spiritual life to which I have committed. During one of my visits to the Big Island, I had the special opportunity to teach, swim, and learn within the context of the ample metaphors the sea provides, my real-life situations corresponding directly to these images and metaphors.

This trip in particular, though it had been beautiful and exciting, had also been quite full of emotion: frustration, confusion, anger, and sadness. The surf of my own mind had been tossing me around, and I had moments where I doubted my ability to swim it. While on this trip to Hawaii, a difficult family situation consumed much of my energy and thought and tested my deepest reserves of love, compassion, and clarity. I felt myself contracting and reacting, suffering, punishing and being punished. It was difficult to see the other with that impartial eye, to see that unfettered soul referred to as Atman, especially through the murky viewfinder of my stance of righteousness and sense of superiority. In my initial hurt and angry view of this situation, I could see two distinct waves with no ocean to connect us. I could not conceive of any reality in which we shared a common divinity — in fact, I believed I could not be more different from this person, who I was sure caused my suffering.

Every day in Hawaii, I was consumed by this situation, and my mind was in a constant swirl of questioning and evaluating, devising and weighing responses and trade-offs. The best respites I could find were through teaching and swimming. One day, with a few hours of free time, Sasha and I headed to the beach to relax and reflect. The surf was crashing and there were several people on the beach just looking out at the ocean, not daring to jump in. With abandon and thoughts of cleansing, ignoring the size of the waves and the cautious assessment of the other swimmers, we ran in and dove under the biggest wave, a beach break, allowing it to carry us back out beyond the tumult and crashing of the surf. We swam around a bit, feeling triumphant and strong—we were the only ones who had dared to brave the waves!

After about ten minutes of being tossed around in the clear blue water, I decided I was ready to go in to shore. I waited for a wave to bring me in, but the next wave that came was so huge I couldn't get on top of it and had to dive under just to stay where I was, neither going in nor being pulled any further out. Then it happened again, and again. I looked toward the beach and saw the others standing on the shore; I reached my feet as low as they could go but could not find the bottom. I turned back toward the sea just to see another huge wave coming toward me. Each time I tried to swim in, the surf would turn around and pull me further out. I caught Sasha's eye and could tell in an instant that he too was struggling. He said, "Don't panic Molly; we're going to make it in." Sasha reached out his hand and grabbed my wrist to pull me toward him. Just then another powerful wave came and pulled us both under, and his hand, which had just a moment before comforted me, now seemed to be holding me under; I instinctively wrestled myself free to come up for air. Sasha was now about six feet in front of me, closer to the shore. I said, "I'm scared Sasha. Someone is going to have to come get me. I can't get in." Sasha repeated calmly, although I could see the fear in his eyes, "Don't panic. Swim when the waves move you toward the shore and don't resist when they pull you back out. Conserve your energy. You are going slowly toward the shore, I promise." Don't resist? When I feel as though I am being pulled out to sea? And yet I had no choice. I was becoming increasingly fatigued and increasingly inwardly focused. Nothing mattered except getting to shore. Finally, I saw Sasha touch the ground. The surf was so strong that even that didn't mean a speedy exit; although his feet were finally on the ocean floor, he still struggled against the waves that were pulling him forcefully back out to sea. Finally, I saw him reach the sandy beach, standing with whitewash up to his knees. A moment of security flooded me. He is there; I can make it too or he can get help for me. I returned all my thoughts and energy to focus on myself, repeating Sasha's instructions: "Swim in when it's easy; let it take you when it's pulling you away. You will eventually get in. Conserve your energy. Focus."

I had a momentary thought of how terrible it would be for my students if their teacher drowned while leading their retreat, a moment of defeat—perhaps I wasn't really as good a swimmer as I fancied myself to be—and then came the realization that I really was on my way in to shore. Within the next several waves, I finally dragged myself out, to the encouragement and praise of people on the beach. I walked over to where Sasha lay exhausted on the black sand and dropped down beside him. We both looked out at the surf, noticing the sets getting smaller and easier, and finally the people on the beach running in when it was safe and splashing around with ease.

In my favorite commentary on the Bhagavad Gita, Mahatma Gandhi acknowledges how difficult it is for us to really see others with an impartial eye. How difficult it is for us to see ourselves and to see others as both the wave and the ocean. In my mind, it is as difficult as swimming against a huge wave. We flail and flounder with great effort, only to meet resistance and exhaustion. Gandhi said, "The yogi is not one who sits down to practice breathing exercises. He is one who looks upon all with an equal eye, sees all creatures in himself. Such a one obtains moksha (liberation)....It is not easy to see all creatures in ourselves...we must see them in ourselves by seeing them and oneself in God....He is a true yogi who is happy when others are happy and suffers when others suffer. He alone may be said to be a person who has dedicated his all to God; but this is a difficult state to achieve."

I understand Gandhi to mean that our practice of yoga is not what we do on our mats or in our yoga classes, but how we approach all of life and especially those situations that challenge us. Much like swimming in the big surf, we must see that each wave is only that, a single wave, and that all waves belong to the more powerful force of the ocean itself. In this way, we really can work with the total power of the ocean, and not get lost in the fear of the single big wave. In this way too, we can see ourselves in others, by seeing we are all part of a larger whole. To me, this ocean, this wholeness, is God, or an infinite opening of the heart to love and grace. It is easy to feel connected like this when things are going our way, but so hard to hold on to when we are faced with a spiritual or relational challenge. I think we all have the instinct to swim against the current, to push up against it, force requiring more force. But like my experience at the black sand beach, in fact we move with more ease, and in the direction we really want to go, when we do not resist what is challenging us, but swim mightily with the current of our spiritual lives.

Many years ago, in a workshop with Richard Miller, PhD, on the deep meditative practice of yoga nidra, I recall him telling us, "Don't be angry or irritated when someone snores, disrupting your practice; instead, thank them for their gift. They are bringing you back to awareness, waking you up to go more deeply into the practice. Offer gratitude, for gratitude is the soaring emotion." I have repeated this phrase, gratitude is the soaring emotion, many times over the years, and it has helped me immensely in my yoga nidra practice. But what of the day-to-day situations, where someone's actions are causing us disturbance and anguish?

On our retreat in Hawaii, my students and I discussed the mission of The Samarya Center — to foster individual growth as a means to radical social transformation — and all its implications. Ah, but sometimes that individual growth is so hard. We miss multiple opportunities when we take a stand for one thing against another and delude ourselves that we are only the wave, separate from the ocean. We discussed the wonderful work of yoga and social justice and how noble and satisfied we feel when we lend our hands and our hearts to those in greatest need: children who have suffered abuse; victims of domestic violence; the homeless. But we also thought about how easy it is to forget the perpetrators, those who are the instigators of domestic violence, the abusers, and the oppressors. Don't they too need our love? Does any of this happen in a vacuum? Are these people not a part of the ocean we all share? What if we could open our hearts to these people in the same way and offer compassion and even gratitude, the "soaring emotion," for their part in igniting our continued spiritual awakening? What if, in fact, we were able to see all people who bother us, offend us, hurt us, as people in the greatest need of our love and openness. What if we did not resist our natural capacity for love, but moved with the current toward those who hurt us when our hearts were the most open? This might require us to swim in the big surf, and yet, with practice, we gain confidence, strength, and ultimately liberation from the fear that we might be washed away, despite our greatest efforts.

my difficult family situation, I made many of the same mistakes I made while swimming. I saw myself as separate. I saw myself as both more and less powerful than I actually am. I jumped in without looking, without assessing the readiness of the person with whom I was engaged in conflict. I was ready to "swim," but the "ocean" was not in any condition to receive me safely, and rather than waiting for the natural moment of calm, I jumped in when it was the most tumultuous. I wanted to move quickly, to change the course of the interaction to my version of what seemed right; I pushed back when I felt I was being dragged away from the shore of my own center. And, like my situation in the surf, I became increasingly fatigued, confused, and despairing.

But the big surf taught me how to navigate those errors. Don't resist the push back. Let it flow over me. Respect the timing of others even if I don't understand it. Move slowly and thoughtfully. Open myself to grace, and trust that with this clear intention, I will be held in safety and steadiness.

I got myself to shore. And I resolved, in my own heart, my family conflict. This does not mean that everything was the way I wanted or hoped it would be. It means only that by opening my heart, even when it is most difficult to do so, I find the clarity and contentment that yoga practice offers as the reward for dedication to it. I get to rest easy on the shores of my own heart. I find stillness and presence. And I have learned. I am still learning.

I am glad I am a strong swimmer, because I get to tell my story — of challenge, fear, and triumph — and I hope that it will touch or ignite something in all of you. But my confidence in swimming comes from practice, courage, and reflection on my most difficult situations in the water. It is the same with yoga. In the Bhagavad Gita, when Arjuna complains to Krishna how hard it is to stay focused on his practice and how "fickle, unruly, overpowering and stubborn" the mind is, Krishna responds, "Without self-restraint, yoga, I hold, is difficult to attain; but the self-governed soul can attain it by proper means, if he strive for it."

Practice is not always fun or easy. We love it when we are not asked to push ourselves too much and when we get the results we want. It is infinitely more difficult when we are presented with a challenge that takes us to the edge of our capacities. But with dedication, trust, and thoughtfulness, such challenges are the very opportunities to strengthen our practice, our hearts, and our minds. Less resistance, more grace. We will always find our way safely back to shore.

In yoga, one should no longer care for what people think or say - this is an absolutely indispensable starting point.

~ The Mother, Sri Aurobindo Ashram

MOLLY LANNON KENNY

In-flight Insight, a First Class Epiphany

On my most-recent flight down to Mexico, I was thrilled to get the notice that I was upgraded to first class. I love being in first class in general, but especially when I am going to Mexico, because it means I'm one of the first people off the plane and that I will be one of the first people through customs. Now, it may seem that this is just a desire to be "first" at everything, but, in fact, one of my very most anxious times when flying is when I am sitting toward the back of the plane, the plane has landed, and people are getting their stuff together to get off the plane. This particular ten or fifteen minutes seems almost unbearable to me. I mean, we've sat on the plane for five hours or more, and now it's time to get off and people just seem to be so sloooooooow. I find myself fidgeting and antsy and creating my own little world of impatience and irritation. So, when I combine that with then getting off the plane in Mexico and standing in the very chaotic and random line to go through customs, it feels like hours are added to the trip. In the world I have created for myself, I've done the hard work of flying and now I just want to be there. These last trials seem unbearable.

I love to observe the little moments in my life when I realize that, as a result of my yoga practice, I am doing something differently than I used to. It could be the way I am moving, the way I'm speaking, my reaction to something, or a choice that I am making about health and wellbeing at any level. These times remind me that my practice is working—that it is meaningful and it is bearing fruit.

One such time for me is when I am traveling—and by traveling, I specifically mean traveling by plane to teach somewhere. It is only since I started The Samarya Center and began teaching Integrated Movement Therapy nationally and even internationally that I have become a person who seems to always be in an airport or on a plane. Maybe it's just that over the past eleven years I've simply gotten better at traveling, or more used to it, or just more grown up, but I also think I've gotten better at just being myself. And that, I believe, really does come from my yoga practice.

See, when I first started to travel I would get pretty anxious whenever there was a change in flights, a delay, a cancellation, or some other eventuality of air travel that was not in my plans. My plans were always the same: to get there and get back as efficiently as possible. I would get seriously thrown off balance if I had to wait, or if I missed a connection, or if my seat was changed. I have many memories of running through airports, sweating, disheveled, toting heavy bags, trying to rush to a gate so I could get on the flight I was supposed to take. I have as many memories of crying in airports, or on airplanes, depending on whether I missed the plane or caught it.

Now, I still don't like missing flights, or flights being delayed, or getting in really late at night, but I don't cry over it. And I don't freak out. I still don't like it when my seat gets changed, but instead of stewing the rest of the way home, I just kick back with a glass of wine and open up my Life and Style magazine.

I have thought and taught often about this particular benefit of our yoga practice—the ability to be comfortable in a place of discomfort. My students often hear me refer to yoga as "the life of leisure," a life we can cultivate in which we are able to be at ease in more and more situations, including ones that are challenging to us. It doesn't mean that it's suddenly easy; it takes practice, discipline, and patience, but it is worth it. We become people who, although we might like the creature comforts and have our own preferences about our environments and accommodations, are also totally OK without them. Well, mostly totally OK. We can manage. We're fine.

Having taught hundreds of students specifically in teacher training, this is one of the issues I see as the most deeply challenging for many people—the ability to let go of their "little thing" that they need. We convince ourselves of all sorts of stories about what we need, and what we cannot function without, and what brings us happiness. In truth, I have occasionally found myself feeling frustrated with students and impatient with both their "needs" and their process. Sometimes I feel as if I am up against a wall of self-imposed suffering in the student, and I can't understand why they don't see it too. Of course, they're not the only ones – it's often said that we teach what we most need to learn. All the same, there are times when I just want to scream, sometimes even to myself, "You don't need that thing! Just let it go! Why can't you just be OK without that; you don't need it!"

But, as it turns out, screaming and shaming and impatience don't work so well, and they look really bad coming from a yoga teacher (although it certainly doesn't deter some — but that's another story...) So I just try, with the help of my own practice, to be patient with their process, to try to guide them as best as I can, and to lead them gently into the realization that they could have more freedom and ease if they could just loosen their grip on getting what they think they need.

As for myself, and my own "little things," I try to recognize and remind myself that I too experience more freedom and ease when I am not subjugated by the tyranny of my own various desires. But sometimes it seems that the very act of trying to subvert or divert those desires or so-called needs is in service of another dictator — that of my yoga practice or, more accurately, my own false idea of what it means to be a good yogi.

So, back to my delight in the moments of clarity, and back to the ever-steady and exacting teacher of air travel.

When I get upgraded to first class, not only am I one of the first people off the plane, but if I am in seat 1C, I am the first person off. And so, my great delight on this trip was not simply that I was in first class, but that I was, in fact, in seat 1C. Until, that is, a couple asked me to move.

Arrgh! I felt that familiar anxiety coming back — I "need" to be the first one off the plane, I can't wait in that unbearably long customs line! – and yet, what am I going to do? Am I really going to tell a couple traveling together that they cannot sit next to each other because no, in fact I don't want to be in 4A, I want to be in 1C. 'Cause that's my seat! So, being a good yogi, and a good, reasonable person, I got up and moved back to 4A. But I couldn't settle in, and I kept thinking of ways I might be able to get back up to 1C. I decided that, since the plane made a stop in San Francisco, I would find the couple at the gate and let them know that I wanted to be in my own seat when we landed; that they could sit in it up until that point and then we would have to switch. It seemed like a good compromise.

After we deplaned in San Francisco, I decided to call my husband, Sasha, to tell him the story and to get a little outside perspective, to check in if I was making a good decision. Sasha, in his ever-generous way said, "I guess that seems like an OK thing to ask." Eagerly, I checked in further: "Would you do that?" Sasha laughed kindly and said, "No, I would never do that Molly, but I suppose you could."

OK, well, not the resounding endorsement I had hoped for, but I was feeling OK in my decision. I even searched around in the airport and at the gate for the couple to tell them my decision and to make sure they would be alright with it. After all, it was my seat, and I was being very generous with this compromise, wasn't I? (Amazing what we can convince ourselves of!)

But I couldn't find the couple, and when the flight attendant began to call up the first class passengers, I realized that they were not there anymore. They were only going to San Francisco anyway! The whole awkward situation averted! I settled into 1C and watched the other passengers file in. Relief! No one was going to sit in 1A, or at least no one was going to ask me to move from my seat. That is, until someone did. Just as the flight attendants were preparing to close the doors, two people rushed onto the plane, one who was seated in 1A and one who was seated in 2C. And of course, they were a couple. And they wanted to sit together. However, this time it was the flight attendant who came up to me and very discreetly asked if I would change my seat. I told her I had been asked to change seats on the several previous flights I had been on and was reluctant to do so again. She immediately and emphatically assured me that it was no problem and I should just stay where I was. Great! And I didn't even have to say it to the couple myself.

So, the man settled in next to me, and his wife settled in behind me. The man was friendly and funny, and before the flight took off, turned back to his wife and said, "This is fine, right? We can play cards through here," gesturing to the space between our seats. Of course, in that moment I felt ridiculous and knew I could not stay in my seat. I turned to him and told my story. I told him that I had been moved a bunch of times and that, for some silly reason, I wanted to be the first one off the plane. (I can hardly believe I am admitting to this story!) I asked him if we could switch back right at the last minute. He smiled with a generosity that lit up his whole face, "I totally get it," he said, "we all have our own little things, and it is completely fine that you are asking." I felt even sillier. I said to him, "It's not really fine, it doesn't make any sense, and I'm sorry to have even asked—I must be crazy!" He laughed heartily, "Not at all, it's just your thing and it's no problem," he said again, "we all have those."

Humbled and grateful, I moved back a row. The man kept turning back to me and smiling, and even said to the flight attendant, "Take good care of her, she has been so generous and has had to move so many times. It was so nice of her to move for us."

Of course, the first class flight attendants are always nice to us, and what more could they really offer—did I really need more wine or a free cocktail, the usual bribes from the flight crew? And did I even deserve anything "nice?" I felt so silly.

By the time we were approaching the ground, I said to him, "I don't need to move, this is fine, I really don't know what's wrong with me." His easeful, kind smile was all the response I needed. When the flight landed, he and his wife hung back so I could be the first person off the plane... only to get detoured to a shuttle bus that in fact, waited for all the passengers, and where I had no "rightful seat." Oh, the wisdom and wry humor of the universe.

But, in fact, maybe it was the wisdom of the universe. Because this is what I learned: that perhaps we can allow people to have their quirks and funny little "needs" and odd little desires. That maybe it is OK, and that we don't actually "need" to take something away from someone just because we think it is unreasonable. I think of how often someone will say about someone else, "She's just doing that for attention," as if the appropriate response to that is, "so let's not give it to her." What if part of our yoga practice is actually to yield a bit and to accommodate another person's wish if we can, no matter how silly it seems to us? And that maybe, in fact, if we share what we need or want more openly with others, we can have that need met, and we won't have to feel ridiculous for being human or suffer unnecessarily for something we could have just as easily have had, if only we had asked.

I think the practice then, really, is to be able to both ask for what we want and to be OK if we don't get that thing too. We can hold both ways, at the same time, as equally valid and helpful. We might just be able to accommodate other people's quirks, unless we really can't, and then let them know lovingly that it's not that they are bad for wanting it, it's just that their need can't be met right now, and that they are still OK. And when they're not OK because they can't have what they want? We could be patient with that process too. And that might just really be the yoga. That might be the stilling of the "mind stuff" and that might be just the way that we, and by extension those around us, are able to really experience a sense of peace — that same sense of peace that makes it easier for us to be comfortable with discomfort, and the same sense of peace that allows us to be generous and accepting.

Sigh. I love yoga. And seat 1C.

MOLLY LANNON KENNY

Take up one idea. Make that one idea your life; dream of it; think of it; live on that idea. Let the brain, the body, muscles, nerves, every part of your body be full of that idea, and just leave every other idea alone. This is the way to success, and this is the way great spiritual giants are produced.

~ Swami Vivekananda

Juniper Pruning, Campfire Singing and a Red Winged Blackbird — a reflection on faith and family or Tapas, Svadhyaya, Ishvara Pranidhana

It seems as if whenever I am talking about yoga — and that is a lot of the time — I find myself saying things like "this is the greatest gift yoga has to offer" or "this is my favorite thing about yoga" or "this is the most foundational aspect of yoga." It seems I'm always caught in superlatives, always finding a new way in which yoga is informing, even driving, my thoughts, my actions, and my perspective. Although I sometimes feel silly when I catch myself in the midst of such outpourings, I also feel gratified and reassured — my yoga practice truly is my life. And yet, at the very same time, with all my great proclamations about yoga, I just as often doubt that I actually know anything about it at all. Is this really yoga? Is this the correct interpretation? Did that actually come from the Vedas? Could I pass an exam on the Upanishads? The honest answer is, I don't know. But what I do know is that whatever began as a practice and study of yoga as a physical discipline evolved into a spiritual lens through which I understand, or seek to understand, my place in the world, my relationship to others, and my heart's deepest desire for the only thing I believe really matters in this life at all — to become kinder, more expansive, more open minded, and more open hearted. It is this same lens that illuminates my longing to live with integrity within a great paradox: my own profound ability to influence others through my words and actions and my total insignificance in the great wonder of life.

It is in this spirit that I have been thinking about tapas, svadhayaya, and Ishvara pranidhana, the last three of the niyamas, or observances, as defined by Patanjali in his Yoga Sutras, which he collectively describes as Kriya Yoga, the yoga of action. At The Samarya Center we have the "topic of the month," our community's opportunity to learn about yoga as a real, living practice by discussing various aspects of yoga and understanding how it is influencing our everyday lives.

When it was the month to discuss tapas, I said, "Tapas is the most important of all the niyamas, because it refers to hard work, discipline, and perseverance. If we didn't have this dedication to the hard work of our practice, we wouldn't be able to really commit to any of the other restraints or observances." When it came time to talk about svadhyaya, I said, "Svadhyaya is the most important of all the niyamas, because it refers to self-study. If we didn't have this commitment to self-inquiry, we wouldn't be able to really see how we are in the world or how to clearly see our relationship to any of the yamas or niyamas." When it was time to talk about Ishvara pranidhana, I said, "Ishvara pranidhana is the most important of all the niyamas, because it refers to surrender, to trusting in something mysterious and wondrous, something beyond our limited view of life. If we didn't have this sense of trust in the hard work of our practice, we wouldn't really have any reason to orient ourselves so fully toward expansion of heart and mind."

This is, in fact, just another way of saying that all three observances are of equal importance, and they have a special relationship to one another, which is likely the reason Patanjali grouped them together for us in his classical text. These are my favorites of all the basic tenets because, for me, even though they are more often thought of as the inner-directed tenets, they are in fact the essential ingredients for positive harmonious relationships. And the quality of our relationships, I believe, is the single most important measurement of the value and effectiveness of our spiritual life and growth. I truly believe that If we could see how important our individual roles are in creating positive interactions in our lives and in the world, while simultaneously accepting and even celebrating how totally insignificant we are in the great wonder of all life, we would have the ability to influence the world around us in a profoundly positive way. We would put forth real effort (tapas) to create, mend, evolve, and heal our personal relationships; we would contemplate and evaluate (svadhyaya) our own role in the relationship; and then we would let go (Ishvara pranidhana) and allow ourselves and others to be on their own path, their own continuum for growth. This, in my view, is radical social change.

In my role as spiritual director of The Samarya Center for Humankind (ness) and as a yoga teacher and therapist, I have the privilege, and often feel the sadness, of hearing people's stories of challenge in relationship, whether it be with family, friends, co-workers, a significant other, a partner, or a child. Of all these, I believe family gives us the greatest opportunity to challenge our internal status quo. Contemporary American spiritual teacher Ram Dass says, "If you think you're enlightened, go home for thanksgiving." With family, more than with almost anyone else, we have the greatest desire to be connected, the greatest capacity to be wounded, and the greatest facility to reveal both our best and worst behaviors. In my own family, with four brothers and two sisters and their partners, fifteen nieces and nephews, and two parents still living and still married, you can imagine that we have a lot of fun, a lot of stories, and a lot of opportunity to challenge and be challenged, as well as many opportunities to heal. My family history includes, depending on which day and who you ask, tons of shared love, laughter, regret, resentment, loyalty, blame, anger, hurt feelings, misunderstandings, great pride in and encouragement of one another's accomplishments, deliberate exclusion, and deep wounds. In short, I think, much like any other family. And like any other family, there are certain times when we revisit our past together and again, depending on the day, the circumstance, the mood we are in, these times can provide both opportunities to deepen our relationships through that shared history or to deepen the chasms and wounds that come with that history.

One such time for my family is when we return to the cottage where we spent every summer of our childhood. In fact, we kids don't return all together; we've actually learned that we do better when we have focused individual time with each other, whether it be with siblings or parents. My husband, Sasha, and I make a point of spending at least ten days with my parents at their lake house every summer. My brothers and sisters, as much as they are able, also try to take time at the cottage with their own children in the summer. I think for all of us this is a time to relive the most idyllic aspects of childhood and to spend time connecting with my parents in the place they are most relaxed. But, like any family, or any human being, along with connecting and sharing good times, there is the possibility of recalling, whether revisionist or not, the less-than-idyllic aspects of our shared history. We recall the time that, as little kids, dad made us prune juniper bushes for hours or yelled at us for not putting the sailboat away right, or how mom would interrupt the deepest outpouring of our soul to point out some mundane detail around us: "Look at that red-winged blackbird!" or how our brother did this thing that hurt us, or our sister reacted in this way that made us feel small, or whatever it was that however tiny or however huge, found its way deep into our being to create the many deep and lasting wounds that open anew by some real or imagined slight in the present.

Of course, hurting is always hard, but it is in our hurts that we can also often find the most significant opportunities to heal, and within those opportunities we have the chance to test our yoga or whatever spiritual orientation to which we have collectively committed.

And so I return to tapas, svadhyaya, and Ishvara pranidhana and to the supreme importance of relationship. For us to make the choice to stay in our relationships, to see what might be revealed by that commitment, we need tapas, the determination that keeps us coming back and trying again, even when we do feel hurt or slighted, because we have some belief that the relationship is worth it. In my view, family, barring some egregious and dangerous situations, is always worth it. And in my experience, most people want to come back to family, even when they are conflicted. I, for one, am infinitely sentimental that way. If I walked away every time I felt dissed by my parents or one of my brothers or sisters, I would have walked away a thousand times and eventually ended up so far away I might never find my way back. And so I use my tapas, my fiery determination, to keep returning to the relationship. But let's not get too idealistic, right? Many of us have families in which our brother or sister or mom or dad continually returns to the relationship but with the same resentments, the same attitude, the same anger, and, in fact, makes the revisiting miserable, even dangerous, for everyone.

This is where svadhyaya comes in. I have to be able to look at myself, courageously and lovingly, and say, what was my part in that? What am I doing that is perpetuating this pain or discomfort? What can I do, what would I like to do, or to be, that would change the way this communication goes down? One afternoon, as I sat with my dad in the last sunlight of the day, watching the lake and the breeze coming across it, talking about all the great times we had at the cottage as kids, building bonfires, singing together as a family, he suddenly shifted the conversation back to the pruning of the juniper bushes. In a precious moment of uncharacteristic and unselfconscious reflection, my dad said quietly, "I did so many stupid things back then. I didn't even have any reason; sometimes they didn't even make any sense." It was a small thing, and in reflecting on the hard times we had as a family, barely worth mentioning compared to the bigger hurts. Yet it was a symbol of self-study on the part of my dad and an opportunity for self-study on my part as well. My dad was showing, in however apparently small a way, that he took responsibility for some of the pain we recalled from our childhood, along with the joy. I was offered a chance to study my own ability to take this tiny grain and make it meaningful, an opportunity to use this forgiveness as a stand-in symbol for all other things I might have resentment about towards my dad, or my mom, or my family, or any of my life experiences or relationships.

Which brings us back then to Ishvara pranidhana — surrender and trust. This is the greatest tenet of all. This one asks us to let go and let people be themselves. To stop trying to make other people be the way we want them to be and instead to trust in our own ability to be the way we want to be. To surrender to the idea that there may be some grand divine plan to which we are not privy. To trust that this commitment to the relationship will yield some benefit, either internal or external, that we may not yet be able to imagine, but for which one day we will be infinitely grateful.

We are all in this together.

"Juniper Pruning" by Patricia Clauhs (then Kenny), age 7.

Above all, trust in the slow work of God. We are quite naturally impatient in everything to reach the end without delay. We should like to skip the intermediate stages. We are impatient of being on the way to something unknown, something new. And yet it is the law of all progress that it is made by passing through some stages of instability-and that it may take a very long time. And so I think it is with you; your ideas mature gradually-let them grow, let them shape themselves, without undue haste. Don't try to force them on, as though you could be today what time (that is to say, grace and circumstances acting on your own good will) will make of you tomorrow. Only God could say what this new spirit gradually forming within you will be. Give Our Lord the benefit of believing that his hand is leading you, and accept the anxiety of feeling yourself in suspense and incomplete.

~ Pierre Teilhard de Chardin

The Ideal of Satya~
or the Reality of Lying, Conniving, and Thieving

Not so long ago, while down at my home in Mexico, I was ripped off. No, not robbed or mugged, but ripped off, cheated out of about $150 at a "reputable" franchise. Now, yoga is really good for me, because I can have a tendency to get all uppity and irritable way before I consider slowing down. This is a lot harder in Spanish, because somehow the effect just isn't the same when you have to say, "Listen, you lying thieving....hold on, let me get my dictionary....tramposo!" I can pepper in swear words as breezily as a local at the cantina, but they just don't sound quite as forceful coming from me as I struggle for what should follow. This is tough for me, because one thing I do not have trouble with in English is opening up a can of Whoop Ass. Further complicating my ability to be taken really seriously is the reputation I have acquired in my little town as the peace-loving, fun-loving, outgoing, Spanish-speaking *gabacha* English teacher who never really gets mad at anybody. So turning on the Jersey girl really is a tough switch.

But anyway. I went to a Telcel franchise to buy a modem for my computer so I could get online at home instead of whiling away my hours in a dark Internet "café," a café that didn't actually offer any coffee, food, lighting, assistance, or reliable connection. The first store I went to told me that I could not purchase any such thing in the pueblo but would have to go to the flagship store in Puerto Vallarta for my modem. Luckily you can't swing a plate of ceviche without hitting another Telcel, so I just moved on down the block to find someone with a different answer—the answer I wanted, that I could buy a modem for my computer and use it reliably in my tiny town. To my great good fortune, or so I thought, the very next store told me what I wanted to hear. Of course they had a modem for me. And it should work in my little pueblo about 10 kilometers down the road. Our new fast friends, a manager and two employees, at the shop then proceeded to sell me a phone, saying the only way I could get a decent rate to the United States was to buy this new phone that had a promocion on it. OK, that all sounded fine, as did their suggestion to take the chip out of my old phone to power the modem, instead of using the chip that actually came with the modem. They were so smiley, so helpful, and I was very pleased with my purchases. When neither the phone nor the modem worked when I got home, I went back to the store. My friends were very helpful, messed with the phone and modem a bit, told me what great Spanish I spoke, and sent me back home. The modem worked for about a week, but I could never get the phone to register the promotion, the main reason I had bought the phone. I went back to the store again, and they called Telcel's main office for me, gave me back my phone, and said I just had to wait 48 hours. They asked me how my banda ancha, or broadband, was doing, and I told them, "Great."

And it was doing great, until the modem refused to work on the eighth day after I bought it. I went back to the store one more time, to ask for a receipt (I had not received one when I bought it), because I was going to Puerto Vallarta and would return the modem myself, as well as get my phone registered in person. The folks in the store looked furtively at one another, sort of mumbled something, then said that they could give me a receipt for the phone, but they had a better idea for the modem. The manager himself was going to Puerto Vallarta the next day and would personally bring our modem down and get it exchanged. How friendly! How thoughtful! What excellent customer service! Since we hadn't brought the modem with us, the manager took down my husband's phone number and said he would call him at 7:00 the next morning to pick up the modem and get it all sorted out for us. When we triumphantly returned to our hometown and told some of our local friends of our success, they just laughed and said, "Yeah, right! Buena suerte! Good luck!" But I knew they were wrong. That guy was gonna call us, and we were gonna have a brand spankin' new modem by the end of the next day.

Since we were going to Puerto Vallarta ourselves that day anyway, to register the phone, a dear friend from our town suggested that we take the modem with us, even without the receipt, just in case. Off we went on the hot trek to Vallarta to stand in line at the grand Telcel store. Now, Mexico teaches you nothing if not patience and letting go, and we needed both of those things in spades simply to make it through the wait at Telcel. To make a long story short (always a challenge for me), when we got to the counter we learned several important things about our purchases: 1. We were not eligible for the phone promotion, it was only available to full-time residents; 2. our "new" modem was over three years old; 3. a brand new modem, with a warranty, direct from the Telcel store costs the equivalent of about $70, less than half of what we had paid; and, finally, 4. the employees at the other store had taken the chip from the modem they sold us because it came with a 30-day free Internet promotion that they could then use in their own modem. This is when we realized that we'd been had, and by the very people with whom we thought we had made a friendly connection. Oh, and are you still wondering if that guy ever called us at 7:00 the next morning?

But back to yoga for just a moment.

As we become more familiar with the yamas and niyamas, and especially their application to everyday lives, we start to see how they all overlap and interweave. Satya — translated as truthfulness, honesty, reality, being with what is — is directly linked to ahimsa, yoga's foundational precept of non-harming, just as it is connected to the next yama, asteya, non-stealing, and to all the other ethical precepts of yoga. We start to more clearly understand a pathway that is not so much about remembering this word and that rule, but about pausing and asking ourselves what feels really right, in the deepest, purest parts of our being, and trying more and more to consistently act from that place.

Yoga, remember, is a practice. We are all students of yoga; all we can do is make the effort. Sometimes that effort seems easy and natural, sometimes it's the hardest thing we can think of doing, and sometimes we just don't know in what direction to make the effort — it remains completely hidden from our conscious view. When we practice together, make a commitment together, in sangha — a community of practitioners — we support and encourage one another. We kindly shed light on difficult situations that the other can't see clearly; we forgive one another, and ourselves, for our inevitable lapses in judgment, forethought, or compassion; and we lovingly inspire one another to keep on keepin' on. With my friends from the Telcel store, I had my practice, but I didn't have my community. I would have to tackle this one on my own.

Satya. Truthfulness, honesty, reality, being with what is. There are so many facets to this apparently simple situation with the phone and modem.

Three dishonest people ripped us off. That seems simple enough.

And when I lay in bed at night thinking of how I could get back at them — maybe I could make fliers and hand them out to all the gringos shopping in the town, letting them know not to shop at this store; maybe I could make giant posters and post them outside the store; maybe I could take pictures of them and say I was going to send them into the local paper — my mind spinning with the sweet glory of revenge, I felt I would only be standing up for myself, doing what was natural and, in fact, righteous.

But, really, it is more complicated than that....and it is always more complicated than that. Three dishonest people ripped us off. But were they truly dishonest, that is, were they habitually dishonest people, or were they dishonest just in this situation? Is there a difference? Were they equally dishonest? Were the two employees as dishonest as the manager or were they doing what they had been taught to do to keep their jobs? "It's not that bad, Americans have plenty of money, they are only here seasonally; what harm will it really do if their modem doesn't work? They can just buy another one." And, in a sense, that is true. I did just buy another one. So, although it is clearly still dishonest of the employees, they also probably had some justification that made sense to them somehow, as most of us do when we too are lying or being less than truthful.

Were they lying when they were helping me, being friendly to me, complimenting my Spanish? Or were they, like all of us, able to compartmentalize their behavior, so that they could at once be "good" people and still be lying to me about the modem and the phone? And did they once consider that perhaps there was much more damage done by their simple lie than simply ripping me off for $150? What about my time, my energy, my good faith and feelings about them and indeed the reputation and trustworthiness of all of Mexico's merchants? How often do we convince ourselves that our lie or half-truth is harmless because we can justify it somehow, but neglect to look at the subtle ways it might deeply and profoundly disturb the peace of another? And what of my rumination about ways to exact revenge? Was I really going to act on them? Was I really going to take time to write, print, and copy fliers, then stand outside of their store like some crazy sore loser with nothing better to do? Obviously not. And yet how much of my own peace did I disturb when I allowed myself to waste energy on these fantasies, even as I knew I would never carry them out?

If we return to the basic definition of yoga as given by Patanjali in the Yoga Sutras, we find *yogash chitta vritti nirodhah*: Yoga is the restraint of the modification of the mind stuff. *Tada drashtuh svarupe avasthanam*: Then the Seer abides in Itself, resting in its own True Nature, which is called Self-realization. In other words, yoga is a practice of calming and stilling the mind so that we remain undisturbed, and in this undisturbed state we are able to connect more directly with, and abide in, our own true nature. Out of this place arises an experience of deep contentment and peace, an experience that, when we use it as a foundation for our actions and reactions, helps us to pause, to reflect, to use intelligence and discernment to guide our behavior.

In considering satya and all of its many interpretations and challenges to us in our everyday lives, we can apply this simple test: On a deep, unmuddied level, is what I am doing, saying, thinking, bringing more peace or more disturbance to this situation, for myself and for the other participants? If I apply this test to the whole situation above, I can see that there is very little peace for anyone. My anger may be justified on one level (no one appreciates being cheated or lied to), and yet holding on to my anger will not do anything to change the situation — it certainly won't get me online — and it will not punish or teach a lesson to my adversaries. So here, part of satya is acknowledging the situation as it is — I paid three times as much as I should have for a modem — and then letting it go. Sounds easy right? Wrong; but that is why we have each other. That's why we practice. That's why we fall down, get up, try again. That's why we share our stories, even the ones that make us feel foolish. We reveal the agitations of our own mind in order to still them. And perhaps in our sharing, we allow others to be tender to their own agitations and foolishness, and in that tenderness, to also be able to still those agitations and rest in that still point — our true nature.

We are all in this together.

Sometimes resilience arrives in the moment you discover your own unshakeable goodness.

~ Gregory Boyle, SJ

Brahmacharya: Moderation and Restraint Revisited ~ Wake up!

Bramacharya, as noted in previous chapters, is the fourth of the yamas, the first limb of Patanjali's eight limbs of yoga. As such, bramacharya is one of the inner "restraints" that we practice. Infamous for its relationship to celibacy, the idea of this restraint can engender fear, humor, or even aversion in many of us householders. The question was brought up among our teachers: if we are celibate but not by choice, does it still count as a practice of bramacharya?

Like most aspects of yoga, it is complex. I suppose the short answer to that particular question would be no; if you aren't consciously and intentionally restraining yourself from sex then it doesn't count as a practice of brahmacharya. Sorry, it doesn't really seem fair, does it? But, take a moment to consider brahmacharya this way instead. Brahmacharya might be translated as something like "walking with God," or as "a life lived with intention, a desire for and commitment to an awakening to self-realization." In this context, the idea of celibacy, which is not in fact the first listed definition of brahmacharya, even in the Sanskrit lexicon, is simply the notion that we have a limited amount of energy in this mortal coil, and that it should not be squandered on unnecessary or superfluous activities or thoughts. The sex act and all of our planning around it is surely one way that the mind and body use energy, and perhaps at times, this same energy could be used in a more directed and productive way, vis a vis our relationship to God consciousness.

But certainly sex is not the only way we might squander our energy. Energy can be leaked, even hemorrhaged, through all kinds of excesses, through all kinds of addictions and obsessions: from overindulging to overwithholding, from being too careless to being too cautious. The key here always is simply moderation and mindfulness.

So how can we develop this spirit of brahmacharya? What are the simple practices that might help us to develop the mindfulness that brings us closer to God? How do we develop the awareness of what gives us energy and what takes it away, of what adds value to our lives, our partnerships, our communities, and what diminishes them?

For me, the number one practice is simply, continuously, nonjudgmentally, "waking up." Becoming aware of what I am doing and how it is affecting me and the people and world around me. Making the commitment to evaluating my actions and reactions, and asking myself over and over, did that make me feel closer to who I want to be spiritually or did it take me further away from it? We can do this practice all day every day, and we can directly observe the positive changes that it makes in our lives in a very real way.

I cringe to recall an experience I once had of writing two specific e-mails of apology. Both were an effort to counter the effects of reactive emails that I had sent earlier. Mad and frustrated, feeling righteous and challenged, I had lashed out with what at the time felt exactly right: just what those people had coming to them. Damn, it felt good to be right and put those people in their place. Oh, but only for such a short, fleeting moment, soon to be replaced with regret, a desire for connection, and the hope of being able to make it right by explaining what my real feelings were. Turns out, those email recipients were people too! Who knew they also had human feelings of righteousness, of frustration? To me, this is a matter of energy management. Slow down. Take a breath. Consider all sides. Assess where your feelings are coming from. Practice restraint. Seems like a lot, but really, in the end, it clearly would have taken less energy than it ultimately did -- from me and from the others involved -- to have to back-track and struggle to reconcile, to arrive at the very place of connection I believe everyone wanted to reach. In the end, too, I would have felt that I was more the person I am always striving to be, instead of more of the person I already am. The brief "victory" of smug vindication would have been dwarfed by the swelling victory over my reactive self and ultimately the greater contribution to my own development, to my community and world.

So, brahmacharya might not be as difficult as it seems, or it might actually be harder. If you can't get credit for not having sex whether you want to or not, you can "work for credit" by simply waking up, showing up, being present to all the complexity of life. This too is brahmacharya. Simple suggestions for this practice in the studio? Fold your mats and blankets. Wait until the teacher is done talking to enter. Be nice and thoughtful to the people who work so hard to make the studio a beautiful place for everyone. Keep your voices down. Smile at a fellow student. Treat yourself, others, and your communal space with reverence and respect. Leave a contribution when you participate in a community class. Bring flowers to put on the altar. This is a collective call to all of us, every one of us, in the community to wake up, wake up, wake up! This is yoga, and just like waking up, it's both easier and harder than it seems. Your efforts will not go unnoticed!

*P*ractice

Take some time to simply notice your own practice. What is it? How is it serving you? Is it still serving you now the way it was when you started it? Is it time to reevaluate? What are the specific, tangible acts you perform every day to keep you on track, to keep you oriented toward the spiritual life and its fruits? Think about the small practices, the ones that you can touch, smell, count, and feel as much as you think about the grander, more esoteric practices. Consider, for example, reframing a practice of "love and compassion toward all beings," as being a fruit of the small practices you do that remind you of where you are aiming. In other words, focus on the small practices that lead you toward your goal of love and compassion.

For example you might consider a daily "ten things" list of things for which you are grateful. Start every morning by listing those ten things in a journal or sharing them with a loved one. Notice how the ten things get easier and easier to notice and acknowledge. Keep spiritual reading by your bedside — not linear books, but texts you can pick up and jump into at any point — and dedicate five minutes just before you go to sleep and five minutes when you wake up to reading uplifting and illuminating poetry or prose. Keep an altar with which you actually interact — bring it flowers, clean it often, light the candle, ring the bell. Write notes of appreciation and love to the people around you. Smile often. Compliment others. Offer help. Let your practice be a living thing, the way that you are in the world, not something you do a couple times a week. Take time to notice your own evolution when you invite your practice into your life, when you allow your whole life to be your practice.

Healer, Heal Thyself: An Equation for Real Change

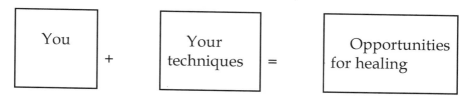

Somewhere around the winter of 2008, I received a phone call that would lead to a pivotal event in my life—as a human being, as a therapist, as a yoga teacher, and as a yogi. When I answered my phone, I heard the voice of the volunteer coordinator at the end-of-life facility where I was a volunteer: "Molly, there's a woman here who is beginning her imminent transition from life. She's scared and calling out and there is no one here to be with her. The nurses have asked for support in her transition. They asked if anyone from The Samarya Center was available to come down and be with her."

I'm not sure what made me respond the way I did--was it because as the person who started the Bedside Yoga program, I thought it was my duty? Was it my ego reminding me of my own great importance in the matter? Was it a real calling from my heart? Was it because of some divine sense that this would be a powerful, and deeply meaningful, moment in my life and growth? I really don't know. Probably a little bit of all of that, but nonetheless, I heard myself saying, "I'll be right there."

When I arrived at the medical center, I was brought to the room of a woman I had never met. Although I had already had the profound, and profoundly humbling, opportunity to attend a scheduled death at the facility, I had never been left totally alone with someone who was in her final hours of life. I had absolutely no connection to the woman in Room 103. I was shown in by Margaret, one of my favorite nurses at the program. "She's transitioning quickly, but she's so afraid, and so alone. She's been crying out and can't seem to get comfortable. I thought you might be able to help," followed by,

"I wasn't sure when you'd get here—I've just administered a sedative to help her relax." I will never forget entering her room. There lay a woman alone, mouth agape, breathing erratically, and for all intents and purposes, completely drugged out of any real sense of what was happening. There was the unmistakable smell of dying. And then there was the music. The staff had put on what I now refer to as "dying music"—insipid New Age pan flutes and waterfalls, intended to create a calming environment. Margaret gazed for a moment at her patient with a look of deep care. She touched the woman on her head and then turned to me with a quiet expression, as if to say, "Here you go," and shut the door. It was just the dying woman, the music, and me. I felt instantly and simultaneously both lost and empowered. I had been with many people in the last days, and even hours, of their lives, but this was different: I had never been with anyone that I didn't know at all, and who, as far as I could tell, was completely unaware of my presence. As the pan flutes droned, and the waterfalls cascaded, I thought to myself, "This is it. This is everything I have ever taught and everything I think I believe. If I believe in my work, and I believe in the power of human connection, then my presence here is meaningful and powerful. I just have to do what my intuition tells me, and I may be able to offer something." With that I placed my hands on the woman's head and began to offer prayers of peace and connection. Drawing from my Reiki training, I moved from her head to her knees, to her feet to her hands. I sat for what seemed like hours with her hands in mine, praying that if I was offering her nothing particularly earth shattering, that I was offering this body, this being, this soul, some humble gift of care and connection in her final moments on this planet.

After some time, I wish I could say it was intuition, but more likely it was when it became too uncomfortable to lean over her body in bed, I quietly disconnected from her and left her room. I was later told that she had passed shortly after I left, and the nurses reported that she seemed to pass in peace. I didn't know what to do with that information. I still don't. Of course, I want to think it was because of me — my presence and my caring had allowed her to transition quietly and seemingly without fear — but the truth is, it could have just as easily been the valium, or the time, or the body's innate wisdom and ability to let go, or some combination of all those things. Whatever the reason, in my own life this was a profound experience I return to again and again in my thinking, in my prac- tice, and in my teaching.

But let me not get too ahead of myself.

Long before I initiated the Bedside Yoga program for end of life, and long before I had any interest in or experience with yoga, I had been employed as a speech pathologist in a conventional setting. I had worked in both the acute care and follow-up units, and had spent several years working with people in challenging health, and life, situations. With my clinical training and experience, I had honed my techniques to the degree I could; I felt comfortable with, and knowledgeable about, best practices and contraindications for a variety of conditions. I existed in a culture that largely rejected the sense that the practitioner, as a unique human being, should be shared too generously with the patient. This is, in fact, in direct contrast to the strong body of research suggesting that the relationship between the patient and the therapist is the single most important element in the process of healing.[1]

I wanted to help people, I cared deeply about their suffering, but I also wanted freedom from my own suffering, and from my own ego, an ego that told me that changing others was up to me— that when people experienced healing, it was because I had done a good job, and that when they did not, I had done a poor one.

At the same time, I witnessed and clearly understood that the equation could be wrongly skewed in the other direction: the archetype of the all-knowing healer who, by sheer proximity to his or her greatness, could fix, cure, heal, or dismiss a patient. This, as I saw it, created disconnection not just between the patient and clinician, but also within the clinician. For my part, the intense pressure and feeling that I should be the one making the changes happen in my patients' lives was manifesting both in my emotions and in my physical body. I was routinely going home at night both depressed and anxious, as well as in physical pain, particularly centered around my upper back, shoulders, and arms. Sometimes the pain would be so intense that I couldn't even lift my arms enough to pick up a dish or wash my face.

I knew intuitively, even before I knew anything about yoga, that in the intention to help and heal, there was some in-between place, a new equation, in which a balance between deep human connection and well-established interventions and techniques would create the optimal conditions in which healing would occur. I longed to understand this place, to be shown this equation, to be able to do the correct math. I wanted to help people, I cared deeply about their suffering, but I also wanted freedom from my own suffering, and from my own ego, an ego that told me that changing others was up to me — that when people experienced healing, it was because I had done a good job, and that when they did not, I had done a poor one.

What a relief it was then, when through my deepening spiritual pursuit through yoga, I discovered a simple truth: that we cannot change anyone or make anyone do anything. That we are not in fact, the "doers," and that to think we are creates confusion and suffering. The best we can do, and the best we can do for others, is to help them set up conditions for change, and to trust in the innate wisdom, desire, and divine timing of the other person for that change to occur, in whatever form it takes. The understanding of this truth led me to the equation I had been seeking, and one I have been passionately sharing for over a decade.

The equation, thankfully, is quite simple, because it requires only two elements. The first is the understanding that our "gift is our presence." In other words, the healing that we hope to facilitate, or the yoga that we share, is within us, not dependent upon the other. This abnegates completely our own agenda, our inflated sense of self and our own importance. It invites an exquisite paradox: on the one hand, that we have a profound ability to influence others and the trajectory of their healing and, on the other, that we don't actually have to "do" anything—we simply have to "be." Of course, although I say that the equation is simple, requiring just two elements, this first one, the true understanding of self, is actually incredibly challenging. We have to first do the hard work of healing ourselves, of understanding our own biases, prejudices, and limitations, as well as acknowledging and developing our greatest gifts, whatever they may be.

Fortunately, the second part of the equation really is simple. Techniques are relatively easy to learn, and will get better and more abundant with time and experience. What makes this part of the equation complicated is the fact that we often rely too heavily on techniques because we don't see a need for or don't trust in our simple presence. We start to allow the techniques to dominate our work, believing more in the techniques than we do in ourselves or in the person with whom we are working. The techniques become the engine driving our work and, in doing so, all but subsume the subtle and powerful force of real human connection and a sense of wonder and divine wisdom.

In my experience, this equation for healing really is like a math equation--it must be balanced on both sides, and for us to make it function, we must be willing to work on both sides simultaneously and to be able to see how and why one side or the other is dominating. It also requires us to check often on the outcome—as we "show our work" we are making sure that we are coming to the same conclusion, that we are setting up conditions for change, opportunities for healing, and not working toward a different outcome, one where we are trying to make a specific change occur.

I have seen, in both the conventional clinical model and in the world of yoga-based therapy, well-meaning interventionists missing out on the best part of healing work by creating more difficulty than is necessary or simply doing less than the best that is possible. I have seen and experienced the opposites of ahimsa, satya, and asteya when the practitioner robs the client or student of his or her own self-efficacy by overreliance on one or the other parts of the equation. To really set conditions for change, to provide opportunities for real, lasting, and empowered healing, we must work dutifully and courageously on both sides. To create the factor of "you," you must be committed to deep self-inquiry and constantly seek to see the other as atman, not less than, but equal to "us." This requires practice, dedication, and total commitment to the power of this part of the equation. At the same time, we must not confuse this understanding of the power and potential of our loving presence with a hubris that suggests we don't need specific techniques. Our techniques give us something concrete to offer, and remind us of best practices and contraindications. Indeed, it is our techniques, not us, per se, that we are promoting and offering when we say we are therapists, start up programs like Bedside Yoga, or endeavor to explain or share what it is that we are doing to create conditions for change.

I didn't have this equation in mind when I met the woman in Room 103; I hadn't yet arrived at this place in my own learning or teaching. And yet that experience was one of the precise moments in time where I understood and trusted in this magical balance. I brought all of myself to the experience, including all of my insecurities, curiosity, not-knowingness, and trust. I brought the sense that, as a human being with the intention to allay another's fears, I would be able to offer something. But I also offered my best techniques. If I hadn't known Reiki, or meditation, or basic Thai yoga techniques, I wouldn't have thought I had anything to offer. And finally, if I thought that I was the "doer," that it was my job to make this woman's transition into death more peaceful, I would have been unsatisfied with just about any outcome. But since I understood that my job was only to set the conditions for change, to offer an opportunity for healing, it was a job I knew I could do, and whatever the outcome was would be more than satisfactory. Of course I'll never know what that woman's experience was as she passed. But I will know my experience: one free from ego and fear, that once again deepened my faith in a human connection so powerful it could be felt and shared, through skillful means, intention, and loving presence, in any situation anywhere — even in a room filled with the oddly sweet smell of death and the warbling sounds of the pan flute.

1. Lambert, M., J. & Barley, D., E. (2001). Research Summary on the therapeutic relationship and psychotherapy outcome. Psychotherapy, 38, 4, 357-361.

This article first appeared in the Winter 2012 edition of Yoga Therapy Today and has been slightly modified. Reprinted with permission from the International Association of Yoga Therapists. Not edited or copyedited for this book.

If God is at the heart of this physical, evolving cosmos, then love is the energy that makes everything precious and alive. God is the ultimate wholeness and depth and love – the inner omega of everything from the smallest quark to the largest galaxy.

~Ilia Delio

Santosha ~ Contentment, or The Fruits of Practice

Do your practice, all is coming. ~ Sri K. Pattabhi Jois

Increase your sweet practice. Your practice will benefit you at another time; someday your need will suddenly be fulfilled.
~ Rumi (from **The Guest House**)

The journey to parenthood has been challenging to say the least. It has been many years of a constantly evolving emotional landscape and a reorganizing of heart, mind, and body. After losing my first pregnancy in Costa Rica, my beloved husband, Sasha, and I moved on to our original plan A: adoption. Adoption had been our intention when we first were together, but over time, that intention turned into a desire to have our own biological child. It was not so difficult, then, to decide that adoption was truly our path.

We began asking people about it, researching it, going to informational meetings, and generally getting excited at the idea that there was some little person out there that we didn't know and who didn't know us but who would come into our lives and forever change the three of us. Then, as it seems to often happen, in the midst of this, we discovered we were pregnant again. With the first pregnancy, it was all excitement and openness and adventure. With this new one, we leaned towards stoicism and reticence. We hardly talked about it at all, and didn't even tell our families until we had passed the timeframe that we thought was most fragile. While visiting my parents at their summer home in Canada, we finally began to settle into the idea that this was really going to happen. My parents were supportive, comforting, and fun. They were optimistic and joyous when I felt good and encouraging and understanding during the times when I felt down. Quite honestly, it was hard for me to believe in the pregnancy, having had only one other experience with it, which didn't turn out how I wanted.

One night when I was feeling especially unsettled, I was sitting with Sasha on the lake, looking at the seemingly infinite array of constellations and shooting stars. I turned to him and said, "I'm really scared, and I'm glad to be here with my mom and dad. It's like I'm a little kid, believing that when I'm with my parents, nothing can go wrong with the pregnancy, that everything is going to be OK." Sasha, in his wisdom, responded, "Or maybe, when you are with your mom and dad, you just know everything is going to be OK, no matter what happens." Santosha: that deep feeling of being OK, of naturally being in the flow of life. I realized Sasha was right. I was going to be OK no matter what, and my relationship and faith in my parents had everything to do with my relationship and faith in God, the Universe, Ishvara, with Life itself. I started to reflect more intensely on this feeling of contentment. Even with the prospect of giving birth well within my mental reach, I also knew that this child, this pregnancy, this one desire, was not the thing that would bring contentment. I knew deeply that as much as I wanted this child, that I would always be, and in fact always was, OK. That even within the heartbreak and loss, there would always be a part of me that could find a deep sense of peace and ease. This overwhelming feeling of contentment, even gratitude, with and for my life as it is, held me in a soft and suspended place of truly letting go.

I recall a few years ago when I was with one of my most treasured teachers, Pam Havig. Pam has one of the most beautiful marriages, families, husbands, and perspectives on life that I have ever known. Several years ago, I was sitting with her and some of her students, and somehow someone asked her if she could be happy if something ever happened to her husband. Pam answered without hesitation. "Of course! I love Don more than anything in the world, but my ability to be happy is not based on his presence in my life." Wow. I was

NO GURUS CAME KNOCKING

stunned. Pam and Don are the kind of couple that makes you happy just to be around them. They love each other so deeply, respect each other so much, and have so much fun together, it truly seems like they were made for each other, that one could not be without the other. I remember thinking, "How can that be so? I want some of what she's got." What she has is contentment. Santosha. That transcendent sense of being at peace, even in the midst of change, disappointment, simple inconvenience, and even heartbreak.

The motto of The Samarya Center's teacher training is "Teach from the heart, teach what you know." I believe that whenever we teach from this place of authenticity and experience, we offer the gift of our own challenges and joys to illuminate some of the more hidden aspects of our spiritual practice. Our practice then, becomes something living and practical, rather than simply a study of philosophy or a lofty idea. It is in this spirit that I sometimes feel that the Universe is speaking to me, through me, pushing me through trying times so that I might offer some bit of wisdom or contemplation to my community.

On that same trip in Canada with my parents, Sasha and I attended Catholic mass with them as we usually do. My parents instilled in all of their children that whether or not we chose Catholicism, as they had, we would benefit from taking some time out of every week just for silent reflection and connection to something greater than ourselves. Although I am not Catholic now, my sense of the presence of God is such that I can see and feel it in most places that are intentionally created for devotion and contemplation. I have also held on to what I feel are some of the best teachings of that faith, and I enjoy going to mass, back to my roots, from time to time, and to showing respect and love for my parents and their path. During the sermon, the priest talked about his work as a chaplain in hospice care. He talked about how he had observed that many people die in fear and isolation, but that those who had made a practice of saying the rosary always died peacefully. He preached strongly to his congregation that they should start saying the rosary and make it a consistent practice. He reminded them that they could take twenty minutes here and there throughout the day to complete the rosary and that they would benefit deeply from their practice. When we left church, I said to my mom, "I didn't really agree with that sermon. I've sat with people at end of life and have observed both of those things, the fear and isolation and also the peace and readiness. And it did not depend on whether or not the person said the rosary." My mom agreed immediately. "A person can do whatever their practice is. It might be saying the rosary, it might be reading the Torah or the Koran, it might be silent sitting, but what is the same is the dedication to practice. That's what develops that sense of peace and ease." My mom is awesome. And she's right. It is the dedication to practice that creates the change. It is the dedication to the idea of contentment, to developing this inner faculty, which creates the feeling of contentment. When we practice, we reap the benefits, and we never know how or when we will most need the fruits of our practice. I think about learning to do a handstand or headstand, and I recall seeing those poses for the first time. They seemed so out of reach, almost impossible. But we dedicate ourselves to the practice, and we see the results. We learn to do headstand, we learn to do handstand, we progress at our own pace, our "success" looks different than anyone else's. But what we have in common is the desire to create that change. In our spiritual life, it is the desire to live in a way that is more fulfilling than what we have done before.

Just after coming home from that trip to Canada, right at the mystical twelve-week mark, Sasha and I lost our second pregnancy. But our experience this time was radically different. We had already been on this ride, and we knew all of the possibilities. We had already committed to our love and gratitude for each other and had reflected deeply on our commitment to contentment, whatever happened. Yes, it is a sad story, but it is not a story of sadness. This story, to me, is one of hope and joy. I know that it is my practice that has allowed me to come through all of these wildly vacillating and rapidly changing emotional states with an intact soul, a joyous heart, and a deep gratitude for the mystery of life. It is a direct experience of going through heartache as OK and emerging as OK. It's not to say that it was easy, nor to say that anyone else's experience would be or should be like ours. But my desire truly is to "teach from the heart, teach what I know." And what I know is that with practice, this contentment is here, already, for anyone. But it comes with a price: practice. So, like the priest said, twenty minutes here, twenty minutes there—do your practice. The gift of contentment is a gift worth working for and waiting for. We believe that the gift of our child—however he or she shows up—will be the same: worth working for and worth waiting for. And that all that we have gone through, and our dedication to our practice, will make us better people and even better parents.

Do your practice. All is coming.

The God, who is greater than God, has only one thing on her mind, and that is to drop, endlessly, rose petals on our heads. Behold the one who can't take his eyes off of you. Marinate in the vastness of that.

~Father Greg Bolye, SJ

MOLLY LANNON KENNY

White Teeth, Bright Lights and a Revelation

In early September 2011, I attended the Symposium on Yoga Therapy and Research (SYTAR) conference, a fabulous and fabulously informative gathering of yoga therapists from all over the world, organized by the International Association of Yoga Therapists. Morning yoga practice sessions ran the gamut from gratitude practices to yoga for chronic pain; mid-days were spent in various sessions, discussing topics as varied as Yoga and Menopause, Yoga for Mental Illness, and Yoga for PTSD; while the evenings were saved for keynote speeches and networking.

On the Saturday evening, IAYT held a lovely, lively reception, complete with wine, delicious dips and cheeses, and scrumptious desserts. Entertainment and edification came in the form of Vedic astrology readings, free Shiatsu massage sessions, Ayurvedic pulse readings, and shopping for various yogariffic delights, such as special holistic face creams, herbal supplements and remedies, and all kinds of yoga-related publications. The entire evening had the feel of a mini carnival; I was enjoying myself immensely, meeting new friends, availing myself of the various offerings, and generally relaxing following the long days of intensive study and practice.

I must have looked like a game participant. As I stood near the light therapy booth waiting for my free Heart Song massage, one of the vendors came up to me and asked me if I would like to have my teeth whitened, using a special intense light process. Either that or he thought my teeth were less than their pearly white potential. In any event, being up for pretty much anything, especially if it panders to my vain side, and especially if it's free, I quickly agreed.

I should have been tipped off by being handed a "finger glove" that was for wiping my teeth off. This most unpleasant feeling was a prelude for what was to come. Next, the technician filled a dental tray, much like the retainer I wore in fifth grade that usually ended up in the school cafeteria trashcan. As I saw the foaming, flowing hydrogen peroxide mixture, I wondered why the light therapy was needed. The tray and its potion seemed plenty. The tech then placed the retainer in my mouth, covered my eyes with dark sunglasses, positioned a very bright light in front of me, and said, "OK, see you in twenty minutes."

Twenty minutes? That seemed like an awfully long time to be sitting in this seat, mouth full of hydrogen peroxide, friends nearby munching brie and tiramisu and exchanging results of their pulse readings. I wanted to be there. I wanted to be talking to my new friend, Stevie, the Kramer impersonator; I wanted to have a glass of wine; I wanted to be anywhere but right there, with that light in my face and that tray in mouth, frothing and foaming and filling my mouth with the chemical promise of a red carpet smile.

Now, at SYTAR I was a medium-sized fish in a smallish pond, but still, I was vice president of the board of directors, one of the presenters, one of the people who looks like she might know something, or so I gathered from the number of people that came up to me and asked me all manner of random questions: "Can we drink the water straight out of the tap?" "What is the weather going to be tomorrow?" "What time does the next session start?" I was someone who was practically supposed to be hosting the party, for all intents and purposes. Instead, I was stuck, mouth filling with foam, and mind filling with thoughts of my gums turning white; of the technician coming and taking the tray out of my mouth and me drooling everywhere; of me ripping the sunglasses off, pushing the bright, magical light away, and spitting the peroxide out of my mouth before my teeth were left permanently aching.

Suddenly, I remembered. I was at a yoga conference, where everyone was talking about yoga, and I was not only a yoga teacher, but also a student and devotee of yoga. Suddenly, I remembered to practice.

I began to remind myself that this was only sensation. That although it was unpleasant, it was just a feeling, a sensation, and one that I knew would not really harm me, and that would soon be over. I sat and breathed. Just a feeling. The lights began flashing brightly; I felt my heart quicken. It was time; I was done! But then they flashed steady again, and I was left with the sensation. Breathe. It's just peroxide, it's just a mouth full of whitener, it just stings, it's just uncomfortable. The lights flashed again, but this time they flashed, slowed down, and stopped. The light was off. The tech came over to me and took the sunglasses off. He handed me a small cocktail napkin, which I looked at with both curiosity and awe. Did he really think that would help? My mouth was filled, filled, with whitener, saliva, and the urge to give some feedback about the whole teeth-whitening system. As he put out his hand for the retainer, I grabbed the cocktail napkin and held it up to my mouth in a woefully unsuccessful attempt to keep myself from getting covered in this mixture of whitener and drool. My pants were covered; the napkin was soaked. I looked anxiously around for another napkin or towel of some sort, and having no luck there, I just pushed away from the table and found my way to the nearest restroom (thank you to the person who looked like they knew something—"Where's the nearest restroom?")

I found some friends and shared my experience. I tried to make the story funny, but what kept coming back to me was the less funny part about simply being with a sensation, instead of trying to get out of it or make up a story about it.

See, this is just what the conference was all about. It was a research-based conference of the benefits of a yoga practice, some that were huge revelations (an alternative to the pre-colonoscopy *Fleet* enema nightmare), some that we knew from experience (yoga can help with the symptoms of menopause), and some that we—or I, in this case—had just forgotten (that our yoga is here for us all the time; we always have the opportunity to benefit from our practice.)

Earlier that same day, my friend and colleague Kelly McGonigal, PhD, had given a plenary session talk that was a highlight of the conference. In presenting research on yoga as an intervention for depression and anxiety, Kelly had brought to light several important studies, one of which stuck with me the most. In this particular study, published by Farb, et al, 2010, and explained by Kelly in her excellent talk, researchers showed a fascinating aspect of our practice, which was in many ways what I had just experienced in my teeth-whitening experiment.

In this study, a group of participants were shown both sad and neutral clips from sad movies (The Champ, Terms of Endearment) following mindfulness-based stress reduction (MBSR) training. Using imaging technology, researchers found that the group who had received MBSR had greater activity than the control group, who did not receive MBSR, in the area of the brain associated with experiencing a feeling; in other words, they were more aware of their own emotions. One might ask, as did some of the veterans to whom I offer yoga classes and with whom I shared this research, "Why would I want to feel something more, especially if it was something that was hard to feel?" The answer, I believe lies in the second finding of the study — although the mindfulness group felt more, they had less activity in the area of the brain associated with narrative, comparison, and analysis. In other words, they felt more, but created a story about it less. In other words, the participants allowed themselves to be fully present to their emotion or sensation (like me and the chemical soup in my mouth) but were not as inclined to make it worse through rumination and aversion (I don't want to be here, I don't like this feeling. What is going to happen because of that peroxide? What am I missing? Will my teeth hurt later, is this working, can people tell this is me over here..... ?) When I told this part to the veterans, one said, "It's like anger, it doesn't have to turn into rage," and another added, "Or anxiety doesn't have to turn into a full-blown panic attack." This reminds me very much of the difference between pain and suffering. Whereas we might think of pain as being the inescapable "what is occurring," we can think of suffering as being our reaction to what is occurring. When we are able to differentiate these two more readily, we are potentially more able to choose to lessen suffering, even in the face of pain.

When we are on our mat practicing, we usually feel like our yoga is good for us. So good that we want to save those moments, to hold that feeling, and to pass it on to others, whether through actually teaching our practice to others or just by allowing others to experience us differently as a result of our practice. And we often notice that in general, our moods, relationships, and overall health are improving.

But I think we all forget, from time to time, that our yoga is always here for us, in the tiniest stories, in the quietest moments of peace and composure, as well as in the biggest revelations. Yoga becomes a practice of life, of increased self-efficacy, of ease. It allows us to be in the moment, truly experiencing all that is joyous, all that is despairing, all that is difficult, all that is icky, all that is sublime, all that is life itself. In the moments when we feel like our yoga is not working — we're not as flexible as we once were, we are not able to practice consistently, we feel like stilling our mind is the hardest thing imaginable — we can remind ourselves that all the little bits of practice are adding up. They are creating a real change, at a neurological level, that has a profound impact on everything we do, the way we view ourselves, and our experiences and our lives and that change, in turn, impacts others and the world around us. This is individual transformation as a means to radical social change.

Look for opportunities to practice, opportunities to use the tools of your practice, opportunities to reap the benefits of your practice, both large and small, to keep you oriented back to it.

Who knows what else you might get out of it? Perhaps your irritation won't turn to anger, your anger won't turn to rage, or your teeth will turn really, really white.

Everyone who is seriously involved in the pursuit of science becomes convinced that a spirit is manifest in the laws of the Universe – a spirit vastly superior to that of man.

~Albert Einstein

Who Do You Think You Are?
God's Gift to the Universe? ~
Cultivating Contentment Through Connection
to our own Divine Presence.

God is present in every Jiva; there is no other God besides that. Who serves Jiva serves God indeed. ~ Swami Vivekananda

The moment I have realized God sitting in the temple of every human body, the moment I stand in reverence before every human being and see God in him - that moment I am free from bondage, everything that binds vanishes, and I am free. ~ Swami Vivekananda

Halfway across the world, a very poor man prays every day to God: "Please help. Please give me something, anything that will help me to support my family and restore my dignity. God, I don't blame you for my difficult situation, for the tsunami that tore through my home making it mostly unlivable, or for giving me only daughters, who I love unconditionally, but who are less able to help support our family, or for the fact that I had to sell my fishing boat to feed my children—I know that you work in mysterious ways. I only ask that you look on me now with generosity and kindness and send some help my way, in whatever form you see fit."

Back in the United States, a privileged, educated, and curious yoga teacher saves up some money (challenging, but hardly impossible) to make a pilgrimage to India, the motherland of the yoga she has practiced and taught for over a decade. She makes the long trek to India and is immediately both overwhelmed and inspired by the profound generosity and religious devotion of the people she meets.

One morning after meditation, she decides to take an early morning walk along the beach. Everywhere there are fishermen preparing for the day, and she is both disturbed and amused by the fact that she has inadvertently chosen the time of day when many men are using the water's edge for morning cleansing. Keeping her eyes down, she tries her best not to make eye contact with anyone in this private, although at the same time very public, moment.

The devotional man has completed his own morning ritual and is now simply walking, open-faced and smiling, along the beach, hoping to connect with a tourist who might be interested in seeing his "small shop" of trinkets, textiles, and clothing sold out of his dilapidated cement home.

His eyes catch hers; his smile draws her in. He is Rama, she is me.

Although it's not even 7:00 am, Sasha and I decide to join Rama in his home, where we are offered tiny cups of chai and seated like royalty on broken plastic chairs, while his wife and daughters and granddaughter, get busy bringing out all of the little objects for sale. We can't communicate much, but everyone's smiles and loving energy seem to transcend words, and we connect deeply. Rama brings me to his puja (prayer) room. I ask him if I can sing for him, and I offer him the Atma Shatakam, Adi Shankara's summation of advaita vedanta, the philosophy that holds that we are all expressions of one divine truth. Rama closes his eyes and sways, his eyes fill with tears; he reaches his hand to his altar and then to my forehead, and he places sacred ash at my eyebrow center.

We become fast friends and Sasha and I visit Rama and his family every day. One day, Rama asks if I can teach him yoga, and I invite him to my morning class at the resort with my American students. He can't join us there he says—as a local, he is not allowed on the resort grounds. We take this in and then, without hesitation, tell him we will meet him on the beach before the class. It is in this yoga class, with Rama, Sasha, and Rama's tiny granddaughter, that Rama then chants for us. At the end of his chant, he tells us of his daily prayer to God, "Please help. Please give me something, anything that will help me to support my family and restore my dignity." I give him the 1000 rupee note that I had literally found on the street the day before, which he at first tries to refuse. We convince him to take it, and he once again begins to cry. "You," he says, "are the answer to my prayers. I prayed to God, and you showed up. I will never forget you. Thank you."

I've been thinking a lot about this idea, about how we really can be, in fact, the answer to someone's prayers. So often we have the experience where someone might say to us, "Oh, that's just what I needed to hear today," or, "You have no idea how much that meant to me," or even, "You are such a godsend."

When we hear these expressions, I'm sure it makes us all feel good, and satisfied that we may have brightened someone's day or given someone some bit of hope or joy. I'm not sure, however, that we actually experience those expressions as true reflections of our own inner divinity made manifest. In my thinking, and in many recent experiences, I have begun to question, or should I say "own" that in fact, it is no simple happy coincidence and that these moments truly are divinely directed. Someone prays or calls out for help and meaning, and we answer: just the right thing at the right time. How are we not, truly, in this moment, God's gift to the universe — a light of hope in the darkness of someone else's despairing or isolation?

Sasha and I couldn't stop thinking about Rama and about this idea that we had been sent to him by God, in response to Rama's own devotion. When we arrived back home in the United States, we received two emails from Rama within a couple of months. The first was mostly a greeting in his broken English: "I never forget you and your goodness and kind talking and also you taught me about Yoga. Now I have remember you. I am happy for your visited to my home and your good friendship. Please keep in touch and let me know about you and your family. I say hello to your family members and friends. Please you don't forget me."

We responded right away:

Beloved friend Rama,
Thank you for your note. We are so glad you were able to contact us. Our friendship with you was one of the very best parts of our whole trip. You are a beautiful man, a beautiful soul, a great yoga student, and a true friend. We will never forget you or the kindness you showed us in those first days of India. We are in love with your country and your people and will return next year, and of course come to see you in your home, and practice more yoga together. We send all of our love to you, and all of our prayers for good health and abundance. You are forever in our hearts. You have true friends all the way across the world who would do anything for you, your light is that bright. Om namah shivaya. Jai Rama!
love,
molly

A month or so later, we received another note from Rama, this one with a slightly different tone:

My dearest friend Molly,

Mail from Rama (Fisherman & Salesman) with heartfelt greetings to you. How are you? How is your family and friends? I received your mail, thank you very much for your kind message and I am very happy about your kind heart. I never forget you till my death. My wife say much hello to you.

My dear friend, I want to say you about my real situation which is nowadays my small business is very bad and no income because of no tourists people and also more business competition here, so I and my family are very critical situation about our livelihood, here I have no any source of income and also nobody support to me.

I could not maintain to my family by this small business. I don't know what I do, I thought you, you are my dear friend so I am frankly say you about my difficult situation, please If you help me to buy small catamaran and fish catch net, I will manage to buy my family food *and necessary expenses. Right now I have no money to buy small catamaran and fish catch net. This cost is: catamaran -Rs. 17,000 and fish catch net- Rs. 5,000. Total= Rs.22,000. [$400 US equivalent]*

Please you don't mistake me and I am sorry for the disturb you for ask help to you. If you can help me, this is your choice. I am very sorry.

I say much hello to your family and friends. Please keep in touch and let me know about your reply. I am waiting for your mail. Please you don't forget me. Take care of your health.

Thank you.

Yours sincerely friend,

Rama & family with heartfelt greetings

For one brief, infinitesimally brief, moment I felt that sense of contraction and suspicion; had we now entered into a relationship where we would be asked for more and more? But the moment passed so quickly, it barely deserves mention, except to remind myself that we, I, am that conditioned to be wary, to second guess, to not trust that in fact, this is God speaking to and through us. I recalled my own words to Rama, "You have true friends all the way across the world who would do anything for you, your light is that bright." I knew I had to see this through.

Halfway across the world, a very poor man prays every day to God: "Please help. Please give me something, anything that will help me to support my family and restore my dignity."

Back in the United States, a privileged, educated, and curious yoga teacher saves up some money to make a pilgrimage to India.

And these two people meet, and we make a connection. And in that moment, we have the very real opportunity to be the answer to someone's prayers. I am given the chance to help a person to maintain a true sense of dignity through a gift of real money, and he is given the chance to help me with a feeling of my own devotional practice come to life, with my very own, and very real, experience of myself as God made manifest.

So, yes, this is a story about Rama, and it is about an inspiring and life-affirming experience we had in India.

But it is also a story, a reminder really, that in fact when we live a devotional life, one of surrender and trust, we can really see ourselves as being God's gift to the Universe, an answer to someone's prayers, in a very real way. It is this experience, and others like it, that lead us again and again back to an experience of contentment, abundance, and devotion. And we are inspired, again, to offer ourselves, our love, our respect, our advocacy, our smile, our generosity, our warm-heartedness, and our open-mindedness, to everyone we meet on every occasion we can. We have no idea when or where or how we might show up as the answer to someone's prayers. We are the Divine made manifest. And what could ever bring us more contentment than that?

As Gandhi is often quoted, "If we could change ourselves, the tendencies in the world would also change. As a man changes his own nature, so does the attitude of the world change towards him...We need not wait to see what others do."

Things do not grow better; they remain as they are. It is we who grow better, by the changes we make in ourselves. ~ Swami Vivekananda

Rama and his boat. Mahabalipuram.

Atma Shatakam: (from swamij.com)

One version of the atma shatakam, Adi Shankara's description of non-dualistic philosophy in which we remind ourselves of our true nature - soul, joy, freedom.
Find it to sing with Molly at www.mollylannonkenny.org

Mano Buddhi Ahankara Chitta Naham
Nacha Shrotra Jihve Na Cha Ghrana Netre
Nacha Vyoma Bhoomir Na Tejo Na Vayu
Chidananda Rupa Shivoham Shivoham

Na Cha Prana Samjno Na Vai Pancha Vayu
Na Va Saptadhatur Na Va Pancha Koshah
Na Vak Pani Padau Na Chopastha Payu
Chidananda Rupa Shivoham Shivoham

Na Me Dvesha Ragau Na Me Lobha Mohau
Mado Naiva Me Naiva Matsarya Bhavah
Na Dharmo Na Chartho Na Kamo Na Mokshah
Chidananda Rupa Shivoham Shivoham

Na Punyam Na Papam Na Saukhyam Na Dukham
Na Mantro Na Teertham Na Vedo Na Yajnaha
Aham Bhojanam Naiva Bhojyam Na Bhokta
Chidananda Rupa Shivoham Shivoham

Na Me Mrityu Shanka Na Me Jati Bhedah
Pita Naiva Me Naiva Mata Na Janma
Na Bandhur Na Mitram Gurur Naiva Shishyah
Chidananda Rupa Shivoham Shivoham

Aham Nirvikalpo Nirakara Roopaha
Vibhur Vyapya Sarvatra Sarvendriyanam
Sada Me Samatvam Na Muktir Na Bandhah
Chidananda Rupa Shivoham Shivoham

Meaning: (from greenmesg.org)

1.1: Neither am I the Mind nor Intelligence or Ego,
1.2: Neither am I the organs of Hearing (Ears), nor that
of Tasting (Tongue), Smelling (Nose) or Seeing (Eyes),
1.3: Neither am I the Sky, nor the Earth, Neither the Fire nor
the Air,
1.4: I am the Ever Pure Blissful Consciousness; I am Shiva, I
am Shiva,
The Ever Pure Blissful Consciousness.
2.1: Neither am I the Vital Breath, nor the Five Vital Air,
2.2: Neither am I the Seven Ingredients (of the Body), nor
the Five Sheaths (of the Body),
2.3: Neither am I the organ of Speech, nor the organs for
Holding (Hand), Movement (Feet) or Excretion,
2.4: I am the Ever Pure Blissful Consciousness; I am Shiva, I
am Shiva,
The Ever Pure Blissful Consciousness.
3.1: Neither do I have Hatred, nor Attachment,
Neither Greed nor Infatuation,
3.2: Neither do I have Passion, nor Feelings of Envy and
Jealousy,
3.3 I am Not within the bounds
of Dharma (Righteousness), Artha (Wealth), Kama (Desire)
and Moksha (Liberation) (the four Purusarthas of life),
3.4: I am the Ever Pure Blissful Consciousness; I am Shiva, I
am Shiva,
The Ever Pure Blissful Consciousness.
4.1: Neither am I bound by Merits nor Sins, neither
by Worldly Joys nor by Sorrows,
4.2: Neither am I bound by Sacred Hymns nor by Sacred
Places, neither by Sacred Scriptures nor by Sacrifies,
4.3: I am Neither Enjoyment (Experience), nor an object to
be Enjoyed (Experienced), nor the Enjoyer (Experiencer),
4.4: I am the Ever Pure Blissful Consciousness; I am Shiva, I

am Shiva,

The Ever Pure Blissful Consciousness.

5.1: Neither am I bound by Death and its Fear, nor by the rules of Caste and its Distinctions,

5.2: Neither do I have Father and Mother, nor do I have Birth,

5.3: Neither do I have Relations nor Friends, neither Spiritual Teacher nor Disciple,

5.4: I am the Ever Pure Blissful Consciousness; I am Shiva, I am Shiva,

The Ever Pure Blissful Consciousness.

6.1: I am Without any Variation, and Without any Form,

6.2: I am Present Everywhere as the underlying Substratum of everything, and behind all Sense Organs,

6.3: Neither do I get Attached to anything, nor get Freed from anything,

6.4: I am the Ever Pure Blissful Consciousness; I am Shiva, I am Shiva,

The Ever Pure Blissful Consciousness.

For the intellectual mind can never behold the depth of God. Only the heart can enter into the incomprehensible mystery of divine Love.

~Ilia Delio

MOLLY LANNON KENNY

Influence of the Confluence
or Non-grasping at Mata Ganga

Some of us think holding on makes us strong; but sometimes it is letting go. ~ Hermann Hesse

Faith is a state of openness or trust. To have faith is like when you trust yourself to the water. You don't grab hold of the water when you swim, because if you do you will become stiff and tight in the water, and sink. You have to relax, and the attitude of faith is the very opposite of clinging, and holding on. ~ Allan Watts

...And I start to think about India again. One moment stands out for me in my rumination: The moment just before I bathed in the Ganges, joining millions of pilgrims over thousands of years in diving into the Divine Mata Ganga and with that act being cleansed and renewed at the level of my very soul. As I stood on the makeshift dock out in the middle of the river, singing and praying, both giddy and serene with anticipation, the atma shatakam came to me, as it often does. This beautiful poem, also known as The Song of the Self, attributed to the Vedic scholar Adi Shankara, is a declaration of the self as love, consciousness, and bliss and is a simultaneous denial of the self as possessing any material or finite form. I have taught this poem to hundreds of students, and many have found, as I do, that the chanting of this powerful prayer alleviates fear and anxiety and brings us to a place of contentment. It permeates my mind and heart spontaneously in almost every situation where I feel overwhelmed by circumstance and allows me to return to the place of equanimity that is the state of yoga itself.

I had been home from India for about three weeks, and everything I had been through was still all just settling within me. Showing photos, telling stories, sharing audio recordings — all of these brought back the powerful experiences that seemed to come daily on that most profound of pilgrimages, my first trip to India. I find myself saying again and again, "This is something I learned that I don't ever want to lose," all the while fighting the loss as the most visceral of feelings related to my experience begin to fade.

My photos, even for me, begin to lose their immediate emotional impact and to transform slowly into just beautiful images. Sometimes I noticed my own fear in this loss; fear that somehow the transformation that took place in me would also fade into mere intellectual truism rather than the deep, soul-shaking affirmation of life, and how I wish to live it, that I realized throughout my travels. This desire to hold on to my India experience, in and of itself, could be the basis for a discussion on aparigraha, non-grasping. In many of my classes over the years, we have talked about holding on to the past, fear of loosening our grip, trading in real experiences for the ones we want to preserve. Through photos and storytelling, we tend to use the moment of true presence not just as the opportunity that it is but also as an opportunity to record, to save, and hold on for some other time when we want to revisit that moment. Ah but alas, we learn over and over that, in fact, those recordings don't ever really evoke the moment as it was, and in a sense they only provide us with a flimsy souvenir, devoid of, or at least, lacking in, any of the real impact of the experience itself.

I have been thinking about my India pilgrimage and the lessons learned, and I have also been thinking about what brings us to this holding, hoarding, and attaching. I have been thinking about yoga and about Patanjali's instructions to us that we are to practice stilling the mind so that we may see and be our true nature, one of original perfection and divinity. I have been thinking about the kleshas, or what Patanjali describes as the five obstacles to happiness, including fear and desire but especially ego-identification. I have been thinking about all of this in relation to aparigraha and our reasons for holding on in the first place.

Standing perched over Mata Ganga, I sang a song, the "Song of the Self," and I did indeed in that moment feel utterly connected to the river, to myself, to God, to the people around me, to all of humanity, and to the cosmic continuity of life itself.

That, I believe, was truly a moment, an experience, that I will never forget — a feeling of connection so profound and strong, the memory of which still ignites in me that deepest sense of steadiness and contentment.

And yet again, I have to remind myself, not just of that instant, captured in my heart — and yes, in photos — but also of the deeper meaning, the deeper experience of that moment.

When I came back, and indeed whenever I return home after a trip, there is the inevitable task of coming home to responsibility, to the menial duties of the day, to the organizational structure that keeps the material life functional and sane. When I am thrust back into this parallel life, the life of practical obligations and challenges, I am tested, or reminded, almost daily of the challenges of being human and living an everyday life.

One of the challenges I see, one that always agitates my mind and pulls me away from the exquisite serenity of the deeper Self is the universal tendency to hold tightly on to the "currencies," that prove one's "worth" on the material plane. This quality of mind is supremely skillful at creating distraction and dissatisfaction,

Whether it is recognition for a contribution made to one's profession, acknowledgement of a skill or gift we might bring to an organization, a monetary "stamp" — compensation for the effort of carrying out work — I notice that I hold on tightly to the things that appear to affirm my value. Of course, it is natural to feel pleasure and satisfaction with professional recognition or a fat paycheck. Yet, in these circumstances of achievement, I also feel the holding, the grasping, the hoarding, not as something ultimately productive, but something instead that actually stirs in me the very opposite: the feeling that I am somehow not valued or valuable without these external markers of achievement and therefore I must be prove otherwise through these various means of recognition. In these moments, I am telling myself the exact antithesis of the atma shatakam. I am telling myself that I am only what I appear to be and that if those appearances are not upheld, I will lose my value. This is unquestionably a moment of sadness and fear that leads me to hold on to an individual identity and away from the sense of myself beyond those confines.

It is not unlike holding on to a photo to affirm the reality of a moment captured in time. We hold on to some external "proof" to affirm our own value, our own preciousness.

My mind drifts back to that moment, standing on a floating dock, surrounded by the Ganges, bright in my sari, bright in my intention, with that supreme feeling of oneness, of ultimate and never-changing value, not subject to the whimsical tyranny of ego gratification. In that moment, I felt no need for recognition, as I knew deeply that I was already and always would be a manifestation of the Divine, an undeniable beloved of the Universe itself, as love, consciousness, and bliss. So I recall this moment to steady my mind. I don't need the photo; I don't need anything else to know the magnitude and reality of this experience and the ultimate truth of its message.

Today, as I reflect on the concept of aparigraha, I pray that I will return over and over to this truth: that we grasp and hold and hoard out of a feeling of essential unworthiness or lack and that in letting go, we affirm our basic perfection and unquestionable value, irrespective of how much we are paid, where our name is recorded, or how many medals or acknowledgements we have received.

In India I rediscovered one of my very earliest and most beloved teachers, Swami Vivekananda, a giant of fearlessness and unfailing affirmation of Self. I have thought of this particular quote many times in the context of this reflection on aparigraha.

Above all, beware of compromises. Hold on to your own principles in weal or woe and never adjust them to others' "fads" through the greed of getting supporters. Your Atman is the support of the universe — whose support do you stand in need of? ~ Swami Vivekananda

May we affirm for one another our essential worth. May you always know the value of your very being. May you always feel the support of the universe — your own soul — and in this knowing, let go into a deeper peace.

Tapas - The Agony and the Ecstasy of Hard Work

Not long ago I spent many hours reading various wonderful stories on Hindu mythology. I especially loved reading the Shiva Puranas, a series of stories about Shiva, one of a trinity of Hindu gods, often considered to be the "original yogi," and the one who actually created the other two, Brahma and Krishna. One of these stories in particular has stuck with me, the story of Parvati, Shiva's consort, and the crazy intense tapasya (austerity) that she undertook to draw Shiva toward her as her husband — an effort that lasted thousands of years and nearly killed her. Nothing would budge her from her intention. Instead of becoming discouraged when Shiva appeared to not notice her, she only intensified her work, first eating nothing but wet leaves, then only dry leaves, and finally only taking in air. Finally, in the end, she gets the guy, and becomes one of the supreme beings in the Hindu pantheon. There are references in all the stories to similar feats of will and devotion, mainly by bhaktas (devotees) who are hoping for the good will, or boon, of one of the gods. It seems that these tapasyas were always rewarded with the very gift that was most precious to the student performing them.

Let me take a moment to remind you of the essential meaning of tapas. The word is derived from the Sanskrit root tap, meaning "to heat," which is often used to mean a sort of austerity or penance. According to Sri Aurobindo, it implies "a fierce and strong effort of all the human powers towards any given end. It is a tremendous concentration of the will which sets the whole being aflame, masses all the faculties in close ranks and hurls them furiously on a single objective."

Indeed, especially in the mythology, the efforts that were required to receive those rewards were extremely challenging, and often the seeker nearly gave up from exhaustion or frustration. OK, so now this sounds more like what you think of when you hear about tapas — this intense "burning" effort.

But in our own efforts, we sometimes forget about the reward, and just how powerful and meaningful it will be for us, and we give up too easily.

I was thinking of this recently while talking with a friend about skiing versus snowboarding. We are both skiers and figured that most likely, with some effort, we could also be good snowboarders. But when we get to the mountain, and pay our money, and then start to snowboard, it's really hard. We're falling down and hurting ourselves and quickly decide, "This is no fun" and go right back to skiing, which we already know we are good at. But, I'll bet, if I could just stick with snowboarding long enough, I would actually be good at it, and maybe I'd even like it more than skiing, but I may never give it a chance because what I already do is easier.

This simple example reminds me of how we so often stay with what we know because whatever is new is too hard, or we fear it will be less interesting, or less fulfilling, so we end up staying the same, and not reaping the benefit of the discipline to stay with it. What are we missing out on by not persevering?

As I write this particular piece, it happens to be my birthday, and I happened to be able to spend it with a very dear friend of mine, who at 95 is just about twice my age. I asked my friend, as someone who has seen a lot of life, what advice she would give me on my birthday. She replied, "Molly, it seems like whatever you have done for the past 47 years has worked. Do that for 47 more." I loved that response. At the same time, I know that "what I have been doing," in terms of what is working, has not actually been for all of those 47 years; in truth it has been for just a bit over a decade. So what have I been doing? And what has the reward been?

I believe that since I began practicing yoga seriously my life has a deep multidimensional beauty to it, and I can feel that in the way I see people, the way I see my life, the better choices I make, the kinder and more forgiving my words are, the ever-increasing spaciousness of my heart, the deepening simultaneous sharpness and humility of my mind, the advancing confidence of my teaching, and the love I can show through my hands. And that, I know, is due to my practice.

There have been so many times over the years when I have wanted to give up on my asana practice, on my meditation practice, on my relationships, on my work, on my devotion, on my life focus. But something has always spurred me onward, even if only in fits and starts. I have always managed to return to that "fierce and strong effort of all my human powers." Toward what end? To embodying the deep belief that I have just this one life, this one body, this one shot to become the very best human I can be, to offer more love, more joy, and more hope to a world in need. To living fully my belief that life is wonderful, and also very challenging, and I can choose to move through it with ease or with fear and contraction, and that given those choices, my desire is clear. Of course, it's not always easy, and of course I sometimes slow down or swerve off the path from time to time. But it is my practice and above all my teaching and my community that keeps me coming back. And the boons keep rolling in, along with continued challenges. But when I open my eyes and really see myself and how I am growing and changing, I am able to continually reorient myself to my "tremendous concentration of the will which sets the whole being aflame."

As one of my dear students wrote to me so, so sweetly on my birthday, "You have stood in the mud and are now the Lotus." I take this to be a powerful reminder for all of us: no mud, no lotus.

We are all in this together. If there is ever anything I can do for you, or give to you, to remind you of how your efforts are paying off, even when you doubt yourself, or to encourage you back on your path, or to give you understanding and solace when you are feeling defeated, I am here. That is the fruit of my practice. May I offer it to you, joyously, humbly, from the bottom of my heart.

Bottoms up!
On Colonoscopies, Yoga and Deep Insight ~
Another Look at Tapas

Here is a return to the topic of tapas. It seems a running joke in talking about this precept – the tenet of hard work and determination – is whether we are talking about the little plates of culinary delights we might find at a downtown happy hour.

As I think about that well-worn idea today, it seems particularly ironic. I am thinking about the idea of tapas – hard work – while also deeply involved in a major transition and relocation of The Samarya Center, and about my recent (and first) experience with a colonoscopy. Believe it or not, I saw many parallels in that experience that seem to speak quite directly to the process and rewards of hard work.

In the colonoscopy there is first the inevitability to be considered: something I have to do that I don't want to – something that seems scary, unpleasant and bit unmentionable. I fear the process, but even more, I fear the outcome – what if, even if I get through this horrible thing, it doesn't turn out the way I wanted. In my case, it did turn out the way I wanted, in other words - no news is good news. But in fact, even if the results had been different, then I would know what was happening, where I stood and what to do next.

This was much like finding out that the building that housed The Samarya Center had sold – at first scary, unpleasant and a bit unmentionable. Again, I notice that I fear both the process and the outcome. How should I reorganize, how will we make decisions, who will come with me? And, what if I make it through the move, but somehow it doesn't work? What if the community can't, or doesn't, support it? What if we can't find the "perfect" new space? In fact, much like with the colonoscopy, no matter what the outcome, I would now have information that is clear- information that allows me to make a new plan based on what I know, rather than what I just assumed, was happening. This seems to me to be a good thing, and although it requires hard work and courage, the possibilities are greater than the simple not knowing. Kind of like a colonoscopy.

As I started to prepare for my colonoscopy, I began to understand why people always say, "The preparation is way worse than the procedure itself." How could that be true? One involved me drinking a huge jug of clear liquid, while the other involved me going under anesthesia and having a long probe inched into my colon. Without having had prior experience, the comparison of those two activities seemed ludicrous – the latter obviously seemed far worse than the former. But now I do have experience, and what they tell you is the truth: the prep is indeed much worse. And yet, for me it also offered several illuminating metaphors that again remind me very much of the preparations we are now doing to move The Samarya Center – metaphors that I believe speak to any major undertaking we must face.

First there is the gathering of information (the pre-op visit) and of necessary related items (that giant jug of liquid that you have to drink within 24 hours of the procedure.) Then there is the planning and anticipation (the fasting and the preparing of the solution). When I picked my big plastic bottle up at the pharmacy, I was feeling pretty relieved – it was a lot of liquid, but hey, it was just liquid, and not only that, it is colorless and odorless. How bad could it be?

I began my fasting on Saturday evening, with my colonoscopy set for Monday. So far, it wasn't so bad. The hunger was "just a sensation" as we at The Samarya Center like to say about challenging sensory experiences. I was actually kind of looking forward to starting with the liquid, I was doing so well with the fasting, and I had an idea that I would be really good at drinking the concoction, and was set to debunk the myth of its foulness.

It was a huge surprise then, when I poured myself the first tall, cool glass and went to down it all in one gulp. It is hard to describe the taste and consistency of that potion. It has a bitter chemical flavor and worse than that, a viscosity that makes it almost impossible to chug. I tried my best to drink the whole glass down, and was horrified when I stopped to look at how much I had actually gotten down in what felt like a mammoth gulp. The glass was barely half empty, and in this case, I most definitely wanted to be a "half empty" kind of person. I looked at the glass, then back at the jug and then at my husband Sasha. I could feel tears forming and a sense of frustration and defeat washing over me. "I can't drink all that," I said, "there is no way I will be able to drink that all down." Sasha looked at me with kindness, and firmly said, "You can, and you will. You can do this Molly." With that he filled my glass and handed it to me. "Drink up." I looked at the glass, picked it up and took a sip. As my gag reflex kicked in, the tears in my eyes rolled down my cheeks. I put the glass down again and looked at the jug. "I can't drink all that Sasha." Again with kindness, Sasha simply responded, "Molly, don't look at that huge bottle and all that is in there. Just look at the glass in front of you and focus on that. Get that down, and then see where you are."

Truer words have indeed hardly been spoken. Like the magnitude of change that is the new Samarya Center, when I look at the whole process at once, it feels totally overwhelming and almost immobilizing. When I attend, however, to just one doable task in front of me, no matter how challenging it might be or seem, I am able to focus my energy and determination and complete that one thing. With each item completed, I am able to reassess and determine what's next. Knowing that I have only to complete that one thing at that one time, I am able to act with clarity. Little by little, the magnitude of the larger task diminishes and I begin to see results.

But how big of a task can I handle without becoming overwhelmed? I learned this too through the magic colonoscopy potion. I noticed that whenever I would pour myself a glass to drink, I would use a tiny glass. It seemed like then there was not that much to get down. When Sasha would pour for me, he always chose one of our larger water glasses. At some point I said to him, "Would you just pour me tiny glasses? They are easier for me to wrap my mind around." Sasha's response? "If I pour you just a tiny glass, the jug seems like it's never actually draining, so you won't see the results of your efforts, but it will feel like you are drinking a lot of tiny glasses. If I pour you one big glass, you will have to work a little harder on that one glass, but you will be able to look at the jug and see how it is emptying, and you will be motivated to get through."

That also turned out to be true – there was some balance to be had between not looking at the total volume of the solution when drinking just one small glass, while at the same time choosing a glass large enough that I could see real progress based on my effort. In the same way, as we undertake any seemingly huge task, we will have to continually strike a balance between feeling paralyzed by the magnitude of the task, and taking bold steps to move discernably closer to our goal.

This was turning out to be the best colonoscopy prep ever: I was learning so many things about myself, including the way I, and many of us I'm sure, approach things that are difficult and I had even more to learn. Let me pause for a moment here and tell you two things: one - if you have never had to drink this stuff that I am referring to, it is difficult to convey just exactly how nasty it is, and two – I am, in general, a pretty sensitive person, which includes a very strong gag reflex. So, the sum total of these two facts is that for every swallow I would take of the solution, I would have not only the horrible experience of the liquid itself, but also an equally dramatic gag reflex. My eyes would tear, my stomach would lurch and my throat would close spasmodically.

I soon found that the reaction to the liquid was as bad, if not worse, than the liquid itself. This one I figured out by myself, I didn't need Sasha to tell me. I realized that while I was not in control of whether I had to drink the liquid, I was in control of my own reaction to it, as much as I would have liked to tell myself otherwise. This time I created my own solution. My job became not to get the potion down, but to control my reaction to it. It became a mind over matter exercise of trial and error, until I found that I could exhale completely, take a huge gulp, hold my exhale and drink some bubbly water right away. Then I would inhale and bypass the reaction. This insight became so exciting to me that soon I was drinking the liquid just to see how well I could control my reaction.

The knowledge that even when we cannot control an event, we can control our reaction to it, and in doing so makes the situation much easier was nothing short of revelatory. Again, I think about making any huge change. I see how much our reaction to the news of the change shapes the whole experience. In our case with The Samarya Center, I can't change that we have to move, but I can decide to react any way I want. I get to choose to react from a place of excitement, curiosity, generosity, ownership, agency, focus and above all, community.

I drank the whole jug down; I was prepared in every way for the colonoscopy. While I was nervous for the procedure, I also knew I was in good hands, and that as big as this all seemed to me, it was just a part of life, something that happens every day. I was in and out of the clinic within a couple of hours, and life goes on. I have the knowledge I need now to attend to my health and well being as best I can. If not for thinking about the whole ordeal to write about it and the lessons learned, I would probably have forgotten about it by now. I am at peace with the present.

I know we will have a similar process and a similar outcome at The Samarya Center. We will do the work. We will learn the lessons. We will manage our reactions and trust that together, we know what we are doing. Life goes on. We will have the knowledge and tools we need to attend to the continued well-being of our beloved center, or whatever big project we are taking on, and all too soon, we will mostly forget about the process. No matter what happens, and in every moment, we can be at peace with the present.

Cheers! Bottoms up! We are all in this together.

Satya,
or, the Truth of the Matter: Your Gift is Your Presence

The holiday season is always an opportunity to experience the full spectrum of emotions, which also means it's a great time for us to examine how we respond to a full spectrum of situations. It also happens to be a time when many of us are invited to, or sometimes confronted with, an opportunity to connect with family, and as we all know, there's nothing like family to bring up a whole lot of joy and a whole lot of discord. With so much sensory overload that occurs during the holidays, and with so much to think about and get done and get through this month, I'm going to keep it short and sweet and to the point -- the greatest gift you have to give is your own loving, accepting and gracious presence.

Being loving, accepting, and gracious can be really hard when we enter into situations where we see some dysfunction or difficulty and we want to change it. Perhaps we have a sister or an aunt who is struggling with a loss, or a cousin or parent who is overbearing or controlling, or an uncle or family friend who is mired in addiction— and then we come home to visit. And we are yoga people, so we want to help and we want to be yogic and we want to let people know what would be good for them, or what we can or can't accept because we are so good at setting boundaries. We could speak the truth to them (whatever that is), we could teach them about yoga and tell them they should just relax and meditate, we could insist on the time we need and the space and trappings we need to do our practice, or we could just be there. What if we could imagine that instead of our job being to create a change by doing, we could create a change by simply being. What if we could see that by simply being a sweet, easy-going, light presence amidst chaos and discord, that we are contributing a far greater gift than the gift we think we are giving when we stand up at the dinner table and pronounce the family dysfunctional or enabling or dishonest or whatever might be the words seemingly appropriate to the situation?

Try it. See what happens when you just let go of trying to fix, or change, or illuminate something you think people don't see or don't acknowledge, and instead be the beacon of joy and ease in an environment rife with disharmony. It's hard; believe me, I know. I can sometimes be pushy, bossy, and a know-it-all. I work on that every single day. But here's one thing I really do know -- that when I act from this part of myself, even when I tell myself my intentions are good and my actions therefore correct, that I often only add feelings of shame, anger, and exclusion to the situation at hand. When instead I tap into that part of me that has been polished by my practice, the part of me that can just be with people without trying to change anything and show my love through acceptance and not adding harm, I ease suffering or, at the very least, I don't add to it.

I am reminded today of a story from Father Greg Boyle where he recalls the Christmas Carol, "Oh Holy Night," one of my favorites ever since I was a little kid singing away in church, although I didn't understand then the full power of the message - "Long lay the world, in sin and error pining, till he appeared and the soul felt its worth. A thrill of hope, the weary world rejoices, for yonder breaks a new and glorious morn.'"

"He" is you. And me. Whether you believe in any kind of "God" or not, you can believe in Love. To me, they are the same thing. And every one of us who acts as that light and loving presence for another offers that thrill of hope – that place to rejoice, that place where every single one us can know, finally, the essential and unchanging worth of our own soul. Thank you for being that.

We're all in this together!

When I dare to be powerful-- to use my strength in the service of my vision, then it becomes less and less important whether I am afraid.
~Audre Lorde

Afterword
September 12, 2015

Aparigraha - letting go
The fruits of the season

Om Tryambakam Yajamahe
Sugandhim Pushtivardhanam
Urvarukamiva Bandhanan
Mrityor Mukshiya Maamritat

We Meditate on the Three-eyed reality
Which permeates and nourishes all like a fragrance.
May we be liberated from death for the sake of immortality,
Even as the cucumber is severed from bondage to the creeper.

I just got back from Mexico to enjoy a few weeks of this beautiful Seattle weather, to visit friends and family, to check in on The Samarya Center and to prepare for Samarya Yoga Teacher Training.

As I was driving to the Central District from Vashon Island the other day, I passed a big handwritten sign that said: Fresh Peaches! Heirloom Tomatoes! Oh yes, I thought. I haven't had either of those things yet this summer, both delicious fruits that I wait all year to eat. While I wasn't able to stop right there and then for the bounty, it did make me think about the fruits of the season, and the season itself.

I remember being a kid and, with a June birthday, always requesting Breyer's Peach Ice-Cream for my celebration - it was a seasonal item that only showed up on the store shelves in June and was gone by September. That peach ice-cream represented everything about the beginning of summer - swimming, playing with friends, staying out late, fireworks, corn on the cob, barbeques and lots of sunshine.

But I also remember, even as a kid, toward the end of summer feeling ready to go back to school - to meet my new teachers, reconnect with school friends, wearing some new outfit that I had been planning for weeks. The summer would be gone, but the fall would be here, bringing it with its own special gifts, not the least of which was paving the way for winter and the holidays. The peaches and tomatoes would be gone, but pumpkins and then even, eventually, hot chocolate would be on its way.

It's kind of the same now. When I was in Mexico I had so many mangoes dropping from my tree, I had to eat a couple a day just to stay on top of what I couldn't give away. As my time there progressed, the mangoes became more sparse and I mourned their waning abundance. But then, one morning, I found an avocado on the ground. As mango season ended, it made the way for avocado season. And avocado season means moving away from the stifling heat of the height of summer, and into the electric beauty of tropical thunder and lightning.

One season gives way to the next.

I remember many years ago sitting in my office with friends and talking about the day that The Samarya Center would eventually close. I remember saying that, when I opened it in 2001 as a sole proprietor business, I always assumed that I would just close it when I was done. But then, as the seasons of the center progressed, I came to realize that it wasn't mine to close - that in fact, The Samarya Center belonged to a community and it would be up to the community to decide how to transform it once I was ready to move on. That was another season.

Now, almost fifteen years later, the season has changed again. And what I have learned through the process of the last several years is that the center is indeed mine to close. While it belongs to and benefits a community, it does not have the available leadership to continue. So many people have come through, stepped up, given so much to try to steward its continuation, but at the end of the day, the season has shifted. It is time. So someone has to be the one to say it. To change the page on the calendar. To acknowledge how letting this season go will only yield a new season, with new opportunities and new fruits.

This makes me think of the stunningly beautiful *maha mrityunjaya mantra*- or the great death conquering (sometimes called the great fear conquering) mantra - one of the most precious Vedic mantras. In this short chant, the devotee invokes Shiva and especially his powers of transformation. The chant includes a reference to a cucumber - asking to be freed from the bondage of the vine once it has reached its peak. In learning this from my teachers over the years, I have always learned the great significance of the creeper vegetable in the chant. Fruits that grow on trees fall to the ground when ripe - they become their maximum selves and then they drop at that point of full maturity - much like the mangoes and avocados in my backyard. But creeper vegetables - cucumbers, squash, melon - will stay on the vine, rotting into the ground if they are not picked or severed. They will pass their prime and simply decompose, never having been liberated in fullness.

The idea of the *maha mrityunjaya* is that we are like these creeper vegetables, and that we in fact pray to be released at that very point of fullness, not languishing in torpor. We want to realize our own fullness and in that state of brilliance, move on to the next phase of our cycle.

The Samarya Center has reached its full potential and maturity as it exists right now. It is time for this season to end and for us to open ourselves up to what's next - focusing on trainings, on spreading the work of the last decade and a half to an even greater community, for me to move to my home in Mexico, for the beginning of the Loma Indra Ashram that we are building in the mountains there.

Like the *maha mrtynujaya*, this is a time of celebration and exaltation, not fear and not mourning. The fruit has ripened, the season has turned and the new cycle is under way. Let us join together in joyful anticipation of the bounty yet to come.

~

It will have been just about three years to the day between the time I first approached my editor to work with me on this collection of essays and the time it was finally published. Throughout that three year process I was by turns excited, overwhelmed, and embarrassed. It seemed like every time that I said the book was going to come out, something got in the way to delay it. At first I apologized, and then I just stopped talking about it, but every time someone would bring up the book I would find myself cringing, feeling guilt ridden and anxious. Why hadn't I been able to finish? What was wrong with me?

My day-to-day work with The Samarya Center always seemed to take precedence over finishing the book, and yet the prospect of the book always loomed over me. I knew that some ay I would finally finish, but by the end, I gave up wondering when and decided I needed to be simply content with the process as it was unfolding.

Then, just last month, after almost fifteen years with The Samarya Center, I closed the center down to move on to new adventures of my own, without the additional work and responsibility of stewarding the center. In a sense, the completion of this book also marks a sort of closing scene for The Samarya Center. This book is a collection of the essays I wrote for The Samarya Center community newsletter over many years, and it seems so divinely fitting that the very last newsletter for the center featured this essay about letting go.

As you close this book, I close this chapter of my life. Thank you for being on this journey with me, thank you for your patience and your practice, and thank you for joining me for the next phase of evolution. We're all in this together.

Sometimes the lights all shinin' on me;
Other times I can barely see.
Lately it occurs to me
What a long, strange trip it's been. ~ Grateful Dead

SEVEN SIMPLE DRAWINGS:
I always use these simple line drawings in my teaching to illustrate these seven powerful concepts. I call them my "seven yoga drawings," and I wanted to share them with you here. They are elementary and unedited, but they have been very useful over the years as they are. I hope you enjoy them.

STILL POINT

One way we can think about our yoga practice is just to think about quieting the mind so we can listen to our heart.

We can think of our heart as being a still, quiet point, the place where our most authentic self, our soul, resides. Sometimes the mind is so noisy, its like it is drowning out our heart with all its chatter and hum. Our mind is pretty much constantly agitated - like a washing machine - in constant motion.

We can think of our thoughtstream as waves on the ocean surface. Sometimes they are so big or so unpredictable; they keep us from being able to find the STILL POINT of the ocean floor.

when those waves are REALLY
big, we can become completely
tossed around and lose sight

STILL POINT

of the fact that there even
is a still point. We are tumbling,
we may even feel like we are
drowning. **The practice of
YOGA**, the practice of stillness,
the practice of becoming aware
of our thoughts, of the waves,
and learning to manage them,
will help us to always get back home-
to our heart, to that still
point, to our soul. It's a little
like a road map. If we know

where we are now....,

● ← YOU ARE HERE

and we know where hOMe is..

and we have
lots and lots

of experience getting from

Here

to

there

it will be easier
and easier for us
to return, and we
will have less and less
experiences of feeling lost or
confused. **Practice quieting**
the mind, come home to the
still point of your heart.

THE GARDEN

i like to think of all the different aspects of "us" as different seeds and flowers or other plants in a garden.
i think about all of our possibility, all our potential, like a handful of seeds thrown into fertile soil.

They are ALL there, just with different potentials to grow.
envy) jealousy kindness
athleticism musicality patience

Some have been seeds, and the tendency to cultivate them, passed down for many generations.

Some are brand new, experimental.

Some we nurture, and are pleased with their growth, some we nurture inadvertently and we don't like them ~

Sometimes we wanted vegetables but we ended up with flowers. there's nothing wrong with the flowers, or with the vegetables. its just that one might feed us more, and help us to grow. When I think of the saying, "Fake it till you make it," i think - we're not really faking it, we're just tending to a seed, a sprout, that we want to nurture, that will enhance our relationships. Sometimes we need to prune, sometimes we need to water, sometimes we need to allow "volunteers" to grow and wonder and delight in potential we didn't know we had. Tend your garden. Not "good" and "bad," but what nourishes your body and soul?

FILLING THE CUP

Sometimes in our roles as teachers or as therapists, in our friendships or in family relationships, or even in our own process of growth and change, we might feel like we are not making an impact and become frustrated or discouraged ~ we don't have enough time with a person, someone moves on, and we wonder if we have contributed anything. **What** we have to remember is that whatever we have done or contributed has laid a foundation, added to the whole. **Remember** that the next therapist, the next teacher, the next opportunity, will contribute something new and that whatever that is, is directly impacted by all previous contributions. **Finally,** whether it is in thinking of our own evolution or that of someone in our life, we have to know that at some point, there will be a filling up, an overflowing, a tipping point. We must recall and acknowledge that the tipping point only occurred because of **ALL** the contributions, no matter how small, over time. **This is helpful** in at least two important ways.

1. it helps us to let go of the need to **SEE** the result of our actions, we can trust that whatever we have offered - "good" or "bad" - will have an impact and we can stay dedicated to **presence** - and accountability - of what we are contributing **NOW.**

2. we can remain humble, open and curious when we know that even when a big shift happens "on our watch", it doesn't make us the hero - or the villian. And that the same contribution, the same effort, in a

different situation, may
yield very different results.

What if what you
are contributing this
time around, even if
it is the very same
thing, is just drops into an
empty cup rather than the
little bit that caused the cup
to overflow?

Stay present.

Stay humble.

Stay curious.

Stay accountable.

Stay patient and loving.
The cup will fill!

MOLLY LANNON KENNY

THE FOREST

The heart chakra, called anāhata, is said to have the color green. अनाहत The word anāhata means something like "unstruck." Having my two homes in the Pacific Northwest and in the jungles of Mexico, I like to think of that color green as the lush layered green of a rainforest. This image is perfect for me in thinking about the heart and its infinite capacity for love, kindness, compassion, forgiveness and non-judgement.

just like the canopy of the rainforest doesn't discriminate what it holds within, every single thing about us has its place in the delicate eco-system of the heart. The rainforest has plants that are medicinal, and plants that are poisonous, and many that are both.

It has animals that are predators, and ones that are prey, and many that are both. There are flowers that we think look, or smell, beautiful and others we may think look, or smell, ugly.

The rainforest doesn't care. The rainforest doesn't exclude or judge. It accepts and protects everything under its cover. The heart chakra, anāhata, is the same. It accepts, forgives, loves, offers tenderness and care to ALL the parts of YOU. unstruck. infinite. spacious. LOVE.

You are perfect and whole, just the way you are!

THE CAR AND DRIVER

One way to think of soul, or the part of us that is eternal, unchanging, divine.

The car and driver!

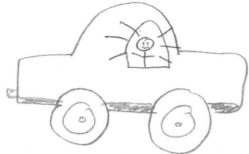

You are perfect and whole exactly you as you are - nothing to change, nothing to fix.

"But how can that be true? I have a chronic pain condition, I am an addict, I am a survivor of trauma, I have a broken leg, and, and, and..."

STOP Here's a new way to think about it - I hope it's helpful.

You can think of yourself (and everybody else) as a car and its driver. The car is your vehicle, your body, your life, your incarnation - we could refer to this as an aspect of prakriti. The driver is consciousness, soul, divine spark - we could call this purusha. Soul is always perfect, unstuck, impervious to the rapid changes, desires, traumas and even joys and sorrows of our life. The driver is the essential YOU, who is always whole and free from suffering.

Think of this: maybe you drive an old broken down jalopy. You may have an identification with this, and surely many others will make assumptions about you too, because of the car you drive.

But one day, you win a raffle and suddenly, you are driving a fancy sports car!

Now you may have a different identification, and others also have a different idea about you. But YOU are the same. Nothing about YOU has actually changed. We can even start to think of all people this way: simply as souls in a vehicle, but at the core all the same and all perfect. BUT WHY DO WE TRY TO IMPROVE THEN? AND WHAT ABOUT THE VERY DIFFICULT THINGS THAT HAPPEN TO US- DO WE JUST SAY, "OH WELL, IT'S JUST THE VEHICLE?" Well, yes and no. You can think of that this way: there is a saying, "God loves you just the way you are, but too much to let you stay that way." The truth is, we do come in this vehicle. And the vehicle should be cared for and optimized, since it is what carries us through this life. Sometimes the vehicle has specific challenges that it is necessary to address. If you were driving down the road and suddenly your clutch went out, or you got a flat tire, you wouldn't just keep driving and say "Oh well, my car is perfect." No. You are perfect. Your car has a flat. So change it! It is an impediment to joy! But don't try to change it into a Maserati, just change the flat. Your vehicle. Change what impedes your sense of forward motion, your sense of ease and freedom, in whatever way you can. Sometimes that is changing your body, sometimes that is changing your mind.

One more thing to think about: Sometimes your car, or someone else's, has a big scratch, but it works just fine. Do you have to fix that scratch? Do they? Maybe we can get better at tolerating scratches and dings and put our energy toward something more important, more impactful. We can stop judging others for their little "imperfections." In the same way, sometimes those little scratches really affect us. We think about them a lot and we can't just stop. Then we can also be tender towards that. If we can, maybe it's ok to address something even if we "know" it doesn't really matter. And we can be loving and patient to another who is consumed by their "scratch" (body image, ageing...) even if we don't see it as an issue. Car and driver - all on a unique journey... TOGETHER.

THE MOUNTAIN

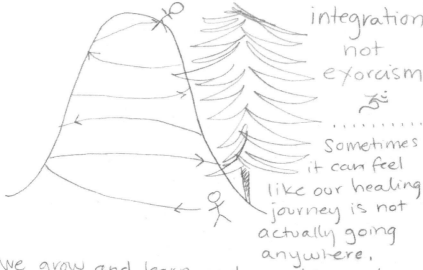

integration
not
exorcism

Sometimes
it can feel
like our healing
journey is not
actually going
anywhere.
We grow and learn and practice and
evolve but those early issues just
keep coming back. "why do i have
this same fear, this same insecurity,
this same reaction?" "i really thought
i had moved beyond that, but here
it is again. Maybe i will never fully
heal, maybe i won't ever really
transform." But you are transforming.
You are evolving. You are changing!
we think we will be healed when
our greatest challenges are a thing
of the past - disappeared - exorcised.
But healing is not a process of

exorcism. Those patterns, those challenges, those traumas will always be a part of our unique experience and narrative. Our work is to integrate, not exorcise. We bring in new joys, new perspectives, new experiences that change our relationship to those past traumas in such a way that they become part of our healing story, part of the wholeness of our being. I like to think of the spiritual life like climbing a mountain. It is not a linear process. There are a lot of switchbacks, daunting climbs, vistas, resting points, and even sites where we camp out for awhile. I see our core issues, our biggest challengest, our darkest traumas as a giant tree. At the outset of our journey it looms large over us, casting a shadow and darkening our path.

But as we move up the mountain, we don't just move away from it. No, we keep coming back around to it, but each time we have a different relationship to it. We see the tree - the challenge - from a new perspective - one where we can see light through the branches, all its nuanced colors, all of its own process of aging and evolving. We have grown. We have learned and evolved through our practice. The tree becomes an integral part of the journey, maybe even in some way a touchstone, rather than a thing to be felled. Spiritual life and healing into wholeness from our challenges and traumas is like that. It is about integration, not exorcism. Look for the new perspective, not the absence of the tree.

THE STRAIGHTAWAY

Practice in the straightaway what you'll use in the curve.

Many many years ago i had a grad school professor- I can't even remember his name - who would say this to us often in reference to working with people who stutter. Practice every day, in the smallest and most available moments, that which you will need when things get really tough. Our spiritual practice is like that. I often encourage my students to attend the series classes we offer at The Samarya Center, even if they think the topic doesn't apply. Yoga for Grief Recovery, Yoga for Chronic Pain, Yoga and End of life, Yoga for Anxiety or Depression, Yoga and Addiction. All of these are issues that we will face, directly and indirectly, at some point in our lives - why wait until we are facing these challenges to figure out how to work with them? Why not create patterns, strategies and practices NOW to prepare us for the inevitable hardships of life? Why not use our every day interactions, our meditations, our sadhana, as a training ground for the greatest challenges in our life? Why not create simple, every day SMALL PRACTICES that will serve us well on the arduous journey of life and healing - and consciously acknowledge them as a continuum of that which we'll need the most when

we're climbing the biggest mountains?
Practice in the straightaway
what you'll use in the curve.
Practice everyday gratitude,
Practice connecting,
Practice slowing down.
Practice forgiving,
Practice that one some more.
Practice breathing,
Practice being with
What is,
Practice LOVE,
Practice being spacious.
Practice NOT being who you think
you are.
Practice when things are
easy-let that same practice
serve you when things get hard,
Hundreds of my students use
this mantra because it works,

Practice in the
straightaway
what you'll use
in the curve.

=♡=
/ \

the time is now.
your time
our time.
don't wait until it feels
like too much.
the time is NOW.

Molly Lannon Kenny is the founder and director of The Samarya Center for Humankind (ness), a 501 c 3 non-profit service and training organization dedicated to individual transformation and radical social change.

Having received her master's Degree in Speech Pathology and working for over six years at a large HMO, she left her position to create, publish and trademark a unique therapy method, Integrated Movement Therapy®, built on the principles of acceptance, inclusion and healing of self as a means for healing others and our communities.

She has written and taught extensively on the topics of Yoga as Therapy and Yoga as a means to individual and social change, and has taught many hundreds of students in her specialized yoga teacher trainings both locally and internationally. She has been featured in Yoga Journal, MSNBC, Yoga Chicago, Yoga Northwest, Wisdom Magazine, and The New York Times, among many others.

She is past Vice President of the International Association of Yoga Therapists, and was the board liaison to the international committee on educational standards for the field of yoga therapy. She is currently an advisor to the Yoga Service Council.

In her other life, Molly has been the bass player and front person for several local bands over almost twenty years, and is a part of a large, raucous, multi-ethnic and culturally and socially diverse family of origin. She spends about a quarter of each year at her home in a small fishing village in Mexico, thinking about things like cultural relativism, paternalism, social change, and delicious food.

Molly is widely known as a vibrant, funny, accessible and super knowledgeable teacher, with a heart of gold and a spirit of fire.

www.mollylannonkenny.org
Facebook: Molly Lannon Kenny, Teacher

Molly Lannon Kenny ~ Somewhere in India